This is cutting edge work, which addresses current debates in the fields of criminology, victimology and social psychology. A must-read for anyone interested in justice issues.

Jo-Anne Wemmers, Professor, *School of Criminology, Université de Montréal, Canada*

Using detailed, open-ended interviews with victims and offenders, this book expands the widely used but conceptually limited framework within which researchers have explored procedural justice issues. It reinvigorates the field with a new and broader conceptual framework through which to understand how fairness is defined by those involved in the criminal justice system.

Tom R. Tyler, Macklin Fleming Professor of Law and Professor of Psychology, *Law School, Yale University, USA*

The insights of procedural justice research are of crucial importance for most fields of law, yet they are hardly integrated into current legal discourse and practice. In order to make procedural justice operational, we need to know what people experience as fair or unfair in a wide range of different circumstances. It is therefore my sincere hope that this book will set a trend of qualitative research in the field of procedural justice.

Eva Brems, Professor, *Law School, Ghent University, Belgium*

This illuminating volume contains important messages for all those involved in procedural justice research. Interviews with defendants and victims within the Belgian criminal justice system demonstrate the complex, multi-dimensional nature of people's "justice judgements", and underline the need for a more detailed conceptual and empirical understanding of the idea of procedural justice. Everyone interested in moving this exciting area of research forward should read this book.

Ben Bradford, Departmental Lecturer in Criminology, *University of Oxford, UK*

Perceptions of Criminal Justice

In recent decades, research into the legitimacy of criminal justice has convincingly demonstrated the importance of procedural justice to citizens' sense of trust and confidence in legal authorities and their resulting willingness to conform to the law and cooperate with the legal authorities. Reversing the age-old question 'why do people break the law?', theories of procedural justice have provided insight into the factors that encourage people to abide by the law, suggesting that experiences of procedural fairness are crucial to achieving compliance with the law and to enhancing the legitimacy of criminal justice.

While these studies are important in showing that legal authorities need to pay attention to the fairness judgements of the people involved in legal procedures, the focus on showing the importance of procedural justice has had the ironic consequence of distracting researchers from studying the equally important question of what fairness means to the people involved in legal proceedings.

In one of the first studies on procedural justice to use a qualitative research design, the author provides the reader with detailed and insightful descriptions of the elements that determine how victims and defendants assess the fairness of their contact with the police and the courts. Focusing on both the pre-trial and the post-trial phases, this book will be of interest to academics and students engaged in the study of the psychology of law, procedural justice and the legitimacy of criminal justice.

Vicky De Mesmaecker obtained a master's degree in Criminology, a master's degree in International Relations and Conflict Management and a Ph.D. in Criminology at the University of Leuven, Belgium. She worked as a doctoral researcher, postdoctoral researcher and affiliated researcher at the Leuven Institute of Criminology (University of Leuven, Belgium) and has been a visiting researcher at Yale University in the United States and at the Netherlands Institute for the Study of Crime and Law Enforcement in the Netherlands. Her main fields of study include theories of procedural justice, the legitimacy of criminal justice and legal authorities, victimology and restorative justice.

Routledge Frontiers of Criminal Justice

Perceptions of Criminal Justice

Vicky De Mesmaecker

Routledge
Taylor & Francis Group

LONDON AND NEW YORK

First published 2014
by Routledge

Published 2014 by Routledge
2 Park Square, Milton Park, Abingdon, Oxfordshire OX14 4RN

and by Routledge
711 Third Avenue, New York, NY 10017

Routledge is an imprint of the Taylor and Francis Group, an informa business

First issued in paperback 2015

British Library Cataloguing in Publication Data
A catalogue record for this book is available from the British Library

Library of Congress Cataloging in Publication Data
Mesmaecker, Vicky De, author.
  Perceptions of criminal justice / Vicky De Mesmaecker. -- First Edition.
    pages cm. -- (Routledge frontiers of criminal justice ; 16)
  1. Criminal justice, Administration of--United States--Public opinion.
I. Title.
  KF9223.M47 2014
  345.73'05--dc23
        2013036195

ISBN 978-0-415-70859-3 (hbk)
ISBN 978-1-138-96128-9 (pbk)
ISBN 978-1-315-88596-4 (ebk)

Typeset in Times New Roman
by Taylor & Francis Books

Contents

List of Tables

Foreword

By Tom R. Tyler

Macklin Fleming Professor of Law and Professor of Psychology at Yale Law School

Procedural justice is a well-established concept within the literature on criminal justice, yet this book makes clear that there are important aspects of the meaning of procedural justice which can benefit from being further explored. One is what people mean by fairness. Using detailed open-ended interviews with victims and offenders this book expands the widely used but conceptually limited framework within which researchers have explored procedural justice issues. There are several consequences of this re-examination. One is the identification of additional aspects of the lay meaning of fairness that have fallen outside the scope of the usual measures of procedural justice. For example, this study finds an important role for quality of treatment by the other parties to a crime, while the prior literature focuses upon treatment by authorities. In addition, by examining a large set of open-ended narratives a better understanding has been gained of the traditionally studied concepts of neutrality and standing. Readers of this book come away with a richer and more nuanced awareness of the concerns which motivate the considerable attention that people involved in the criminal justice system pay to the fairness of the procedures they experience.

Why is a book of this type important? Although there have been many prior studies of procedural justice the framework for this research has been heavily shaped, some might say constrained, by the research paradigm of the early researchers John Thibaut and Laurens Walker. These early researchers focused their research narrowly upon issues of control and within that focus used experimental research methods to demonstrate the importance of the perceived justice of legal procedures in shaping people's reactions to their experiences. While this experimental approach played an important role in establishing the importance of the field of procedural justice, it also led that idea to be widely associated largely or even solely with issues of participation, voice and control. Lost in the evolution of the field has been a broader conceptualisation of issues potentially related to the perceived justice of procedures, issues such as those outlined by the early researcher Gerald Leventhal. This book is an important and necessary effort to correct this narrowness of focus and reinvigorates the field with a new and broader conceptual framework through which to understand how fairness is defined by those involved in the criminal justice system.

The key to this effort is the use of detailed qualitative interviews that explore in depth people's understanding of and reaction to their experience. Such efforts are seldom undertaken because of the time and effort they require but this volume illustrates why they are important. The use of detailed and open-ended interviews reveals issues in people's understanding of their experience that have been neglected in prior studies. The author's effort to explore fairness concerns from different perspectives, i.e. from the point of view of the victim and of the criminal, and at different points in the criminal justice process, i.e. ranging from pre-trial mediation to the post-trial period, are especially important since these structural variations have been largely ignored by prior researchers. Beyond its contribution to our understanding of the perceived fairness of criminal procedures this volume is a wonderful illustration of how the use of qualitative interview methods can reopen and expand thinking in fields that already have strong and active quantitative research programmes.

Preface

In 1979, Malcolm Feeley published one of the first elaborate empirical studies on the operation of the criminal courts in the United States. In his book, Feeley focused on the lower criminal courts in New Haven, Connecticut, concluding that 'in the lower criminal courts the process itself is the primary punishment' (199). The book, then, carries the telling title *The Process Is the Punishment*. Extensive courtroom observations and discussions with defendants and attorneys led Feeley to contend that from a defendant's perspective, the (pre-)trial procedure is fraught with complexities, obstacles and psychological and financial costs which, according to Feeley, affect defendants' experience to a much greater degree than the sentence does. Though throughout his analysis, Feeley made no mention of procedural justice theory – an emerging field of study at the time – the argument he set out clearly appeals to the propositions put forward by procedural justice researchers.

I worked on this book, covering a study aiming to extend our understanding of the procedural justice notion, in the same town where Malcolm Feeley conducted the research that so poignantly illustrates some of the central assertions of procedural justice theory. I performed the study that is presented in this book as a doctoral researcher at the Leuven Institute of Criminology at the University of Leuven in Belgium. During my time as a postdoctoral visiting researcher at Yale Law School, in New Haven, Connecticut, I revised the dissertation into this book.

With this book, I endeavour to illustrate the procedural justice notion by describing the real-life experiences of victims and defendants on their journey through the criminal justice system. I am greatly indebted to many people who have aided my work. I am very grateful, first of all, to the people whose stories form the basis of this book. I have often been amazed by their willingness to share their story with me – an outsider after all – and have felt like a privileged witness on many occasions. I have learned a lot from them, and I thank them for giving me that opportunity. Furthermore, I would like to express my gratitude to the supervisor and co-supervisor of my dissertation, Prof. Dr. Ivo Aertsen and Prof. Dr. Johan Goethals of the Leuven Institute of Criminology. They have provided vital advice and support all throughout the study. I also owe thanks to the members of the supervisory committee and the examining committee: Prof. Dr. Kristel Beyens, Prof. Dr. Stefan Bogaerts, Mr. Dr. Marijke Malsch, Prof. Dr. Tom Tyler and Prof. Dr. Frank Verbruggen. I would also like to express deep gratitude to the staff and secretariat of Suggnomè, the NGO organising victim–offender mediation in Flanders, the Dutch-speaking part of Belgium where the study took place. I could not have conducted this study without their cooperation. I thank each of the mediators and the Suggnomè coordinator and secretariat for their support and advice. I would also like to thank the Belgian American Educational Foundation and Prof. Dr. Tom Tyler for giving me the opportunity to spend a year at Yale as a visiting researcher. It has been a wonderful experience to live and work there. I would also like to thank all at Routledge for bringing this book into existence.

On a personal note, I'm very grateful to the wonderful colleagues that I have had the pleasure of working with at the Leuven Institute of Criminology. It has been very rewarding for me to work with the great people at the Institute, and I am happy to be able to say that I made great friends there. Finally, I would like to express special thanks to my family. They are, and always have been, an invaluable source of encouragement and support.

Part I
Setting the stage

1 Introduction

Improving understanding of the lay meaning of procedural justice

> In important respects we are on the cusp of a shift from a post- to a pre-crime society, a society in which the possibility of forestalling risks competes with and even takes precedence over responding to wrongs done. In consequence, the post- crime orientation of criminal justice is increasingly overshadowed by the pre-crime logic of security.
>
> (Zedner, 2007: 262)

After increasing sharply in the four decades before 2000, and culminating after the September 11, 2001 terrorist attacks in the United States, fear of crime has become a prominent issue on political agendas worldwide (Simon, 2007). Scholars report a shift from a post-crime society to a so-called pre-crime society, where popular discourse and political agendas are increasingly oriented towards surveillance, crime prevention and 'the pursuit of security' (Zedner, 2007: 262) and individual life choices such as where (not) to live, travel or send one's children to school are made to a large degree on the basis of the perceived risk of crime (Simon, 2007). Risk calculation has become a central feature of daily life as traditional crime control models have been exposed as inadequate to the goal of crime prevention and policy-making in domains not directly related to crime – such as health, education and the environment – increasingly focuses on issues of safety too (Beck, 1992; Giddens, 1999).

Mainstream academic discourse has it that in this 'new securitized environment' (Simon, 2007: 7) the responsibility for security and risk management, in particular in the domain of criminal law, is no longer solely in the hands of governments (Garland, 2001; Simon, 2007; Zedner, 2007). In reply to the privatisation tendencies that emerged as part of the neo-liberalist philosophy that has come to dominate societies in recent decades, individuals and communities are called upon to do their part of the 'crime prevention job'. While the quest for security leads individual communities to take private initiatives, such as setting up a neighbourhood watch system, and leads families to take measures to protect their homes and belongings, private security service suppliers conquer the market of security services.

While these privatisation tendencies are incontestable, a second, equally important shift in approaches to crime prevention has taken place recently. This second development concerns an evolution with respect to the particular state actors that are considered responsible for maintaining societal security. The continuous emphasis on the importance of increasing the costs of crime in order to prevent people from committing crime has led to the conventional notion that legislators bear the responsibility for crime prevention, yet in recent decades research has pointed out the role of law enforcement agencies in crime prevention.

Beyond privatisation: new perspectives on the role of law enforcers

In the past, a getting tough on crime approach governed efforts to discourage crime. The belief in the capacity of punishment to deter crime put the responsibility for crime prevention in the hands of legislators who, through legislative acts, were expected to increase the threat of punishment. Nowadays, the role of law enforcers – particularly the police – in crime prevention and regulation is increasingly emphasised (Tyler, 2007; Meares, 2013; Tyler and Jackson, 2013). The rise of stop-and-frisk policies in some of the major cities of the United States – New York, Chicago and Baltimore to name just a few – is one of the most visible illustrations of the contemporary view that the police too have a role to play in crime prevention. Originating in Wilson and Kelling's (1982) Broken Windows theory (Collins, 2007; Fagan et al., 2009), aggressive and profound stop-and-frisk tactics have been advanced as the prime manner in which the police can contribute to the prevention of disorder. Yet these stop-and-frisk policies, Collins (2007: 420) argues, have led to the development of 'bad blood' between the police and 'large segments of the communities they seek to serve' (see also Hough, 2013 and more broadly on the negative effects of aggressive crime control approaches Howell, 2009 and Tyler and Jackson, 2013). Stop-and-frisk policies seem antithetical to the development of good relationships between the police and the community because of the selective enforcement of these policies, with systemic racial disparity in the implementation of stop-and-frisk policies being the principal problem (Geller and Fagan, 2010; Fagan et al., 2012).

Research on institutional legitimacy advances another, more helpful approach to the role of law enforcers in crime prevention. This line of research suggests that in order for citizens to voluntarily defer to the law, they need to believe that the law and those enforcing it are just. To the degree that they do, they will feel personally obligated to defer to the legal authorities and to the laws that these authorities are enforcing (Tyler, 2006a). The legitimacy of criminal justice and citizen willingness to conform to the law, then, do not primarily depend on governmental effort to raise the costs of crime or increase the risk of getting caught but on the perceived legitimacy of those enforcing the law (Tyler, 2007, 2009a). It is the manner in which the police and the courts perform their duties and behave towards citizens that determines people's willingness to comply with the law (Tyler, 1990, 2003). As such, these authorities have an important responsibility in the prevention of law-violating behaviour. Tyler has taken this argument to proclaim that everyday encounters with the police and courts are 'socialising experience[s] that build or undermine legitimacy' (2013: 17). The adoption of community policing and neighbourhood policing as models of policing as from the 1980s attests to law enforcers' present awareness of the importance of good police–citizen relationships to police legitimacy (Skogan and Hartnett, 1997; National Research Council, 2004; Tuffin *et al.*, 2006; Tyler, 2007; Quinton and Morris, 2008; Myhill and Quinton, 2010). As it turns out, people with a more positive perception of law enforcers have more positive perceptions of the law in general, which in turn promotes compliance (Papachristos *et al.*, 2012) – both compliance with particular decisions of legal authorities and general, everyday compliance with the law (Tyler, 2007).

The crucial feature of law enforcers' behaviour that determines citizen perceptions of these actors and, consequently, citizens' inclination to live by the law and defer to law enforcers, is the degree to which these officials perform their jobs in a procedurally just manner (Tyler and Huo, 2002; Tyler, 2007, 2009b). Social psychological research on citizens' sense of trust in the police and the courts demonstrates that people judge the behaviour, actions and decisions of law enforcement agencies against the criterion of procedural fairness. Procedural fairness refers to the quality of the interpersonal contact between citizens and the law-enforcing authorities, the quality of the information that citizens are supplied with, the chances that they are given for offering the authorities their own point of view on the matter and the objectivity and neutrality of the law-enforcing agencies. These aspects of procedures determine citizens' perceptions of the procedural fairness of their contact with the police or judicial authorities (Tyler, 1989; Tyler and Lind, 1992; Malsch, 2009). Together these factors – which will be elaborated upon more extensively below – constitute the basis for legitimacy-based compliance. By respecting these factors, law enforcers can lead citizens to be more willing to defer to their requests, accept their authority and live by the law in their everyday life. Importantly, the fair exercise of authority also makes citizens more likely to cooperate in crime fighting. Citizens who experience procedural fairness become more willing to assist the police in their job of crime fighters by, for example, informing the police when they witness a crime, helping the police to find a suspect or reporting suspicious activity (Sunshine and Tyler, 2003), which may contribute to reducing crime rates too (Meares, 2013). There are, then, two ways in which procedurally fair law enforcing advances the goal of crime prevention.

Procedural justice in contemporary criminological discourse

Procedural justice theory is grounded in a Benthamian view on justice, i.e. the view that whether or not justice is done is decided upon by those on the receiving end of justice, not by those who are supposed to 'do' justice (Burns and Hart, 1970; Rosen, 1993; Young, 1994). It is no coincidence, then, that procedural justice has become a much-pursued area of research in the last decades. The model's focus on the relation between the state as represented by criminal justice authorities and individual citizens has been much welcomed by the relational models of justice that made their way into the criminological mainstream during much the same time period. Foregoing the traditional rational choice perspective on humans that provides the basis of Western criminal justice systems (Norrie, 1996), relational models of justice press for replacing traditional trial and punishment practices with a justice process that is 'shared' (Norrie, 2000). The very nature of the idea of alternative dispute resolution, for example, as described by Resnik (2013), is that 'from policing, prosecution, and punishment to civil litigation, ideas about what various government officials do have been built, reformatted, and are now under revision again. Whether it was ever credible to talk as though the state monopolises the functions of maintaining order, enforcing criminal law, and imposing civil liabilities, it is not so today' (187). Relational approaches to justice, examples of which are 'alternative dispute resolution', 'neighbourhood justice', 'community justice' and 'restorative justice' (Pavlich, 2005), look for ways to deal with conflict that include repairing the harm caused by the conflict and the relationships that were breached with a strong focus on participatory approaches and involving communities (Schluter, 1994). They have in common the conviction that people involved in a conflict caused by, for example, a crime, a neighbourhood dispute or a school fight should have the opportunity to actively participate in the resolution of the conflict. Keywords of relational approaches to justice are 'collaborative', 'inclusive', 'engagement', 'participation', 'mutual agreement' and 'meeting' (Zehr, 2002: 25–6). Interventions based on restorative justice principles, for example, provide people involved in conflict caused by crime (victims, offenders and their communities) with the opportunity to take the resolution of the conflict that arose between them into their own hands, provided that they want to, and with the caveat that sometimes a state intervention does still follow the restorative intervention. Restorative scholars argue that the parties to a conflict should be allowed to define 'justice' for themselves and collectively decide how justice can be done, 'rather than [to] simply provide offenders with legal or formal justice and victims with no justice at all' (Morris, 2002: 598). Menkel-Meadow (2010: 597) writes that the field of alternative dispute resolution 'has more recently been called "appropriate" dispute resolution, or just dispute resolution'. Notions of procedural justice have indeed been very important to the development of methods of alternative dispute resolution (MacCoun, 2005) and are often referred to by restorative justice scholars and those evaluating restorative justice programmes too (e.g. Peachey, 1986; Braithwaite, 1999; Sherman, 2003; Tyler, 2006b; Tyler *et al.*, 2007; Van Camp and Wemmers, 2013).

Debates on the degree to which diverse forms of dispute resolution, including the crime–trial–punishment approach, deliver procedural justice and fairness now permeate the literature on the legitimacy of Western criminal justice systems. The economic conception of humans that suggests that justice is achieved when those guilty of breaking the law have been adequately punished has been dismissed. It has been substituted with a conception of humans as moral entities behaving in accordance with the law and social values about what is right and proper voluntarily, provided that the authorities enforcing the law are perceived to be legitimate (Tyler, 1990; Tyler and Jackson, 2013). Ascriptions of legitimacy, in turn, are tied to perceptions of procedural fairness.

Procedural justice theory: a brief overview

The history of procedural justice research extends back to the mid-1970s, when John Thibaut and Laurens Walker presented their seminal work *Procedural Justice: A Psychological Analysis* (1975; see also Thibaut and Walker, 1978). Through a number of laboratory studies set up so as to examine participants' preferences for different dispute resolution procedures (e.g. arbitration, autocratic decision-making, mediation), Thibaut and Walker discovered that people judge dispute resolution procedures not only with reference to the outcomes they receive; the perceived level of fairness of a dispute resolution procedure, so they found, to a large extent depends on the characteristics of the dispute resolution procedure itself. In particular, Thibaut and Walker found that those dispute resolution procedures that allow the conflict parties a certain degree of process control, that is, control over the development, selection and presentation of evidence, are considered the most fair. The reason, so the authors argued, is an instrumental one: Thibaut and Walker hypothesised that people value process control because having some control over the process increases the likelihood of achieving a desired outcome. The authors also introduced the concept decision control, pointing out that in particular circumstances, litigants also like to have control over the actual outcome of the dispute resolution procedure, yet argued that, overall, process control is more important to litigants than decision control.

Thibaut and Walker were not the first to suggest the importance of procedures to fairness judgements. John Rawls (1971) and Gerald Leventhal (1976a, 1976b, 1980) too should be credited for their contribution to the development of the notion of procedural fairness. Likewise Rawls and Leventhal explicitly abandoned the material description of fairness that was widely adhered to by other justice researchers at the time (e.g. Adams, 1965), suggesting instead that perceptions of fairness depend on the procedures characterising decision-making and governing social institutions. Both researchers have inspired subsequent research; Tyler's (1990) landmark empirical study on procedural justice for example was heavily influenced by Leventhal's work. Yet Thibaut and Walker were the first to provide empirical evidence for the ground-breaking statement that fairness judgements are not determined exclusively by outcome concerns but also by the procedures used for reaching outcome decisions.

Thibaut and Walker's research received some criticism because of its narrow focus on control issues and for ultimately defining procedural fairness in terms of outcome fairness. Subsequent researchers included non-control variables in their analyses, theorising that relational concerns, that is, characteristics of the relationship between decision-makers and conflict parties, also affect fairness judgements. The very premise of subsequent research indeed was that procedural justice judgements are important because procedures communicate symbolic information not about profit or gain but about self-esteem, self-validation and identity. Arguing that people are, by nature, affiliative individuals who attach great importance to social inclusion and group membership, it was hypothesised, and later empirically verified (see Tyler *et al.*, 1996), that procedural justice matters to people because of its centrality to issues of identity and status – 'what people get from groups in the form of acknowledgement and recognition of their identities' (Tyler, 2012: 356). More specifically, being treated in a procedurally just manner conveys to people the message that they are a respected group member and that they can take pride in their group membership (Tyler *et al.*, 1996; Tyler, 1999; Tyler and Blader, 2003).

The most notable among the studies extending Thibaut and Walker's research are those reported on in Lind and Tyler (1988), Tyler (1989, 1990) and Tyler and Lind (1992). Though these date back to the late 1980s/early 1990s, contemporary understanding of the meaning of procedural justice and the antecedents of procedural justice is still based on these studies (see, e.g. Tyler, 2013). Variations on the initial model of procedural justice have been proposed, but these have never touched the fundamentals of the model or questioned the determinants of procedural justice that the initial model advanced; rather, they ascertained assertions about the *consequences* of procedural justice. The group engagement model demonstrates that perceptions of procedural justice positively influence group-oriented attitudes and behaviour (Blader and Tyler, 2003a, 2003b; Tyler and Blader, 2000, 2001, 2003) and the process-based model of regulation shows that experiences of procedural justice facilitate acceptance of authorities and authorities' decisions (Tyler and Huo, 2002; Tyler, 2003).

Tyler and Lind advanced four key determinants of perceptions of procedural justice. These are voice, standing, neutrality and respect. The first, 'voice' or participation, to a certain degree resembles Thibaut and Walker's process control variable. Tyler and Lind's studies indeed confirmed that the degree to which conflict parties are involved in the decision-making procedure has a significant influence on their perceptions of procedural justice (see also Folger, 1977; Folger *et al.*, 1979). Being awarded an opportunity to express one's own opinion and arguments about the decision-making procedure and preferred outcome and being allowed to participate in evidence presentation was positively valued by Tyler and Lind's study participants; procedures that offered the conflict parties a possibility for voice were regarded as more fair than procedures that did not. Yet, importantly, Lind and Tyler found voice to have a non-instrumental value. This means that voice had an effect on fairness judgements irrespective of whether by voicing their opinion the conflicting parties felt that they had had an influence on the outcome. For this reason, the effect of voice was called a 'value-expressive' effect (Tyler *et al.*, 1985).

Standing, neutrality and trust are usually mentioned in one breath, as Tyler and Lind grouped them under the label 'relational variables'. Standing refers to the conflict parties feeling respected and acknowledged by the decision-maker. Tyler and Lind (1992) subdivided standing into (a) decision-makers treating conflict parties in a polite manner, respecting their dignity; and (b) decision-makers respecting conflict parties' rights. Trust points to the degree to which conflict parties feel that they can trust the decision-maker to act in good faith. Tyler and Lind (1992) broke this concept up into two key features: (a) decision-makers displaying a sincere concern for conflict parties' needs; and (b) decision-makers considering conflict parties' views. Neutrality refers to the absence of discrimination and the impartiality of the decision-maker; it is based on judgements about (a) decision-makers' honesty; (b) the extent to which decisions are based on facts rather than prejudice; and (c) the absence of bias or prejudice in decision-making (Tyler and Lind, 1992). Tyler (1989) empirically demonstrated that, together, these three variables explain more of the variance in dependent variables such as perceptions of the fairness of procedures and outcomes, affect towards the authorities and perceptions of the fairness of the authorities than control variables. Most importantly, Tyler found that people valued each of these criteria irrespective of their effect on the outcome.

Evaluations of experiences of authorities, then, are based first and foremost on the degree to which authorities act in accordance with these four antecedents of procedural justice. In the context of criminal law and criminal procedure, perceptions of procedural justice have been demonstrated to be the prime determinant of the perceived legitimacy of the legal authorities among the public at large and among conflict parties and of support for and trust in the legal authorities (Tyler and Lind, 1992; Tyler and Huo, 2002; Tyler and Fagan, 2008; Mazerolle *et al.*, 2012; Jackson *et al.*, 2013a, 2013b), of the public's willingness to cooperate with the legal authorities (Sunshine and Tyler, 2003; Murphy *et al.*, 2008; Tyler and Fagan, 2008; Hough *et al.*, 2010; Tyler, 2011; Levi *et al.*, 2012; Mazerolle *et al.*, 2012) and of rule-following behaviour (compliance with the law), voluntary acceptance of legal authorities' decisions and deference to the legal authorities (Tyler, 1990, 2009b; Tyler and Huo, 2002; McCluskey, 2003; Tyler *et al.*, 2007; Hough *et al.*, 2010; Levi *et al.*, 2012; Jackson *et al.*, 2012; Papachristos *et al.*, 2012). Moreover, people have been found on several occasions to react more positively to both desirable and undesirable outcomes after fair procedures as opposed to unfair procedures (e.g. Walker *et al.*, 1974; Folger, 1977; this is the so-called fair process effect). Perceptions of fairness, then, affect a range of attitudinal and behavioural responses (Gonzalez and Tyler, 2007).

Purpose of the book

Despite the overwhelming evidence on the importance of procedural fairness to the legitimacy of authorities, rule-following behaviour and cooperation with authorities, the concept of procedural fairness has remained quite abstract. While prior studies have convincingly demonstrated that legal authorities need to try to establish procedural fairness in order to resolve conflicts in ways that are acceptable to the parties, they have not paid sufficient attention to fleshing out what fairness means to the people involved in legal proceedings. It is often unclear what people mean when they say that they have or have not experienced the varying elements of fairness. This is because the typical way of gauging the extent to which people feel that they have been treated in a fair way is by way of items such as 'How fairly were you treated?' or 'Were the authorities neutral?', answers to which need to be indicated on Likert scales (e.g. Tyler, 1987). There is little more open-ended research exploring the details of what people actually mean when talking about fairness. When reflecting on the question 'Were the authorities neutral?', for example, which situations exactly are crossing people's minds? What behaviours are they thinking of when they say that an authority was neutral or otherwise fair?

This is the question that drove the study reported in this book. Legal authorities, not least the police, have repeatedly been encouraged by procedural justice researchers to adapt their policies, procedures and practices and the way they deal with citizens and conflict parties so as to promote perceptions of procedural justice and as such encourage citizen compliance, cooperation and perceptions of legitimacy (e.g. Sunshine and Tyler, 2003; Tyler, 2008, 2013; Gau and Brunson, 2010; Schulhofer *et al.*, 2011). Yet the vagueness of the concept of procedural justice – it is, for example, not clear what exactly people expect from the police when they say that they want them to be neutral or what they expect from the courts when they argue that they want to be heard – makes it hard to adapt criminal procedures with a view to enhancing perceptions of procedural fairness. The results of the study reported in this book provide justice researchers with a richer understanding of what people mean in concrete terms when they talk about (procedural) fairness. Based on in-depth interviews with victims and offenders involved in a criminal trial, this study makes the core procedural justice concepts (standing, trust, neutrality, voice) more tangible, illustrating them with concrete examples and broadening our understanding of these concepts. The study for example shows that a number of the concepts have been interpreted in too narrow a sense, which has important consequences for the way they are conceptualised in quantitative research studies. While MacCoun (2005: 174) argues that 'few areas of socio-legal research can boast a comparable level of attention to measurement reliability and construct validity', others have criticised the procedural justice literature for not providing strong measures of its key theoretical constructs, urging procedural justice researchers to 'refine the way procedural justice is measured' (Henderson *et al.*, 2010: 386; see also Reisig *et al.*, 2007; Gau, 2011; Van Damme *et al.*, 2012). The interview data reported in this book may inspire future studies that are set up with a view to bringing more clarity on how the indicators of procedural justice should or could be conceptualised.

This study does not only stand out from previous studies because of its methodology. It is also among the first to systematically examine perceptions of procedural justice in a European legal culture. While recently important efforts have been made for testing the procedural justice model in a large number of European countries by means of the European Social Survey (see Jackson *et al.*, 2011, 2013c; Hough *et al.*, 2013a, 2013b), the academic literature on procedural justice is based mainly on studies conducted in Anglo-Saxon countries, chiefly the United States. Allan Lind, one of the founders of procedural justice theory, in the 1980s did pay attention to the theme of cross-cultural generality of the assertions of procedural justice theory, but attention to the issue weakened and the further development of the theory was based mainly on studies among American subjects. Notable exceptions are Wemmers' (1996) study on perceptions of procedural justice among victims of crime in the Netherlands, research among Japanese citizens by Ohbuchi *et al.* (2005) and among Chinese citizens by Leung and Lind (1986) and Leung (1987), Lind *et al.*'s (1997) study including Japanese and German respondents, Meško *et al.*'s (2012) study on Slovenians (see also Reisig *et al.*, 2013) and Levi *et al.*'s (2012) study among citizens of eighteen sub-Saharan African countries. Yet these studies are based on quantitative designs and some of them were conducted in the context of civil litigation, not criminal litigation. Moreover, as Kautt (2011) points out, findings from one country cannot be assumed to be applicable to other countries – specific research needs to be set up before making generalisations. The current study is the first study that was explicitly set up so as to investigate perceptions of procedural justice of the criminal justice system in Belgium.

Study context and setting

This book focuses on the experiences of those who encounter the criminal justice system as a victim or defendant in Belgium. The Belgian criminal justice system as any other has its distinct features and the results need to be related to the specific context in which they were obtained.[1] Furthermore, as Belgium belongs to the European legal tradition, whereas the bulk of procedural justice research has been carried out in Anglo-Saxon jurisdictions, it is important to be clear on the differences between Anglo-Saxon 'adversarial' criminal justice systems and the Belgian 'inquisitorial' criminal justice system.

The Belgian criminal justice system differs from common law legal systems in four important respects. First, in Belgium, criminal trials are not bifurcated. There are no separate hearings for determining guilt and for determining the sentence. The pleas concerning the determination of guilt and the determination of the sentence take place during the same hearing. In the judgment, the judge decides on the question of whether the accused is guilty and pronounces a sentence in case the defendant is indeed deemed guilty. Therefore, when the term 'judgment' is used in this book, what is referred to is both the determination of guilt and the determination of the sentence. The judge's decision is usually communicated two to four weeks after the trial. Second, it is important to describe the way that trials are conducted in Belgium. In procedural justice literature, the distinction between adversarial systems and inquisitorial systems has been of great importance ever since the first studies by Thibaut and Walker (1975). Many of Thibaut and Walker's experiments were devoted to comparisons of the inquisitorial and the adversarial system of decision-making; Thibaut and Walker experimentally demonstrated people's preference for adversarial procedures. Yet those well acquainted with Thibaut and Walker's research may find themselves misunderstanding the Belgian system. The Belgian criminal justice system, which is routinely described as an 'inquisitorial' one, does not function the way inquisitorial experimental conditions were designed by Thibaut and Walker. In fact, Thibaut and Walker's conceptualisation of the adversarial condition – '[r]epresentatives will be chosen by plaintiff and defendant. Each will present facts favorable to the side he represents' (1975: 79) – exactly matches the way that adjudication in Belgium works. Parties may choose to defend themselves or appoint a lawyer to defend their case. The way the inquisitorial system was described in Thibaut and Walker's studies – people not being allowed to choose their own lawyer or not being represented by a lawyer at all – is not the way the Belgian system actually works.[2] Third, in Belgium, the large majority of trials are bench trials. No system of plea bargaining exists, and jury trials are only conducted occasionally. When the public prosecutor decides to file charges against a suspect, the case is usually disposed of by bench trial. The only exceptions are murder trials, which do involve a jury, and those cases that do not go to trial because they are eligible for penal mediation. The latter are cases involving crimes that should, according to the prosecutor, not be punished by a sentence of two or more years of imprisonment. It is important to keep in mind, then, that bench trials are the norm in Belgium. Finally, the role of judges in the Belgian system is to be clarified. Judges play a more active role in Belgian trials than they do in Anglo-Saxon legal cultures. The judge is the one who actively interviews the parties in court; (s)he is actively engaged in truth-seeking. Since there is no system of plea bargaining and few trials involve a jury, judges in Belgium play a bigger part in trials than do judges in adversarial systems dominated by plea bargaining and jury trials. This explains why in the results chapters more attention is given to interviewees' impressions of the judge dealing with their case, and less to their impressions of the prosecutor, than might be expected by readers coming from an adversarial legal system.

Chapters outlined

This book is divided into six chapters. This chapter set the theoretical stage for the book, introducing the relevance of procedural justice theory as a strategy for law enforcement in contemporary society yet pointing out our limited understanding of what procedural justice means in very concrete terms to those citizens involved in a criminal procedure as a victim or defendant. The chapter furthermore outlined the specific context of the study that is presented in this book. The second chapter is concerned with the methodology of the study. This chapter presents the data collection methods, the motivations for using a qualitative research methodology, the criteria for participant selection and the characteristics of the sample. Chapters 3 to 5 are devoted to the results of the study. Chapter 3 focuses on participants' experience of the police; Chapter 4 describes their experience of those magistrates that they encountered in the pre-trial phase. Chapter 5 explores participants' experience of the criminal courts. These three chapters set out to investigate the concrete meaning of each of the antecedents of procedural justice and to identify elements that have not so far been categorised as antecedents of perceptions of procedural justice. The final chapter contains a discussion of the results of the study. It provides an overview of the manner in which the current study offers insight into existing concepts of procedural justice and of the manner in which this study extends theories of procedural justice.

In a 2011 book bearing the ominous title *The Collapse of American Criminal Justice*, Harvard law professor William J. Stuntz wrote the words, 'We have built a justice system that strikes many of its targets as wildly unjust' (2). The theory of procedural justice has been demonstrated by many to explain in large part why this is the case, yet has so far mainly looked into citizen evaluations of the police and has done so primarily by means of quantitative research methods. The current study aims to contribute to this rich tradition of research by providing a comprehensive description of those issues that are considered by litigants involved in a criminal procedure, focusing not only on their experience of the police but also zooming in on their day in court, and employing qualitative interview techniques. The result, then, is an in-depth picture of how victims and defendants experience the Belgian criminal justice system.

Notes

1 An excellent outline of the structure and basic principles of the operation of the Belgian criminal justice system can be found in Brienen and Hoegen (2000, ch. 4). Though obviously changes have taken place since Brienen and Hoegen published their study, it is still a valuable source for those looking for an introduction to the basic structure and principles of the Belgian criminal justice system.

2 The only exception to the rule that people choose their own lawyer is the case where people do not have the means of hiring a lawyer and are assigned a pro bono lawyer.

References

Adams, J.S. (1965). "Inequity in social exchange." In Berkowitz, L. (ed.), *Advances in Experimental Social Psychology vol. 2* (267–99). London: Academic Press.

Beck, U. (1992). *Risk Society: Towards A New Modernity*. London: Sage.

Blader, S.L. and Tyler, T.R. (2003a). "A four-component model of procedural justice: defining the meaning of a 'fair' process." *Personality and Social Psychology Bulletin*, 29 (6): 747–58.

——(2003b). "What constitutes fairness in work settings? A four-component model of procedural justice." *Human Resource Management Review*, 13 (1): 107–26.

Braithwaite, J. (1999). "Restorative justice: assessing optimistic and pessimistic accounts." In Tonry, M. (ed.), *Crime and Justice: A Review of Research vol. 25* (1–127). Chicago, IL: University of Chicago Press.

Brienen, M. and Hoegen, E. (2000). *Victims of Crime in 22 European Criminal Justice Systems*. Nijmegen: Wolf Legal Productions.

Burns, J.H. and Hart, H.L.A. (eds) (1970). *An Introduction to the Principles of Morals and Legislation: The Collected Works of Jeremy Bentham*. Oxford: Oxford University Press.

Collins, R. (2007). "Strolling while poor: how broken-windows policing created a new crime in Baltimore." *Georgetown Journal on Poverty Law & Policy*, 14 (3): 419–39.

Fagan, J., Davies, G. and Carlis, A. (2012). "Race and selective enforcement in public housing." *Journal of Empirical Legal Studies*, 9 (4): 697–728.

Fagan, J., Geller, A., Davies, G. and West, V. (2009). "Street stops and broken windows revisited: the demography and logic of proactive policing in a safe and changing city." In Rice, S.K. and White, M.D. (eds), *Race, Ethnicity, and Policing: New and Essential Readings* (309–48). New York: New York University Press.

Folger, R. (1977). "Distributive and procedural justice: combined impact of 'voice' and improvement on experienced inequity." *Journal of Personality and Social Psychology*, 35 (2): 108–19.

Folger, R., Rosenfield, D., Grove, J. and Corkran, L. (1979). "Effects of 'voice' and peer opinions on responses to inequity." *Journal of Personality and Social Psychology*, 37 (12): 2253–61.

Garland, D. (2001). *The Culture of Control: Crime and Social Order in Contemporary Society*. Oxford: Oxford University Press.

Gau, J.M. (2011). "The convergent and discriminant validity of procedural justice and police legitimacy: an empirical test of core theoretical propositions." *Journal of Criminal Justice*, 39 (6): 489–98.

Gau, J.M. and Brunson, R.K. (2010). "Procedural justice and order maintenance policing: a study of inner-city young men's perceptions of police legitimacy." *Justice Quarterly*, 27 (2): 255–79.

Geller, A. and Fagan, J. (2010). "Pot as pretext: marijuana, race, and the new disorder in New York City street policing." *Journal of Empirical Legal Studies*, 7 (4): 591–633.

Giddens, A. (1999). "Risk and responsibility." *Modern Law Review*, 62 (1): 1–10.

Gonzalez, C.M. and Tyler, T.R. (2007). "Why do people care about procedural fairness? The importance of membership monitoring." In Törnblom, K. and Vermunt, R. (eds), *Distributive and Procedural Justice: Research and Social Applications* (91–110). Aldershot: Ashgate.

Henderson, H., Wells, W., Maguire, E.R. and Gray, J. (2010). "Evaluating the measurement properties of procedural justice in a correctional setting." *Criminal Justice and Behavior*, 37 (4): 384–99.

Hough, M. (2013). "Procedural justice and professional policing in times of austerity." *Criminology & Criminal Justice*, 13 (2): 181–97.

Hough, M., Jackson, J. and Bradford, B. (2013a). "Legitimacy, trust and compliance: an empirical test of procedural justice theory using the European Social Survey." In Tankebe, J. and Liebling, A. (eds), *Legitimacy and Criminal Justice: An International Exploration* (246–65). Oxford: Oxford University Press.

——(2013b). "The governance of criminal justice, legitimacy and trust." In Body-Gendrot, S., Lévy, R., Hough, M., Snacken, S. and Kerezsi, K. (eds), *The Routledge Companion to European Criminology*. Abingdon: Routledge.

Hough, M., Jackson, J., Bradford, B., Myhill, A. and Quinton, P. (2010). "Procedural justice, trust, and institutional legitimacy." *Policing*, 4 (3): 203–10.

Howell, K.B. (2009). "Broken lives from broken windows: the hidden costs of aggressive order-maintenance policing." *New York University Review of Law & Social Change*, 33: 271–329.

Jackson, J., Bradford, B., Hough, M., Kuha, J., Stares, S., Widdop, S., Fitzgerald, R., Yordanova, M. and Galev, T. (2011). "Developing European indicators of trust in justice." *European Journal of Criminology*, 8 (4): 267–85.

Jackson, J., Bradford, B., Hough, M. and Murray, K.H. (2013a). "Compliance with the law and policing by consent: notes on police and legal legitimacy." In Crawford, A. and Hucklesby, A. (eds), *Legitimacy and Compliance in Criminal Justice* (29–49). Abingdon: Routledge.

Jackson, J., Bradford, B., Hough, M., Myhill, A., Quinton, P. and Tyler, T.R. (2012). "Why do people comply with the law? Legitimacy and the influence of legal institutions." *British Journal of Criminology*, 52 (6): 1051–71.

Jackson, J., Bradford, B., Stanko, B. and Hohl, K. (2013b). *Just Authority? Trust in the Police in England and Wales*. Abingdon: Routledge.

Jackson, J., Kuha, J., Hough, M., Bradford, B., Hohl, K. and Gerber, M.M. (2013c). *Trust and Legitimacy across Europe: A FIDUCIA Report on Comparative Public Attitudes towards Legal Authority*. Available at http://eprints.lse.ac.uk/50650/.

Kautt, P. (2011). "Public confidence in the British police: negotiating the signals from Anglo-American research." *International Criminal Justice Review*, 21 (4): 353–82.

Leung, K. (1987). "Some determinants of reactions to procedural models for conflict resolution: a cross-national study." *Journal of Personality and Social Psychology*, 53 (5): 898–908.

Leung, K. and Lind, E.A. (1986). "Procedural justice and culture: effects of culture, gender, and investigator status on procedural preferences." *Journal of Personality and Social Psychology*, 50 (6): 1134–40.

Leventhal, G.S. (1976a). "Fairness in social relationships." In Thibaut, J.W., Spence, J.T. and Carson, R.C. (eds), *Contemporary Topics in Social Psychology* (211–39). Morristown, NJ: General Learning Press.

——(1976b). "The distribution of rewards and resources in groups and organisations." In Berkowitz, L. and Walster, E. (eds), *Advances in Experimental Social Psychology vol. 9* (91–131). London: Academic Press.

——(1980). "What should be done with equity theory? New approaches to the study of fairness in social relationships." In Gergen, K.J., Greenberg, M.S. and Willis, R.H. (eds), *Social Exchange: Advances in Theory and Research* (27–55). London: Plenum Press.

Levi, M., Tyler, T.R. and Sacks, A. (2012). "The reasons for compliance with law." In Goodman, R., Jinks, D. and Woods, A.K. (eds), *Understanding Social Action, Promoting Human Rights* (70–99). New York: Oxford University Press.

Lind, E.A. and Tyler, T.R. (1988). *The Social Psychology of Procedural Justice*. New York: Plenum Press.

Lind, E.A., Tyler, T.R. and Huo, Y.J. (1997). "Procedural context and culture: variation in the antecedents of procedural justice judgments." *Journal of Personality and Social Psychology*, 73 (4): 767–80.

McCluskey, J.D. (2003). *Police Requests for Compliance: Coercive and Procedurally Just Tactics*. New York: LFB Scholarly Publishing.

MacCoun, R.J. (2005). "Voice, control, and belonging: the double-edged sword of procedural fairness." *Annual Review of Law and Social Science*, 1: 171–201.

Malsch, M. (2009). *Democracy in the Court: Lay Participation in European Criminal Justice Systems*. Aldershot: Ashgate.

Mazerolle, L., Antrobus, E., Bennett, S. and Tyler, T. (2012). "Shaping citizen perceptions of police legitimacy: a randomized field trial of procedural justice." *Criminology*, 51 (1): 33–64.

Meares, T. (2013). "The good cop: knowing the difference between lawful or effective policing and rightful policing – and why it matters." *William & Mary Law Review*, 54 (6): 1865–86.

Menkel-Meadow, C.J. (2010). "Dispute resolution." In Cane, P. and Kritzer, H.M. (eds), *The Oxford Handbook of Empirical Legal Research* (596–624). Oxford: Oxford University Press.

Meško, G., Reisig, M.D. and Tankebe, J. (2012). "Procedural justice, police legitimacy and public cooperation with legal authorities." *Journal of Criminal Investigation and Criminology*, 63 (2): 112–22.

Morris, A. (2002). "Critiquing the critics. A brief response to critics of restorative justice." *British Journal of Criminology*, 42 (3): 596–615.

Murphy, K., Hinds, L. and Fleming, J. (2008). "Encouraging public cooperation and support for police." *Policing and Society*, 18 (2): 136–55.

Myhill, A. and Quinton, P. (2010). "Confidence, neighbourhood policing, and contact: drawing together the evidence." *Policing*, 4 (3): 273–81.

National Research Council (2004). *Fairness and Effectiveness in Policing: The Evidence*. Washington, DC: National Academies Press.

Norrie, A. (1996). "The limits of justice: finding fault in the criminal law." *Modern Law Review*, 59 (4): 540–56.

——(2000). *Punishment, Responsibility and Justice*. Oxford: Oxford University Press.

Ohbuchi, K., Sugawara, I., Teshigahara, K. and Imazai, K. (2005). "Procedural justice and the assessment of civil justice in Japan." *Law & Society Review*, 39 (4): 875–92.

Papachristos, A.V.P., Meares, T.L. and Fagan, J. (2012). "Why do criminals obey the law? The influence of legitimacy and social networks on active gun offenders." *Journal of Criminal Law & Criminology*, 102 (2): 397–440.

Pavlich, G. (2005). *Governing Paradoxes of Restorative Justice*. London: Routledge.

Peachey, D.E. (1986). "Restorative justice in criminal conflict: victims' and observers' perspectives." Unpublished dissertation, University of Waterloo.

Quinton, P. and Morris, J. (2008). *Neighbourhood Policing: The Impact of Piloting and Early National Implementation*. London: Home Office. Available at http://socialwelfare.bl.uk/subject-areas/services-activity/criminal-justice/homeoffice/141882rdsolr0108.pdf

Rawls, J. (1971). *A Theory of Justice*. Cambridge, MA: Harvard University Press.

Reisig, M.D., Bratton, J. and Gertz, M.G. (2007). "The construct validity and refinement of process-based policing measures." *Criminal Justice and Behavior*, 34 (8): 1005–28.

Reisig, M.D., Tankebe, J. and Meško, G. (2013). "Compliance with the law in Slovenia: the role of procedural justice and police legitimacy." *European Journal on Criminal Policy and Research*. Available at http://link.springer.com/article/10.1007% 2Fs10610-013-9211-9#page-1.

Resnik, J. (2013). "Globalization(s), privatization(s), constitutionalization, and statization: icons and experiences of sovereignty in the 21st century." *International Journal of Constitutional Law*, 11 (1): 162–99.

Rosen, F. (1993). "Utilitarianism and justice: a note on Bentham and Godwin." In Parckh, B. (ed.), *Jeremy Bentham: Critical Assessments* (3–8). London: Routledge.

Schluter, M. (1994). "What is relational justice?" In Burnside, J. and Baker, N. (eds), *Relational Justice: Repairing the Breach* (17–27). Winchester: Waterside Press.

Schulhofer, S.J., Tyler, T.R. and Huq, A.Z. (2011). "American policing at a crossroads: unsustainable policies and the procedural justice alternative." *Journal of Criminal Law & Criminology*, 101 (2): 335–74.

Sherman, L.W. (2003). "Reason for emotion: reinventing justice with theories, innovations and research." *Criminology*, 41 (1): 1–37.

Simon, J. (2007). *Governing Through Crime: How the War on Crime Transformed American Democracy and Created a Culture of Fear*. New York: Oxford University Press.

Skogan, W.G. and Hartnett, S.M. (1997). *Community Policing, Chicago Style*. New York: Oxford University Press.

Stuntz, W.J. (2011). *The Collapse of American Criminal Justice*. Cambridge, MA: Belknap Press.

Sunshine, J. and Tyler, T. (2003). "The role of procedural justice and legitimacy in shaping public support for policing." *Law & Society Review*, 37 (3): 513–48.

Thibaut, J. and Walker, L. (1975). *Procedural Justice: A Psychological Analysis*. New Jersey: Lawrence Erlbaum Associates.

——(1978). "A theory of procedure." *California Law Review*, 66 (3): 541–66.

Tuffin, R.J., Morris, J. and Poole, A. (2006). *An Evaluation of the Impact of the National Police Reassurance Programme*. London: Home Office. Available at https://www.gov.uk/government/uploads/system/uploads/attachment_data/file/115825/hors296.pdf

Tyler, T.R. (1987). "Conditions leading to value-expressive effects in judgments of procedural justice: a test of four models." *Journal of Personality and Social Psychology*, 52 (2): 333–44.

——(1989). "The psychology of procedural justice: a test of the group-value model." *Journal of Personality and Social Psychology*, 57 (5): 830–38.

——(1990). *Why People Obey the Law*. Princeton, NJ: Princeton University Press.

——(1999). "Why people cooperate with organizations: an identity-based perspective." *Research in Organizational Behavior*, 21: 201–46.

——(2003). "Procedural justice, legitimacy, and the effective rule of law." *Crime & Justice*, 30: 283–358.

——(2006a). "Psychological perspectives on legitimacy and legitimation." *Annual Review of Psychology*, 57: 375–400.

——(2006b). "Restorative justice and procedural justice: dealing with rule breaking." *Journal of Social Issues*, 62 (2): 307–26.

——(2007). *Psychology and the Design of Legal Institutions*. Nijmegen: Wolf Legal Publishers.

——(2008). "Psychology and institutional design." *Review of Law and Economics*, 4 (3): 801–87.

——(2009a). "Legitimacy and criminal justice: the benefits of self-regulation." *Ohio State Journal of Criminal Justice*, 7 (1): 307–59.

——(2009b). "Procedural justice, identity and deference to the law: what shapes rule-following in a period of transition?" *Australian Journal of Psychology*, 61 (1): 32–9.

——(2011). *Why People Cooperate: The Role of Social Motivations.* Princeton, NJ: Princeton University Press.

——(2012). "Justice theory." In Van Lange, P., Kruglanski, A. and Higgins, T. (eds), *Handbook of Theories of Social Psychology vol. 2* (344–61). Thousand Oaks, CA: Sage.

——(2013). "Legitimacy and compliance: the virtues of self-regulation." In Crawford, A. and Hucklesby, A. (eds), *Legitimacy and Compliance in Criminal Justice* (8–28). Abingdon: Routledge.

Tyler, T.R. and Blader, S.L. (2000). *Cooperation in Groups: Procedural Justice, Social Identity, and Behavioral Engagement.* Philadelphia, PA: Taylor and Francis.

——(2001). "Identity and cooperative behavior in groups." *Group Processes & Intergroup Relations*, 4 (3): 207–26.

——(2003). "The group engagement model: procedural justice, social identity, and cooperative behavior." *Personality and Social Psychology Review*, 7 (4): 349–61.

Tyler, T.R., Degoey, P. and Smith, H. (1996). "Understanding why the justice of group procedures matters: a test of the psychological dynamics of the group-value model." *Journal of Personality and Social Psychology*, 70 (5): 913–30.

Tyler, T.R. and Fagan, J. (2008). "Legitimacy and cooperation: why do people help the police fight crime in their communities?" *Ohio State Journal of Criminal Law*, 6 (1): 231–75.

Tyler, T.R. and Huo, Y.J. (2002). *Trust in the Law: Encouraging Public Cooperation with the Police and Courts.* New York: Russell Sage Foundation.

Tyler, T.R. and Jackson, J. (2013). "Future challenges in the study of legitimacy and criminal justice." In Tankebe, J. and Liebling, A. (eds), *Legitimacy and Criminal Justice: An International Exploration.* Oxford: Oxford University Press.

Tyler, T.R. and Lind, E.A. (1992). "A relational model of authority in groups." In Zanna, M.P. (ed.), *Advances in Experimental Social Psychology vol. 25* (115–91). London: Academic Press.

Tyler, T.R., Rasinski, K.A. and Spodick, N. (1985). "Influence of voice on satisfaction with leaders: exploring the meaning of process control." *Journal of Personality and Social Psychology*, 48 (1): 72–81.

Tyler, T.R., Sherman, L., Strang, H., Barnes, G.C. and Woods, D. (2007). "Reintegrative shaming, procedural justice, and recidivism: the engagement of offenders' psychological mechanisms in the Canberra RISE drinking-and-driving experiment." *Law & Society Review*, 41 (3): 553–86.

Van Camp, T. and Wemmers, J.-A. (2013). "Victim satisfaction with restorative justice: more than simply procedural justice." *International Review of Victimology*, 19 (2): 117–43.

Van Damme, A., Pauwels, L. and Haas, N. (2012). "Exploring the factor structure of measures of confidence in procedural justice and performance of the criminal justice system by actor. A latent-variables approach." In Cools, M., De Ruyver, B., Easton, M., Pauwels, P., Ponsaers, P., Vande Walle, G., Vander Beken, T., Vander Laenen, F., Verhage, A., Vermeulen, G. and Vynckier, G. (eds), *Social Conflicts, Citizens and Policing* (119–40). Antwerp: Maklu.

Walker, L., LaTour, S., Lind, E.A. and Thibaut, J. (1974). "Reactions of participants and observers to modes of adjudication." *Journal of Applied Social Psychology*, 4 (4): 295–310.

Wemmers, J.-A.M. (1996). *Victims in the Criminal Justice System*. Amsterdam: Kugler.

Wilson, J.Q. and Kelling, G.L. (1982). "Broken windows: the police and neighborhood safety." *Atlantic Monthly*, 249 (3): 29–38.

Young, H.P. (1994). *Equity in Theory and Practice*. Princeton, NJ: Princeton University Press.

Zedner, L. (2007). "Pre-crime and post-criminology?" *Theoretical Criminology*, 11 (2): 261–81.

Zehr, H. (2002). *The Little Book of Restorative Justice*. Intercourse, PA: Good Books.

2 Methodology and design of the empirical study

The methodological history of procedural justice research is characterised by the use of quantitative methods. The early years of procedural justice research, specifically the work of Thibaut and Walker (1975, 1978) and their associates, were marked by experimental laboratory designs involving graduate students as study participants. As from the 1980s, a number of studies started to explore procedural justice in real-life settings; these studies used either experimental designs or survey methodologies. The subjects involved were still very often students, though a significant number of studies was conducted on citizens (e.g. Tyler, 1990) or people who experienced decision-making procedures that affected them in real life (e.g. Casper, 1978; Tyler et al., 1985; Casper et al., 1988; Tyler et al., 1999).

These pioneering researchers' choice for experimental and quasi-experimental methodologies is to be understood in light of their goal of detecting cause–effect relationships. Yet already in 1982, Greenberg and Cohen (1982) argued in favour of qualitative methodologies, that is, in-depth interviewing of people in naturalistic situations, 'to allow us to determine what people's motives are for behaving fairly or unfairly' (456). Still very few examples of qualitative studies on procedural justice are available; one notable exception is Van Camp and Wemmers' (2013) study among Belgian and Canadian participants in victim–offender mediation. The current study did make use of a qualitative research design. Moreover, participants were studied in a real-life setting. These and other methodological choices will be explained below.

Data collection: a qualitative study in a naturalistic setting

Motivations for employing a qualitative methodology

For four reasons, a qualitative approach was deemed the most appropriate one for this study. First, only qualitative designs allow asking open-ended questions to the degree considered necessary for the study. An important limitation of justice research, which is due to the widespread use of quantitative methodologies, is that participants' answers are generally prompted by the response categories that are offered. Respondents are usually confronted with a pre-set list of aspects on which to rate a procedure. Yet when using response categories, respondents' attention is directed to those aspects of procedures that are advanced by the researchers and were translated into pre-set response categories. Such studies typically fail to determine whether respondents would have taken each of these aspects into account had they not been suggested to them. Also, people are more likely to endorse answer categories that are explicitly listed than to come up with new answers or categories themselves (Foddy, 1993); therefore, quantitative methodologies are not suitable for verifying if there are aspects of procedures that are taken into account when people make fairness judgements *other* than those that are anticipated by the researchers. This is a first reason why this study was conducted using a qualitative methodology.

Second, (quantitative) studies asking respondents to rate procedures on pre-set aspects break up people's experience into different types of justice. Studies investigating the relationship between procedural justice and distributive justice, for example, typically ask participants to rate the importance of both types of fairness. Such studies' results convey the (possibly false) message that people indeed differentiate between the concepts of distributive justice and procedural justice. Yet Lind (2001) suggests that people may not differentiate between these different types of justice the way justice researchers do. In order to construct an integrated, holistic picture of how people make fairness judgements, participants were invited through open questions to reflect about their experience with the criminal justice system. This is not to deny that in the data analysis phase, the stories of those participating to this study too were broken up into categories (see below); this is customary for qualitative interview studies. Yet great care was taken to prevent overreliance on previously defined categories of procedural justice during the categorisation process – as will be explained below, other researchers were for this very reason asked to check or repeat the categorisation process. Furthermore, because participants' full stories were available it was no problem for new categories to emerge from the data. Finally, since the researcher was well acquainted with the totality of each of the participants' stories, links and connections between the categories did not get lost in the categorisation process.

Third, a qualitative methodology was most likely to advance the goal of making the key concepts of procedural justice theory more concrete. The concepts of voice, standing, trust and neutrality have remained quite abstract, as the meaning of the concepts has been determined by researchers. A qualitative approach is more promising in terms of examining lay meanings of these concepts. This point has been elaborated on in the previous chapter.

Fourth, the research concerns an issue that relates to morality, ethics, and difficult and emotional experiences. Qualitative designs allow the researcher to explain why certain questions are asked; this is important when a topic is potentially threatening to participants. Also, they allow the researcher to set people at ease and they allow participants to explain their opinions and clarify why they take the position(s) they take, which is indispensable because moral issues can seldom be explained in black-and-white terms.

All this is not to suggest that other researchers in opting for quantitative designs have selected the wrong designs. In view of the fact that many of them aimed to construct general laws about how people make justice judgements, their choice for experimental designs was understandable and justified. The use of quantitative designs has been crucial to the development of procedural justice theory. Yet for the specific purposes of this study a qualitative strategy was developed.

Participant selection and recruitment

The data for this study were collected from people who personally encountered the criminal justice system as a victim or defendant. Participants were accessed through a victim–offender mediation organisation. In Belgium, different types of mediation exist. The particular type of mediation that the participants to this study had been approached for is called mediation for redress pre-sentence.[1] The reason for selecting participants in this specific type of mediation is that this is the only type of mediation that does not lead to the charges against the defendant being dropped if successful. After the mediation process has been concluded, independent of whether it resulted in a (written) agreement or if the defendant keeps to the agreement, the defendant is brought to trial. This was important given the goal of interviewing victims and defendants both before and after trial (see below).[2] For the sake of this study, data were collected from victims and offenders who were invited to participate in mediation for redress and who decided to take the offer. Those victims and defendants who did not receive the offer and those who received the offer but declined it were not selected for this study.[3]

In Flanders, the Dutch-speaking part of Belgium where this study took place, mediation for redress is organised by the NGO Suggnomè.[4] Suggnomè is recognised and subsidised by the Belgian federal Ministry of Justice and the Flemish Community. Suggnomè operates in each of the fourteen Flemish judicial districts. Four districts were involved in the study – in order to protect participants' privacy, the names of the participating districts will not be disclosed. Since all potential participants in the study (i.e. victims and defendants involved in a case that the prosecutor decided to bring to trial[5] and who were willing to participate in mediation) would encounter mediators working for Suggnomè, sometime soon after the prosecutor had decided to prosecute the defendant, a cooperative arrangement was set up with Suggnomè to approach potential participants.

The selection of participants took place according to the principles of purposive criterion sampling. Purposive criterion sampling entails selecting a number of particularly information-rich cases for in-depth study (Patton, 2002; Hesse-Biber and Leavy, 2010). It is a sampling procedure that allows specifically selecting those cases that the researcher believes will serve the particular purpose of the study, instead of randomly selecting a wide variety of cases, many of which will most probably be irrelevant to the research question(s). The information-rich cases are determined on the basis of pre-set criteria. The first criterion that guided the selection procedure for this study was the potential participant's decision to take the offer of participation in mediation; this was explained above. The second criterion related to the type of cases to be included in the study. All types of violent crime, property crime and sexual offences were included in the study; traffic offences and cases that would be tried by an Assize Court (which implies a jury trial) were excluded. The reason for excluding traffic offences was that in these cases, victim and offender roles are not always clearly discernible, nor are those who unintentionally cause traffic accidents perceived as offenders the way those who intentionally commit crime are. Assize cases (these are generally murder cases) were excluded because of the length of time involved in bringing such cases to court; the likelihood that these cases would be completely processed before the end of the study was small. Note that the types of crime involved in mediation for redress are considered serious crimes.[6] As said, this type of mediation is offered in those cases that the public prosecutor has decided should go to trial. Given the fact that public prosecutors in Belgium have discretionary power in deciding which cases should go to trial, these are the crimes that are considered the most serious. Moreover, defendants who committed crimes that should, according to the prosecutor, not be punished by a sentence of two or more years of imprisonment are offered a different type of mediation that, if successful, leads to the charges being dropped. This is another indication of the gravity of the offences that *are* referred to mediation for redress. Information on the specific type of offences that the participants were involved in is provided later on in this chapter.

As the privacy of all those participating in mediation was to be protected, the selection of cases appropriate for inclusion in the study was not in the hands of the author but of the mediators collaborating in the study. During their first meeting with victims and offenders interested in mediation, the mediators asked these victims and offenders if they would be willing to participate in the study. Those expressing an interest in the study allowed the mediator to pass their contact details to the author and were contacted by the author some days later.

Data collection method: the use of semi-structured interviews

The data for this study were collected through in-depth interviews. To the extent possible, participants were interviewed twice: once before the trial and once after the trial (for reasons that will be explained below, some participants could not be interviewed after the trial). Given the purpose of understanding how people make fairness judgements based on their experience with the criminal justice system, participants were selected at the very start of this experience and were reinterviewed at the end of the experience. Importantly, as Tyler and Lind (2001) point out, few studies on procedural justice studies have used pre- and post-tests (one notable exception is Tyler et al., 1999).

Most procedural justice research has examined only post-experience evaluations. The current study did look into participants' pre- and post-experience
fairness judgements. The interviews were semi-structured interviews. An
interview guide containing the key questions to be posed to the respondents
was used during the interviews. A specific advantage of semi-structured
interviews as opposed to highly structured interviews is that though the
researcher takes care to ask all questions listed in the interview guide, there is
ample room for interviewees to add information on relevant topics that the
researcher had not anticipated (Hesse-Biber and Leavy, 2010). It was indeed
crucial to this study not to exclude in advance any elements that might shape
respondents' evaluations of their experience with the criminal justice system.

The pre-trial interviews focused on four themes: (1) respondents' experience
with the police; (2) respondents' experience with the judiciary; (3) respondents' experience with mediation; and (4) respondents' opinion about the
desired outcome of the trial. Respondents were also invited to talk about their
expectations of the trial. Each interview began with an opening question
asking respondents to inform the interviewer about the crime ('what happened?') and a number of transitory questions meant to gain insight into
respondents' general attitudes towards the criminal justice system and their
prior experiences with the criminal justice system. The key questions focused
on respondents' experiences with the police, with mediation and with the
judiciary. Broad, open questions invited respondents to talk about their
experiences with the people they had met. The interviewer was careful not to
prompt any specific elements that have been advanced by procedural justice
theories. The last set of key questions enquired about respondents' opinions
about punishment. Defendants were asked whether they felt that they
deserved to be punished, and, if so, which punishment they thought would be
the most appropriate. Victims were asked which punishment they considered
the most appropriate for the defendant that was apprehended in their case.
Near the end of each interview, the respondents were invited to reflect about a
number of statements (e.g. 'Regardless of what the law prescribes, I think the
only just verdict/sentence in this case is the verdict/sentence that I consider the
most appropriate'; 'If I feel that I have been treated fairly in this case, it will
be easier for me to accept a verdict/sentence that does not match the verdict/
sentence that I have in mind'). These statements were far from straightfor-
ward and as such served to make respondents' implicit assumptions more
explicit. The interviews were closed by inviting respondents to add extra
topics to make sure that no relevant aspects of their experience with the
police, the criminal justice system or mediation had been overlooked.

The post-trial interviews served to define the determinants of respondents'
evaluations of the trial. The main topics addressed during these interviews
were: (1) the respondents' court experience; (2) the respondents' opinion on
the verdict/sentence; and (3) the respondents' experience with mediation.
These interviews started off with a broad, open question: respondents were
asked 'What would you start with when asked how this experience has been

for you?' Their experiences with mediation and the trial were discussed, as was their opinion on the verdict and sentence. After the concrete events had been discussed, respondents were confronted with more wide-ranging questions. They were asked, for example, which lessons they had learned from their experience, if they had any advice for people who would have to go through the same experience, whether there was something that with hindsight they would have done differently during the process and whether they had any suggestions for concrete improvements to be made to the criminal justice system. Finally, the respondents were invited to add extra topics and asked if they had any questions about the study.

At the end of each interview (both pre-trial and post-trial), respondents were asked to complete a short questionnaire asking them to reflect on a number of elements of procedural justice as they would apply to the court phase. For example, they were asked to indicate, on Likert scales, the importance of the judge respecting their dignity (an aspect of standing) or the judge taking the time to examine their case file carefully (an aspect of neutrality). The analysis of the data gathered through these questionnaires showed no significant differences between victims and offenders as to which aspects of procedural justice they thought were the most important. The quantitative results, therefore, are not reported in this book. Yet participants were encouraged to reflect on the statements aloud while filling out the survey, and their reflections did lead to some useful data and insights. These will be touched upon below in the description of results.

All 79 interviews were conducted by the author and all were conducted in-person. The pre-trial interviews lasted on average 65 minutes; the post-trial interviews lasted on average 76 minutes. All participants were free to choose a time and date for the interview and were offered a choice on where to conduct the interviews. Most interviews took place at participants' homes (N = 62). The other interviews took place either in another participant's home (N = 1; two accomplices were interviewed together), in the author's office (N = 5), in the participant's office (N = 4), in prison where the defendant was in pre-trial detention or imprisoned as a consequence of another crime (N = 5) or in a meeting room in one of Suggnomè's buildings (N = 2). All interviews except one were conducted in Dutch (one interview was conducted in French).

Data processing and analysis

Data analysis started with the literal transcription of the audio recordings of the interviews. All interviews were audio-recorded by means of a digital audio-recording device (all participants explicitly agreed to this) and transcribed by the author. The transcripts were entered into the qualitative data analysis software package NVivo (QSR International). The data analysis proceeded through a method of coding and categorising consisting of three phases called respectively open coding, axial coding and selective coding (see, among others, Flick, 2006 and Kvale and Brinkmann, 2009). In the first phase, all elements that were mentioned by victims and offenders when talking about their experience with the police or the criminal authorities were coded. Next, each of these codes was closely examined in order to decide whether the fragments coded related to one of the antecedents of procedural justice defined by prior research (i.e. standing, trust, neutrality or voice). Additional categories were added when codes did not fit any of these categories. As such, a tree of codes originated indicating which factors had influenced participants' fairness judgements.

In order to test whether it had been justified to use the procedural justice framework to analyse the data (i.e. to find out whether using this framework had hindered the author from being receptive to new categories emerging from the data), four other researchers were asked to check the analysis of the data. The open coding work was checked by one researcher unfamiliar with procedural justice theory; this person was asked to read through the fragments coded under one and the same code and to consider whether the label covered the contents well. The axial coding work was checked by three researchers, in two ways. Two researchers unfamiliar with procedural justice theory organised all the codes emerging from the open coding phase into general categories; the goal was to find out whether these people would come to the same categories that the author had identified. The categories they created indeed turned out to be very similar. Finally, one researcher highly acquainted with procedural justice theory was asked to organise the codes emerging from the open coding process into the categories standing, trust and neutrality and to create extra categories if needed or eliminate redundant ones. Afterwards the coding work was compared; it was found to be highly similar.

Description of the participants

Pre-trial interviews

Gender, age, nationality and victim/offender status

A total of 54 people participated in the study. Sixteen participants were female and 38 were male. Thirty-one of them had been a victim of crime; 23 were to stand trial for committing a crime. Respondents' ages ranged from 15 to 76. All respondents except one were of Belgian nationality (one respondent was a Dutch citizen). Table 2.1 shows this distribution.

Table 2.1 Pre-trial interview participants: gender and victim/offender status

	Victim	*Offender*	*Total*
Male	17	21	38
Female	14	2	16
Total	31	23	54

Table 2.2 Pre-trial interview participants: participation in mediation

	Victim	*Offender*	*Total*
Participant	15	14	29
Non-participant*	16	9	25
Total	31	23	54

*Did not participate in mediation because the other party refused.

Participation in mediation

As Table 2.2 shows, 29 of the 54 participants (15 victims; 14 offenders) participated in mediation for redress pre-sentence. Seventeen of them participated in direct mediation, which means that there was at least one face-to-face meeting between the victim and the offender; 12 participated in shuttle mediation, which means that the mediator functioned as a go-between, communicating messages from the victim to the offender and vice versa. Note that at the time of the study, 20 per cent of the total number of cases dealt with by Suggnomè involved direct mediation (Suggnomè, 2009).

Relationship between victim and offender

Twelve of the 31 victims had been victimised by a stranger; 19 victims had a previous relation with the offender. They had been victimised by their husband (N = 2) or ex-husband/partner (N = 2), their mother (N = 1) or stepfather (N = 2), a friend or acquaintance (N = 5), a love rival (N = 1), their brother (N = 1), an employee (N = 3) or a neighbour (N = 2). Sixteen offenders had victimised a stranger; seven had victimised someone they knew. They had victimised either their wife (N = 1), their child or a stepchild (N = 3), a love rival (N = 1), a friend or acquaintance (N = 1) or their employer (N = 1). This means that overall 28 cases involved a victim and offender who were strangers to each other and 26 cases involved victims and offenders who had a prior relationship. The Suggnomè data for 2008 (Suggnomè, 2009), which is the year this study started, show that 43 per cent of the cases that were referred to mediation in 2008 involved strangers.

Type of crimes

Thirty-one respondents (57 per cent) had been involved in a crime against a person (including sexual offences); fourteen people (26 per cent) had been involved in a property crime. The other nine respondents (17 per cent) had been involved in a property crime involving violence (i.e. street robbery) (see Table 2.3). It is not surprising that most crimes were violent crimes; according to the 2009 annual report of Suggnomè, in 2008 more crimes against a person were referred to mediation than property crimes (N = 577 crimes against a person (including sexual offences) versus 424 cases of property crime). The types of crime that mediators were most often confronted with at the time of the study

Table 2.3 Pre-trial interview participants: type of crime

Type of crime	N
Crimes against a person	*31*
Intentional and unintentional assault and battery	23
Partner violence	2
Sexual offences	4
Stalking	2
Property crimes	*14*
Fraud	1
Burglary and theft	13
Property crimes involving violence	*9*
Violent theft, (street) robbery	9
Total	*54*

were cases of intentional assault and battery (N = 244 out of 1,056 in 2008) and all kinds of theft (including breaking and entering) (N = 282 out of 1,056 in 2008). This distribution is reflected in the current study's group of participants.

Timing of interviews

Due to large differences in timing of decisions on prosecution between judicial districts, the period of time that passed between the crime and the pre-trial interviews varied. Usually the interview took place four to six months after the facts, but there were cases in which more than one year had passed. Each pre-trial interview took place within two to three weeks after respondents had had their first meeting with a mediator.

Post-trial interviews

Gender, age, nationality and victim/offender status

Twenty-five people participated in the post-trial interviews. Fifteen were victims, ten were offenders. This means that the relative distribution of victims and offenders (60 per cent victims, 40 per cent offenders) was about the same as the pre-trial interview distribution (57 per cent victims, 43 per cent offenders). Eight of the participants to the post-trial interviews were female and 15 were male. This distribution too reflects the distribution of the pre-trial interviews. Details can be found in Table 2.4. Respondents' ages ranged from 15 to 76. All respondents were Belgian.

Table 2.4 Post-trial interview participants: gender and victim/offender status

	Victim	Offender	Total
Male	7	8	15
Female	8	2	10
Total	15	10	25

As can be deduced from Table 2.4, only about half of the respondents were reinterviewed after the trial. The most important reason why not all participants could be reinterviewed after the trial was that at the time the data collection for this study had to be brought to an end, several cases had not gone to trial yet. This happened in 12 cases. In three cases, the victim had not registered as a civil party or injured person[7] and was therefore never informed of the day of the trial. For this reason, no post-trial interview could be conducted. Four respondents either said that they were not interested in a second interview or that they wanted to leave everything behind them after the trial and thus preferred not to talk about it anymore. In four cases, the public prosecutor or an investigating court decided to drop the charges after all, which was not anticipated, so there was no trial. In five cases, the author was unable to recontact the respondent, even after several phone calls and having sent a letter. Finally, one of the respondents was to be interviewed together with his wife (a respondent too), but was too busy on the day of the interview to attend the interview.

Participation in mediation

Sixteen of the 25 participants in the post-trial interviews had participated in mediation. Ten of these had met the other party face to face; the other six had participated in shuttle mediation. Table 2.5 shows the detailed results. While the group of participants in the pre-trial interviews was more or less evenly distributed between participants who did and participants who did not take part in mediation (29 as compared to 25), during the post-trial interviews people who did participate in mediation were clearly in the majority.

Relationship between victim and offender

Five of the 15 victims participating in the post-trial interviews had been victimised by a stranger. The other ten knew their offender before the crime. They had been victimised by their mother (N = 1) or stepfather (N = 2), their husband (N = 1) or ex-husband/partner (N = 1), their brother (N = 1), an employee (N = 2), a neighbour (N = 1) or an acquaintance (N = 1). Four of the ten offenders participating in these interviews had victimised a stranger. The others had victimised a love rival (N = 1), an acquaintance (N = 1), their employer (N = 1), their wife (N = 1) or their stepchild (N = 2). Comparing these numbers to those of the pre-trial interviews makes clear that more of the

Table 2.5 Post-trial interview participants: participation in mediation

	Victim	*Offender*	*Total*
Participant	8	8	16
Non-participant	7	2	9
Total	15	10	25

Table 2.6 Post-trial interview participants: type of crime

Type of crime	N
Crimes against a person	*14*
Intentional and unintentional assault and battery	8
Partner violence	2
Sexual offences	4
Stalking	0
Property crimes	*8*
Fraud	1
Burglary and theft	7
Property crimes involving violence	*3*
Violent theft, (street) robbery	3
Total	*25*

participants in the post-trial interviews had been involved in a case where the other party was someone they knew. This is the main difference between the group of participants in the pre-trial interviews and the group of participants in the post-trial interviews.

Type of crimes

As Table 2.6 shows, fourteen of the 25 participants (56 per cent) in the post-trial interviews had been involved in a crime against a person (including sexual offences). Eight of them (32 per cent) had been involved in a property crime and three (12 per cent) had been involved in a property crime involving violence (i.e. street robbery). This distribution reflects the distribution of the pre-trial interviews.

Timing of interviews

On average, one to four months passed in between the trial and the post-trial interviews. One should know that the court pronounces its judgment some two to four weeks after the trial. After that, there was some delay in some cases due to, for example, the respondent not finding the time to go to the courthouse to search for a copy of the judgment, respondent illness, or the respondent being too busy with work, making it difficult to set a date for the interview.

Table 2.7 below offers an overview of the participant group.

Table 2.7 Overview of participant characteristics

	Total group	Status		Participation in mediation	
		Victim	Offender	Yes	No
Pre-trial interviews	54	31	23	29	25
Post-trial interviews	25	15	10	16	9

Notes

1 From here on, the word 'mediation' refers to mediation for redress pre-sentence.
2 For more information on this type of mediation, see Aertsen and Peters (1998) and Aertsen (2000, 2004).
3 This choice was inspired by the aims of the wider study of which this book reports one part. As one of the research questions – that is not reported on in this book – aimed to explore the relationship between participation in a restorative justice programme and perceptions of procedural justice, only those people who accepted the offer of mediation were selected. Those declining the offer or those who did not receive the offer would not sufficiently serve that particular purpose of the study, given their lack of experience with mediation. While this methodological choice may have affected the results of this study that concerned participants' experience with mediation – this issue has been reflected upon in detail elsewhere (see De Mesmaecker, 2013a, 2013b) – it does not discount the value of the results reported in this book.
4 The name Suggnomè is derived from the Greek word sun-gnomè. In modern Greek, it means 'agreement' or 'sorry', but in ancient Greek it was a verb referring to the process of creating a shared understanding of reality. The focus was not on the agreement itself, as in modern Greek, but on the process of creating it. This is the particular meaning of the word that Suggnomè wishes to stress (this information is available at Suggnomè's website, see http://www.suggnome.be).
5 In Belgium, public prosecutors have a discretionary power in bringing criminal charges; they are not obliged to bring charges to all criminal cases that are brought to their attention.
6 Most of the cases that Suggnomè dealt with in 2012 – these are the most recent data available at the time of writing; data of previous years indicate similar trends – concerned crimes against a person (38.4 per cent of the cases; these were mainly cases of assault and battery) and property crimes (31.7 per cent of the cases; these were mainly violent theft cases and burglary cases). Mediation was also performed in sexual offence cases (13.6% of the cases; these were mainly cases of indecent assault of minors and rape of minors), in cases concerning crimes against one's family (mainly cases relating to violations of visitation rights; 1.7 per cent of the cases) and in traffic offence cases (mostly cases of deadly traffic accidents; 14.6 per cent of the cases). See Suggnomè (2012).
7 Victims' right to be informed about certain steps of the criminal procedure depends on whether they registered as a civil party or an 'injured person'. As a civil party, the victim becomes a party in the proceedings. As such, they are informed of all the major steps in the procedure. Victims can also decide to register as an 'injured person'. If they do, they have a right to be informed (1) in case the prosecutor decides not to prosecute the offender; (2) in case an investigating judge is appointed to investigate the case; and (3) about the date of the trial. This is especially helpful for those victims who do not wish to act as a civil party but still want to be informed about the trial and the most important decisions that are taken in their case. Note, first, that unless victims undertake steps to register as a civil party or injured person, they are not by default informed of any of the decisions taken. Note, second, that unlike the original Dutch and French terms ('benadeelde persoon/partie lésée'), the translation ('injured person') may wrongfully give the impression that only victims of violent crime can register as an injured person. Yet all those who have suffered damage of any kind (emotional, financial, physical) can do so.

References

Aertsen, I. (2000). "Victim–offender mediation in Belgium." In European Forum for Victim–offender Mediation and Restorative Justice (ed.), *Victim–Offender Mediation in Europe. Making Restorative Justice Work* (153–92). Leuven: Leuven University Press.

——(2004). *Slachtoffer-daderbemiddeling. Een onderzoek naar de ontwikkeling van een herstelgerichte strafrechtsbedeling.* Leuven: Leuven University Press.

Aertsen, I. and Peters, T. (1998). "Mediation for reparation: the victim's perspective." In Fattah, E. and Peters, T. (eds), *Support for Crime Victims in a Comparative Perspective* (229–51). Leuven: Leuven University Press.

Casper, J.D. (1978). "Having their day in court: defendant evaluations of the fairness of their treatment." *Law and Society Review*, 12 (2): 237–51.

Casper, J.D., Tyler, T. and Fisher, B. (1988). "Procedural justice in felony cases." *Law and Society Review*, 22 (3): 483–508.

De Mesmaecker, V. (2013a). "'Dat we op zo'n menselijke manier hebben kunnen praten'. Ervaringen met herstelbemiddeling in Vlaanderen." *Panopticon*, 34 (1): 19–41.

——(2013b). "Legitimiteit via procedurele rechtvaardigheid: kunnen herstelrechtelijke praktijken de maatschappelijke legitimiteit van het strafrecht verhogen?" *Tijdschrift voor Veiligheid*, 12 (2): 10–25.

Flick, U. (2006). *An Introduction to Qualitative Research.* London: Sage.

Foddy, W. (1993). *Constructing Questions for Interviews and Questionnaires. Theory and Practice in Social Research.* Cambridge: Cambridge University Press.

Greenberg, J. and Cohen, R.L. (1982). "Why justice? Normative and instrumental interpretations." In Greenberg, J. and Cohen, R.L. (eds), *Equity and Justice in Social Behaviour* (437–69). New York: Academic Press.

Hesse-Biber, S.N. and Leavy, P. (2010). *The Practice of Qualitative Research.* London: Sage.

Kvale, S. and Brinkmann, S. (2009). *Interviews. Learning the Craft of Qualitative Research Interviewing.* London: Sage.

Lind, E.A. (2001). "Thinking critically about justice judgments." *Journal of Vocational Behavior*, 58 (2): 220–6.

Patton, M.Q. (2002). *Qualitative Research and Evaluation Methods.* London: Sage.

Suggnomè v.z.w. (2009). *Jaarverslag 2009.* Available at www.herstelrecht.be/jaarver slag/jaarverslagsuggnome_2009.pdf

——(2012). *Jaarverslag 2012.* Available at www.herstelrecht.be/jaarverslag/jaarver slagsuggnome_2012.pdf.

Thibaut, J. and Walker, L. (1975). *Procedural Justice. A Psychological Analysis.* New Jersey: Lawrence Erlbaum Associates.

——(1978). "A theory of procedure." *California Law Review*, 66 (3): 541–66.

Tyler, T.R. (1990). *Why People Obey the Law.* Princeton, NJ: Princeton University Press.

Tyler, T.R., Huo, Y.J. and Lind, E.A. (1999). "The two psychologies of conflict resolution: differing antecedents of pre-experience choices and post-experience evaluations." *Group Processes and Intergroup Relations*, 2 (2): 99–118.

Tyler, T.R. and Lind, E.A. (2001). "Procedural justice." In Sanders, J. and Hamilton, V.L. (eds), *Handbook of Justice Research in Law* (65–92). New York: Plenum Press.

Tyler, T.R., Rasinski, K.A. and Spodick, N. (1985). "Influence of voice on satisfaction with leaders: exploring the meaning of process control." *Journal of Personality and Social Psychology*, 48 (1): 72–81.

Van Camp, T. and Wemmers, J.-A. (2013). "Victim satisfaction with restorative justice: more than simply procedural justice." *International Review of Victimology*, 19 (2): 117–43.

Part II

The perceived fairness of criminal proceedings

3 Perceptions of procedural justice in encounters with the police

The three chapters that comprise Part II of this book provide a description of the criteria used by the participants to assess the procedural fairness of their encounters with the police (this chapter), with those magistrates that play a role in the investigation of the case (i.e. the public prosecutor and the investigating judge; Chapter 4) and with the courts (Chapter 5). The aim of these three chapters is twofold. Their first aim is to make the concepts that procedural justice literature has advanced as the determinants of people's procedural justice judgements (i.e. the concepts of standing, voice, trust and neutrality) more concrete. Their second aim is to detect if any elements of people's experiences that influence their fairness judgements have been overlooked by previous procedural justice research or should be added to a theory of procedural justice as it applies to criminal justice. The findings reported in these chapters will be illustrated with quotes extracted from the interviews. The quotes are accompanied by an identification of the participant by gender, victim/offender status, type of offence and whether or not the participant engaged in mediation. Such participation, as described above, may have taken place either face to face or in an indirect manner (with the mediator going back and forth between the parties). The quotes were translated from Dutch and French, as the interviews were conducted in those languages.

This chapter describes the elements that determined participants' assessments of the procedural fairness of the police. The three elements that were found to determine these assessments were perceptions of standing, perceptions of the neutrality of the police, and opinions about police performance. Below, the detailed results for each of these elements will be described. Note that trust was not retained as a determinant of perceptions of procedural justice; the reason for this will be explained in Chapter 6.

Standing

The two defining elements of standing according to Tyler and Lind (1992: 141), who introduced the concept, are 'being treated politely and with dignity' and 'respect is shown for one's rights and opinions'. The analysis of the interviews conducted for the sake of the current study suggests a different set of subcomponents, i.e. (1) respect for dignity (see Tyler and Lind, 1992); (2) respect for rights (see Tyler and Lind, 1992); (3) concern for needs; and (4) social standing. The latter category is new to procedural justice research. The category 'concern for needs' was also advanced by Tyler and Lind, yet they considered 'concern for needs' to be a subcomponent of 'trust'. The interview fragments relating to the police showing care for the needs of the participants, however, suggest that such an experience is in fact an antecedent of perceptions of standing. This will become clear as the results on this category are presented below.

Respect for dignity

This section presents the elements of people's experience that influenced their perception of whether the police had treated them in a manner that made them feel respected. A first element, mentioned by one victim and two offenders, concerns whether one received food and drinks during the interrogation or, for offenders specifically, while one was held in custody at the police station.

> So then they [the police officers who arrested him] took me to the police station and interrogated me. I have no complaints about them; they gave me something to drink and in the evening they got dinner for me. I hadn't had anything to eat yet, so they went out and got me some takeaway food.
>
> (Male offender, sexual abuse
> (respondent 53), participant)

An event that had had a great influence on several offenders' feelings of dignity is whether they had been handcuffed upon arrest or during transportation from the police station to the prosecutor's office or the investigating judge's office. Seven offenders mentioned this issue; two of them in fact mentioned it in reply to the question which of the events of their pre-trial experience had affected them the most. As to why they thought the handcuffing was problematic, a number of them explained that being handcuffed reduces a person's identity to that of 'a criminal'. One's multidimensional identity of being a husband, a father, a colleague and so on is reduced to a one-dimensional one, marked exclusively by the label 'criminal'.

> R1: [respondent's wife] (...) this has branded him as a criminal, you know, they [the police] made him feel like he's some kind of gangster, being put in jail like that ...
> R2: ... wearing those handcuffs ... That really made me feel ... yeah ...
>
> (Male offender, violent theft and threat of arson
> (respondent 24), non-participant)

One participant said his problem with being handcuffed was that the police officers had insisted on handcuffing him in the presence of his children; they had refused to consent to his proposal to handcuff him outside the house. The same participant associated being handcuffed with a young generation of police officers and with reluctance of the police to resolve the situation in a serene manner.

> Older police officers first talk to people and calm them down and then ask them to come to the police station with them (...). That's not how the younger generation works. The young ones immediately use handcuffs – well, at least if they manage to handle those handcuffs.
> (Male offender, intentional assault and battery
> (respondent 31), participant)

A related issue is offenders' feeling of having been treated in a manner that does not at all match who they are. Seven offenders – mainly people who were accused of relatively minor offences that happened accidentally or unwittingly – felt undignified because they had been treated – in their own words – 'as if I was a big criminal', whereas they actually had a clean criminal record and perceived themselves as law-abiding citizens who just made one little mistake. Some explained that they felt like their one-time encounter with the police had left the stamp 'criminal' on them.

> You know, I never had any contact with the police or anything before, and all of a sudden, because of one interrogation, bam, I get branded as a criminal.
> (Male offender, intentional assault and battery
> (respondent 26), participant)

When asked to describe the attitude of the police officers they had encountered, most victims reported positive attitudes. Offenders' opinions about the police's attitude were more negative. Victims mainly ascribed positive characteristics to the police officers they had met, such as friendliness, politeness, fairness, understanding, compassion and sympathy and being concerned about the victim. Understanding and empathy especially were important to the victims. Some victims said that they could not imagine the police not being polite to them; they said it is police officers' duty to be courteous and respectful to victims.

> I assume police officers are trained to do so. (...) I can't imagine that they wouldn't first of all take care of the victims, offer them a drink and try to put them at ease.
> (Female victim of intentional assault and battery
> (respondent 1), non-participant)

> The police treated me well and really, that is so important. Imagine they would just sit people down somewhere and neglect them or be brutal to people ...
> (Male victim of intentional assault and battery
> (respondent 12), non-participant)

One victim described how a police officer had laughed in her face when she filed a complaint and had treated her arrogantly. She also reported police officers behaving scornfully and condescendingly, judging her lifestyle and her parenting style.

> (...) we really didn't get along, this person [the police officer] and me. At all. He clearly had his own opinion about the matter and he acted all disdainfully.
>
> (Mother of male victim of intentional assault and battery
> (respondent 30), participant)

To victims, the way they are treated by the police is important with a view to acknowledgement of the offence and acknowledgement of their status as a victim. Four victims complained that the police did not take the offence seriously. A victim of stalking explained how the police laugh at her when she reports new facts of stalking. Another victim said that the police had not shown any sense of understanding of her problems, which had the far-reaching consequence that she felt treated as if she was the offender.

> They practically laughed at me each time I went in to report new facts. When I came there to report that he had called me 104 times in 75 minutes, they were like: 'okay, so'?
>
> (Female victim of stalking
> (respondent 18), non-participant)

Another indicator of whether or not the police take the case seriously is whether they put much effort into trying to find the offender. Several victims of offenders whose identity was clear from the start had been stunned by the fact that the police did not arrest the offender immediately after they had reported the offence. One victim explicitly associated this with 'not taking the case seriously'. Another participant explained that she had called the police to report the offence and had agreed to come to the police station in person later on; when she had not arrived at the police station an hour after the phone call the police had called her to ask what was keeping her. To her, this was an indication that they took the facts seriously. Yet another participant stated that the police had only started to take her story seriously after they had visited the offender at home and had been threatened by him themselves.

A second aspect of victim acknowledgement is acknowledgement of the victim as victim. Two victims reported that they had never considered themselves 'a victim' until the police had made them realise that they were.

> They helped me with everything I needed help with and they said: 'this has to stop, you have to get help for yourself and for your kids'. In the past I never did anything about my situation. They really opened my eyes.
>
> (Female victim of rape
> (respondent 38), participant)

Victims furthermore attach great importance to the police believing their story. One victim upon reporting an offence was explicitly asked by the police 'whether she was aware that she could be sued for falsely reporting offences to the police' – the police openly expressed doubt about her story – and a couple that had been burgled described how they went to the police station to recover their belongings but could not recover things that the thieves said were theirs. All three victims were upset by their experience.

> The police came, I opened the door and the first thing they said was: 'so, miss, are you absolutely sure about what you are about to report? You do realise that if you report things that aren't true we can prosecute you for that?'
>
> (Female victim of stalking
> (respondent 18), non-participant)

Another aspect of victim acknowledgement concerns what is known in the literature as 'blaming the victim': six participants talked about whether the police had blamed them for the offence. One person explained that when she had telephoned the police about the offence she had been told that what had happened was her own fault. Being held responsible for the offence had made her so angry that she decided not to officially report the offence (for the sake of clarity: this concerned another offence than the one that led to the interview).

> I called the police (...) and they said 'well ma'am, surely you know you shouldn't exchange money on the street, that's not wise. Everybody knows that.' When they said that to me I got so angry (...). I felt so small. I didn't report it.
>
> (Female victim of burglary and theft
> (respondent 52), non-participant)

The acknowledgement of victim status also relates to the police's attitude towards victims who repeatedly report offences. A couple who were frequently bullied by their neighbour at the time of the study talked about how the police were getting annoyed with them. A victim of stalking too said that the police seemed to think that she was having pleasure in calling them as often as she did, and one person said that the police clearly thought 'that she was calling them every day on purpose'. In this respect, one victim said that police officers are not responsible for victims' healing but do have to consider victims' well-being.

> know that they are not responsible for my healing process, but they do have the duty of showing concern for my well-being. (...) And I think that if they would treat me in an unfriendly manner, I would feel even more victimised.
>
> (Female victim of robbery
> (respondent 47), participant)

The latter quote provides an indication of the effects of (not) being treated with respect: a lack of respect may cause secondary victimisation. Another negative consequence of not being treated with respect concerns willingness to cooperate with the police: one is less inclined to report new offences, one victim said, and another victim mentioned a relationship between how one is treated and willingness to tell one's story in detail. She said that she could imagine that if the police were unfriendly, a victim would decide to get the interrogation over with as soon as possible and consequently not tell the complete story, which is an important observation with a view to fact-finding.

> Since they treated me in a correct manner I felt inclined to tell them my story in full detail, even if doing so was very hard for me. I think that if I would have faced an unfriendly cop, I would only have told him part of the story. I would have thought 'never mind'.
>
> (Mother of female victim of sexual abuse (respondent 50), participant)

One of the victims said that the fact that she had felt acknowledged by the police had made her feel peaceful and calm. She did not have to fight for acknowledgement; she did not have to spend time proving that she had been a victim and that she merited attention. This made her feel at ease and more capable of letting go of the offence and raised her confidence not only in the police but also in the judicial authorities who would try the case.

> At no point did I feel a need to thump the table and say 'hey, I'm the victim!', and at no point did I feel that I had to prove that I was a victim, or that I had to explain how hurt I was because someone questioned my story or anything. I've given this a lot of thought, I've been thinking a lot about the reason for this, and I think it has a lot to do with the fact that they took me seriously. The more one feels acknowledged and that people are taking one's case seriously, the less one feels the urge to thump the table. (...) The feeling of being acknowledged ... it gives me peace. I didn't feel the urge of getting involved in the case or of constantly reminding the authorities 'hey, I'm a victim here'. I was at ease. It enabled me to let go and to put trust in the authorities to do their jobs. It also gave me more confidence in the trial.
>
> (Female victim of robbery (respondent 47), participant)

Overall, the offenders were more negative about police officers than the victims. About half of the offenders said that the police officers that they had met had been friendly and polite, understanding and calm; the other half described the police officers that had been involved in their case as arrogant, pompous, provocative, immature, and as people who made fun of them and insulted them.

> This police officer who is interrogating me comes to stand right in front of me chewing his sandwich with his mouth wide open and then in this very, very heavy dialect he says: 'You don't really think you can get out of

this, do you?' Seriously, for a grown man to act like that ... It's just childish to provoke someone that way. I never thought it possible that an adult would behave like that.

> (Male offender, intentional assault and battery
> (respondent 54), non-participant)

Four offenders reported having experienced physical violence by the police upon arrest or upon being brought to jail. A number of them did mention that they understood *why* the police officers had treated them harshly: as police officers often do not know who they are dealing with, they said, it is understandable that they sometimes act heavy-handed with suspects. Four offenders reported that they had been bullied by police officers. One offender for example explained that during the interrogation the police officers had deprived him of his eyeglasses after he had told them that he cannot see a thing without them. Six offenders had received threats from the police in order to pry a confession out of them. Police officers had for example been bragging about how many years in prison the defendants risked if they wouldn't confess to the crime.

> The way they literally threw me in that cell ... I almost hit my face against the bed. That was really uncalled for.
>
> > (Male offender, violent robbery
> > (respondent 48), participant)

> He told me that the police said that if he didn't confess to being involved he would have to stay in jail for a couple of days. It's not hard to imagine what kind of effect that has on a kid.
>
> > ((Mother of) male offender, theft
> > (respondent 39), non-participant)

Four offenders reported that they had felt emotionally upset after the police interrogation. The police officers had been rude to them, they had been pressured into admitting to crimes they did not commit, or they had been held at the police station for hours on end. Because of being so upset, one respondent signed his statement without reading it – he wanted to get out of the police station as soon as possible to bring an end to the upsetting situation. The effect of being treated in an angry manner was such that when he found out that the statement contained falsehoods he didn't dare go back to the police station to have the statement corrected. He didn't think he could face the police officers again; he said that it would make him feel physically unwell. Another participant said that the treatment he received from the police officers had made him lose his self-confidence; as a result, he had started to neglect his job, go to bed unusually early and so on. He said that the treatment he had received from the police officers had felt like a punishment.

> The way these people treated me ... that in itself felt like a punishment. (...) The way they acted, it's no wonder people crash, and very fast for

that matter. It's this feeling of ... a feeling of powerlessness, of being a nobody.

> (Male offender, intentional assault and battery
> (respondent 54), non-participant)

Markedly, two offenders who had been treated in a friendly manner by the police said that they did not believe that the police officers were *genuinely* friendly – they thought it was just a sham.

> This one cop he said – of course he just said that to appease me – he said in this very understanding manner: 'yes of course, anybody would have reacted like that, you were upset and of course if people act like that it's normal to react the way you did'.
> (Male offender, intentional assault and battery
> (respondent 34), participant)

> One of them [one of the police officers that interrogated him] was super friendly but of course I knew he was just pretending. It's ridiculous.
> (Male offender, burglary and theft
> (respondent 41), participant)

Three participants (one victim and two offenders) felt that their dignity was violated by the fact that the police clearly distrusted them. The offenders for example were perplexed that the police thought that they would flee if they would allow them to take their own car to drive to the police station.

> They put on handcuffs, they wouldn't allow me to drive to the police station with my own car 'cause heaven forbid I would take off ...
> (Male offender, intentional assault and battery
> (respondent 54), non-participant)

Notwithstanding these negative perceptions, many respondents explicitly said that police officers should not all be lumped together. They said that the fact that they had had a bad experience with one police officer does not imply that they regard all police officers as unfriendly and impolite. Also, even those participants with a negative opinion about police officers and their work stressed that the police force is a necessary institution, though one victim unenthusiastically called the police a 'necessary evil'.

> I won't say they're all bad guys. These people [police officers] have jobs to do and I'm sure many of them do a lot of great things, and you know in the end they're only human and we all make mistakes.
> (Male offender, intentional assault and battery
> (respondent 8), non-participant)

A number of participants said that the police are entitled to be harsher on some people than on others. One victim stated that police officers are entitled to be harsher on offenders than on victims – other participants explicitly disagreed with this. Another participant said that the degree to which police officers should show respect for citizens depends on their task: those who need to resolve a crime would be allowed to be less forthcoming than local police officers whose task it is to be available to the local community. Two other participants declared that it all depends on the seriousness of the crime committed: those who committed a severe crime should not be treated with as much respect as those who committed a minor crime. Furthermore, participants agreed that people who behave impolitely towards police officers should not be surprised if those officers do not treat them as respectfully as they treat others.

> To me it's clear that, even if someone has committed a crime against me, that this person should nevertheless be treated in the same way as me.
>
> (Female victim of intentional assault and battery (respondent 1), non-participant)

> They shouldn't make a difference – unless we're talking paedophiles or the like, those, yes, those should be treated harsher than others. Yes, that's a clear difference.
>
> (Male offender, robbery (respondent 27), non-participant)

Finally, participants said that when police officers behave properly towards citizens, these citizens in turn will be forthcoming towards the police officers. Both victims and offenders, ten in total, said that the way they behave towards police officers depends to a great extent on how the police officers behave. Yet the opposite is also true: participants acknowledged that if the police behave badly, that is often due to the behaviour of the person they are dealing with.

> The cops and I, the way we interacted was a little more relaxed than I guess is usually the case. (...) I think that's because I didn't resist when they arrested me, I wasn't aggressive either, I think that has something to do with it.
>
> (Male offender, intentional assault and battery (respondent 54), non-participant)

Respect for rights

The issue 'respect for rights' has not been clearly described in procedural justice literature. Tyler and Lind's (1992) seminal paper seems to suggest that justice theorists strictly conceive of this issue as respect for those rights that are defined by law. Yet the participants of the current study on several occasions had had the feeling that a right had been breached by the police when actually they did not have a legal right to rely on at all. In other words, a *perceived* breach of rights took place. There seem to exist some 'natural' or 'moral' rights that people believe they are entitled to. The category 'respect for rights', then, consists of those interview fragments relating to respect for/ breaches of rights that have been defined by the legislator *and* those examples of situations in which participants mistakenly believed that a right had been breached.

Note that below, mainly *breaches* of rights are described. Throughout the analysis, very few concrete examples of situations in which rights had been *respected* were found. People mentioned a number of things about their experience of the police that showed that the police had respected rules concerning people's right to add documents to the file or to receive a copy of their statement, but these were mentioned in passing, whereas breaches of rights received much more attention. There are several possible explanations for the predominant attention to breaches of rights. First of all, people are known to be more prone to elucidate on negative experiences than on positive ones when evaluating other people's behaviour. This is explained by the fact that in people's minds, losses are more powerful than gains. Tversky and Kahneman (1979, 1984: 342) introduced the concept 'loss aversion' to point to 'the intuition that a loss of $X is more aversive than a gain of $X is attractive'. Further support for this hypothesis is found in Weitzer and Tuch (2004). Building on the literature suggesting that negative experiences with the police lower opinions of the police to a much stronger degree than positive experiences with the police lead to more favourable opinions of the police, Weitzer and Tuch suggest that positive experiences may simply be viewed as normal by those who have positive prior views about the police and discounted as an exception to the norm by those with a negative prior view about the police. Another potential explanation is that people didn't mention those cases where a right had been respected simply because they were not aware that this had been the case, just as many respondents seemed not to be aware of it when a right had been breached. Respondents often did not know that there had been a breach of a right or that a specific right had been given due attention. Sometimes participants mentioned breaches of rights without actually being aware of it, and a number of them remarked that lay people do not know the law sufficiently well to actually notice when legal rules are not respected. In all, then, respondents mentioned (perceived) breaches of rights much more often than they praised the police for respecting their rights.

Below, the focus will mainly be on offenders' perceptions of respect for their rights. The specific rights of victims of crime in Belgium relate to information, to practical and emotional support and to referral to specialised centres for victim assistance. This means that there was considerable overlap between the categories 'concern for needs' and 'respect for rights' for victims. In order to avoid repetition, all fragments from victim interviews relating to these matters will be discussed under the category 'concern for needs'.

Nine offenders mentioned seven examples of how legal rights had been breached, though they themselves did not always realise that this had been the case. They were more likely to say that the police 'did something that was unacceptable'. They mentioned: (1) the police not giving the offender a copy of his statement (which is a breach of article 28 quinquies § 2 of the Belgian Code of Criminal Procedure); (2) the police not respecting their duty for professional secrecy (breach of article 28 quinquies § 2 of the Belgian Code of Criminal Procedure); (3) the police not giving the offender sufficient time to read her statement before signing it (breach of article 47 bis 4 of the Belgian Code of Criminal Procedure); (4) the police dissuading the offender from altering his original statement (breach of article 47 bis 4 of the Belgian Code of Criminal Procedure); (5) the police gaining unauthorised access to the offender's premises (breach of article 15 of the Belgian Constitution (inviolability of the home), of article 18 of the European Convention on Human Rights (right to privacy) and of article 17 of the International Covenant on Civil and Political Rights (right to privacy)); (6) not having received drinks or food during the interrogation or while held in custody (breach of article 5 of the Universal Declaration of Human Rights and article 3 of the European Convention on Human Rights (right to humane treatment and physical integrity)); and (7) the use of physical force by the police (breach of article 5 of the Universal Declaration of Human Rights and article 3 of the European Convention on Human Rights (right to humane treatment and physical integrity)).

Two examples illustrate these offenders' experiences. A first example is that of the mother of a young adult offender who was shocked by the fact that the police had entered her house without permission when they had come to arrest her son.

> They knocked on the door but my daughter was upstairs so she didn't hear the knocks, and they just let themselves in. That's completely inappropriate. My daughter even called me about it again this afternoon, she said, 'mum, is that actually allowed, what they did?' Well I don't think it is.
>
> ((Mother of) male offender, burglary and theft (respondent 43), participant)

A second example relates to five offenders being appalled by the police breaching their duty for professional secrecy. One offender noticed that his ex-girlfriend was familiar with details about his case that not even he was acquainted with, which made him conclude that she had been briefed by a contact person within the police force. He mentioned these leaks seven times during the interview, which is an indication of the importance that he attached to this breach of professional secrecy. Two of the offenders criticising the police for not keeping to professional secrecy said that they did not dare complain about this to the officers' chiefs out of fear of reprisals. They said they were sure that if they complained to the officers' chiefs about it, the officers would take revenge.

> It doesn't make sense that she [the respondent's ex-girlfriend] is the one I should go to if I want to know what the victim told the police. (...) Something's not right here. I guess she knows one of the cops and he thinks he can just tell her those things. But how can I prove that?
>
> (Male offender, intentional assault and battery
> (respondent 54), non-participant)

> Telling this guy's boss is only gonna make it worse, it will make the cops more hostile towards me, the next time I park my car in a place I'm not supposed to I'm bound to get a ticket. I know a couple of cops and they tell me, 'don't go against us, because we can screw you over', that's what they say, they say, 'we can screw you over as much as we want to'. Really? Seriously? Is that the goal of policing?
>
> (Male offender, violent theft and threat of arson
> (respondent 24), non-participant)

Coming then to the category of victims' and offenders' *perceptions* that rights had been breached when in fact there were no rights that they could invoke, these are all examples of respondents condemning an *in se* correct procedure. The procedure just did not *feel* correct to them. For example, a common complaint among the parents of adult (in Belgium, children reach legal adulthood at age 18) yet young offenders still living at their parents' place was that the police had not informed them that they had taken their child to the police office for interrogation or that they had arrested their child. The parents, who had been worried to death as they didn't know where their child was, said that the police have a duty to inform them. In other words, they felt like they have a right to be informed while the police are not required to do so when the suspect is 18 or older. Other things that parents criticised were that they were not informed about what had been said by their child during the interrogation (one victim, one offender) and that they had not been allowed to be present during the interrogation of their child (one victim, one offender).

> So we asked them why they didn't inform us that they had arrested our son, and all they said was 'he's 19 years old, we are not required to inform the parents'. Unbelievable. Children are disappearing every day; he may be 19 but there's so much danger out there on the streets. I was shocked. (...) All it would have taken was just one phone call, that's all.
>
> ((Mother of) male offender, burglary and theft
> (respondent 41), participant)

Two offenders complained that they had been detained by the police and had had to spend the night in a police cell. Although there are no indications that by detaining these offenders the police had broken any rules, it clearly felt unfair to these respondents. They felt that being taken into custody was disproportional to the offences they committed. Another thing that provoked negative reactions from offenders, though from a legal point of view there was no problem, was being handcuffed. This was discussed above, yet it is one more example of an action that is legally correct but may be perceived as unjust. One offender complained about the fact that he had not been allowed to call his family to inform them of his arrest, yet, again, in Belgium suspects do not have a legal right to do so. One last example is that of the victims who were surprised to find that they could not recover their stolen goods because the offenders claimed that they were the rightful owners.

Concern for needs

The police are the first authorities that victims and offenders encounter after what has been a difficult if not traumatic experience. Victims and offenders expressed a variety of needs that they face in the immediate aftermath of the offence. They expressed: (1) emotional needs; (2) practical needs; (3) the need for involvement in the criminal procedure; and (4) the need for the police to be available to citizens. By way of a preliminary remark, it should be noted that, first, where participants' needs could not be met by the police this was not always due to unwillingness or carelessness on behalf of the police. In fact, certain rules pertaining to the criminal procedure prevent the police from meeting litigant needs. This will be explained below. Second, the respondents did not always make their needs explicit, that is, they did not usually say 'I had a need for ... '. Yet the interviews revealed that the police had had attention for participants' needs in many ways without the participants expressing it as the fulfilment of a need. For example, one element that will be discussed is that the police satisfied a victim's need for security by patrolling near her house. The victim did not explicitly state that she had *needed* the police to patrol near her house, yet the police by doing so had obviously met an unexpressed need. This observation is similar to the observation made above with respect to the issue 'respect for rights': people do not explicitly talk about the police having respected their rights or having shown concern for their needs. They talk about what they think the police did well and what they think the police should have done differently, but the contents of what they say do fit the categories defined by procedural justice research.

Emotional needs

As for psychological or emotional needs, several victims mentioned that the police officers who had intervened in their case had done their best to reassure them, put them at ease and calm them down, either immediately after the offence had taken place – at the crime scene or at the police station – or in a later stage of the proceedings. Things the police had done that had been helpful to victims were: taking the offender away from the scene of the crime as quickly as possible, informing the victim that the offender had been put in preliminary custody, staying on the telephone and talking to the victim the entire time from the moment the victim called to report that she had been robbed until the moment police officers arrived at the scene, and explaining to victims why exactly the police officers were asking them certain questions and why they were following certain procedures. For example, a victim who had been driven around town by the police to help them find the offenders immediately after she had been robbed on the street said that what had been really important to her was that the police had explained why it was necessary to start the search for the offenders immediately and why it was crucial that she would be present, as she was in shock and it was hard for her to do what she was asked to do. It seems, then, that being given a good explanation for the police's deeds and information about what happened to the offender after (s) he had been arrested is the common denominator in these stories. Information and explanation seem to be what victims need in order to remain calm.

> Afterwards they called me to say that he [the offender] would have to stay in jail, and they reassured me.
>
> (Female victim of violent theft and threat of arson
> (respondent 28), non-participant)

A female victim of rape was grateful for the fact that the police had appointed a female social worker to support her while telling her story to the police. The mother of a victim whose offender was released from jail praised the police for having helped her with informing her daughter about this. The way two victims of burglary talked about the loss of their goods and the satisfaction they expressed about the police trying their best to recover their stolen goods indicated that the police by doing so had paid regard to an emotional need rather than merely a material need. Finally, all (three) parents who needed to take very young children to the police, either because the children themselves had been victimised or because the parent had been victimised and could not arrange for childcare during the interrogation, talked about the fact that the police had taken good care of their children, giving them toys and keeping them in a separate room.

> I thought it was great that they asked a female social worker to attend the interview. That was really nice of him, the police officer saying, 'I'm a man, I know this must be hard for you, so I'll ask her to come'.
>
> (Female victim of rape
> (respondent 38), participant)

> She said, 'you know what, come to the police station again and I'll tell your daughter, I'll explain to her why he [the offender] was released and what he is and isn't allowed to do.' Because to tell my daughter that

the offender was released ... That was too hard for me to do, so she helped me.

> (Mother of female victim of sexual abuse
> (respondent 23), non-participant)

They [the participant's children] got toys and stuff and they got a room next to the room where I was sitting and the doors between the rooms remained open so I could see them. So that was okay. They were very well taken care of.

> (Female victim of rape
> (respondent 38), participant)

One victim was especially satisfied with the fact that a victim support worker had given her her telephone number for her to call any time. This shows genuine concern for the victim. In this respect, two victims mentioned how helpful it is to have one contact person at the police to whom one can direct all one's questions and who notifies people of important developments in their case. Only after they had finally found such a person had they felt some relief and found some peace. Victims are not happy about encountering a new police officer every time they contact the police, because it means that they have to tell their story over and over again and that nobody really knows their case well.

The police can also satisfy victims' need for security, as said, which also is an emotional need because physical safety leads to emotional safety. The police had for example been patrolling near the house of a victim of robbery the night after the robbery – the offenders had taken her purse and therefore had the keys to the victim's house. Furthermore, a number of victims spontaneously mentioned that the police had provided them with leaflets of victim support organisations, yet there were only five of them, whereas the police are required to provide all victims who report a crime with this kind of information. However, it is not possible to draw any conclusions about the degree to which the police fulfilled this task from this observation, as the other victims may well have received this information but just did not mention it during the interviews.

To conclude, there was also one complaint. The complaint was uttered by the mother of a child victim who felt that she had been neglected by the police when her child was taken for interrogation. She said that she had been 'pushed into a small room, without any explanation' and that her child had been 'ripped from her body'. Another victim was content with the police intervention as such in her case, but she did mention that other victims could have been discontented about a similar intervention because the police upon arrival at the crime scene had first dealt with the offender (it had taken several police officers to calm him down) and only after that had taken care of her. She said that she could imagine some victims being dissatisfied about the police first dealing with the offender and only then taking care of the victim, yet to her it had been good; the fact that the offender had been taken away from the crime scene as soon as possible had allowed her to remain calm.

I can imagine that some people would be upset – they first directed all their attention to him [the offender] before interviewing me, so I might well have accused them of neglecting me.

(Female victim of intentional assault and battery (respondent 32), participant)

It is clear that the list of emotional needs expressed by victims is long. Summarising, fifteen victims mentioned thirteen emotional needs. In sharp contrast, only two offenders mentioned the police paying regard to such needs, though none of them expressed a lack of police regard for their emotional needs. Offenders just did not talk about the police in terms of emotional support that often. One offender who was in preliminary custody expressed approbation of the fact that the police had come to collect him for an interrogation and eventually had held him at the police station for almost a whole day; they had said that they understood how hard it was for him to be in prison and gave him a chance to spend some time out of prison. The participant appreciated that as a very humane thing to do. Another offender, who had burst into tears after a very tough interrogation, said that one police officer had come to him to ask if he was all right and had stood with him for a while.

Practical needs

Moving onto practical needs, two young men who had been detained for 24 hours were offended by the fact that the police after deciding to release them just turned them out on the street and did not in the least care about how the two men would get home. Another practical need expressed by offenders was to recover belongings that had been confiscated. One of them criticised the fact that he had been sent from pillar to post when trying to recover his mobile phone. Another offender was satisfied about the fact that the police had made some effort to make sure he could recover his car.

If I had been alone when they let me go, if I had been the first one to be released for example and they had released me in the middle of the night, I wouldn't have been able to get home. My cell phone battery had gone flat, and there were no busses at that time. I guess I should have walked home. (...) Those are things that are ... They arrested me here [at home], they put me in custody, and then they just put me out on the street. And that's it. They didn't care about how I would get home.

(Male offender, burglary and theft (respondent 3), participant)

The police had provided practical support to at least nine of the victims participating in the study. Six victims mentioned that they had been taken to hospital by the police or that the police had offered to do so. This gesture had a major influence on victims' satisfaction with the police. Other examples of the police offering practical help are: the police removing the offender's belongings from the victim's premises and the police driving a victim who had been robbed in a town strange to her back to her car that had been left in a car park after taking her statement. All these efforts on behalf of the police contributed to a positive evaluation by victims.

> (...) after we found the perpetrators they [the police] brought me to the hospital emergency department, and they waited for the doctors to finish their work before they interrogated me. They handled the situation very well.
>
> (Male victim of intentional assault and battery
> (respondent 12), non-participant)

The need for involvement in the criminal procedure

A third category of needs expressed by victims and offenders relates to their involvement in the criminal procedure. In order to structure these needs, a distinction was made between needs for active participation and needs for passive involvement, that is, a need for information. This distinction is based on Edwards' (2004: 975) typology of victim participation in criminal proceedings and Malsch's (2009: 18) scheme of interactions between citizens and criminal authorities. Both typologies have been created with a view to specifying the potential roles that citizens may assume during the course of criminal procedures, and both stress that any type of citizen involvement in those procedures should only be labelled 'participation' in case there is a two-way contact between the victim or offender on the one hand and the legal authorities on the other hand. In other words, participation requires an active contribution from the victim or offender. To receive information, both Edwards and Malsch argue, lacks this essential element of participation: the victim or offender is relegated to a passive role. Receiving information, then, is a form of passive involvement. Actual participation presupposes that the victim/offender and the legal authorities both actively contribute to the interaction.

Employing this definition of 'participation', it becomes clear that in the pre-trial phase the participants of this study displayed a higher need for receiving information than for active participation. The degree to which they had received information from the police was discussed by fourteen victims; for a fair number (seven) of offenders too this was an issue, but not to the degree it was for victims. Offenders predominantly voiced dissatisfaction about the degree to which the police had given them information; about half of the victims was satisfied about the (amount of) information they had received from the police.

The decisive issues for those victims who were satisfied about the information given by the police were: (1) that they had been informed about what had happened to the offender after the interrogation (i.e. was (s)he allowed to go home afterwards or taken into custody?); and (2) that the police had told them which actions to undertake or who to go to with questions. For example, one victim had been informed as to the importance of going to a doctor to have his injuries recorded, and two employers had been informed on how best to go about catching their employees stealing in the act.

> They [the police] came by to tell me that one of the offenders had been released. (...) I also got a phone call from the police when they [the offenders] had been arrested, so I never had the feeling that I had to ... that I had to move mountains myself to get information about the procedure. Everything was always very clear to me.
>
> (Female victim of robbery
> (respondent 47), participant)

> They [the police] also told me – so I did get the most important information – they told me to see a doctor and go to the hospital to obtain a report about my injuries and to bring the report in case they would call me for a new interview. So I was well informed about the most important things.
>
> (Male victim of intentional assault and battery
> (respondent 21), participant)

Likewise, what victims complained about most was that the police had failed to inform them about whether the offender had confessed to the crime or about what the offender had said during the interrogation. They felt left in the cold after they had filed their complaint.

> But afterwards [after filing the complaint] they should have given us more information. I don't know the legal regulations concerning who is allowed to communicate information and what they are allowed to communicate, I don't know these things, but I was not informed at all about what the offender told the police.
>
> (Male victim of theft
> (respondent 37), non-participant)

> Once I had done everything the police had asked me to do, I felt like garbage. They didn't seem to care anymore. They didn't ask me how I was doing anymore, they didn't ask how things were going for me or if there was anything they could do for me or if I needed any information.
>
> (Mother of female victim of sexual abuse
> (respondent 23), non-participant)

The offenders discussing the issue of receiving information from the police mainly expressed discontent. Their frustration was chiefly due to the police's failure to inform them: (1) about the reason for arresting them or taking them to the police office; and (2) about what would happen after the initial interrogation. Also, they displayed a need for the police to explain the procedure of being arrested, being interrogated, being taken to an investigating judge, being taken into preliminary custody, et cetera. Most of them didn't know what usually happens after an arrest and where thus drifting in uncertainty.

> My son asked them [the police] 'what is going on, what is this about', and they said 'we don't know, all we know is we are supposed to come and arrest you'.
>
> ((Mother of) male offender, intentional assault and battery (respondent 26), participant)

> I didn't know what was happening, I didn't know what was going to happen, they [the police] simply took me with them; they said you have to go to the prosecutor and stuff, and they put me in the car and handcuffed me.
>
> (Male offender, burglary and theft (respondent 41), participant)

Six participants referred to what was defined above as a need for active participation. These participants had looked for opportunities for contributing to the police investigation. In offenders' cases, the underlying reason for their need for active involvement in the investigation was to make sure that all relevant information would be available to the judge at a later stage. They wanted to reassure themselves that the judge's decision would be based on accurate and complete information. Four offenders, for example, had looked for a way in which to add to the evidence gathered by the police. To one of them it had been very important that she had been allowed to attach an extra document to her statement in which she explained at length what had induced her to commit the offence. One offender's mother planned on taping a conversation between her son – the alleged offender – and the actual offender, who in a previous conversation with her son had confirmed her son's innocence. One alleged offender considered the police investigation so poor that he started a search for evidence himself, sending the police pictures that he found on the alleged victim's Facebook page disproving her side of the story. Finally, the mother of an adult yet young offender felt a great need to tell the police officers investigating her son's case about his home situation and to tell them that his accomplices were not really friends of his in order to make sure that the judge would know that her son comes from a respectable family.

> So in the end I got the opportunity to tell them [the police] about our situation and to give my point of view (...) I think they should always hear young suspects' parents, just so they know what the situation at home is like and who their friends are.
>
> ((Mother of) male offender, burglary and theft (respondent 41), participant)

The day after [the interrogation], he told my son 'well yeah of course I lied, did you really think I would tell them [the police] the truth?'. I would want to record that and take it to the police – but it's not allowed as evidence. We really thought about setting that up, we said to each other let's buy a recorder, let's go see that guy again and get him to repeat what he said before. But it's not allowed in court.

((Mother of) male offender, intentional assault and battery
(respondent 26), participant)

Only one victim expressed a need for active involvement in the investigation. This person regretted that he had not been allowed to participate in the search that the police had conducted in the homes of the thieves who had stolen many of his belongings during a burglary. Markedly, throughout three victim interviews negative consequences of being involved in the criminal proceedings were detected. Two victims expressed distress about the fact that the police had asked them to come to the police station for an additional interview some months after the offence; they had just recovered from their experiences and were then forced to relive them. One victim had felt forced to try to take some control over the proceedings because the police in her view had not taken any action in her case. She had taken great pains to get things moving herself; this, so she said, had made her feel like she had been victimised twice: first by the offender, then by the fact that she had to work so hard to get the police to do their job.

I feel like I have to fight so hard for this, it's ... I feel like I have been a victim twice: once by the perpetrator and then with the police and all the hassle.

(Female victim of stalking
(respondent 18), non-participant)

The need for the police to be available

The fourth category of needs concerns the need for a police intervention in a particular situation – two offenders and four victims complained that the police had not been available to them at a time when they had needed them. For example, one victim had informed the police that her neighbours had regularly seen her offender hanging around her flat and had asked them to talk to him in order to prevent future victimisation. Yet they had told her that they would only take action if she were actually victimised, and that in that case she would need to call the emergency services. Three more victims made remarks about the police's unavailability.

Things like, for example, he [another victim of the same perpetrator] works late, the police office is open until 10 pm, one time when we arrived there at 10 to 10 they said they couldn't talk to us anymore. That happens all the time.

(Female victim of stalking
(respondent 18), non-participant)

Two offenders suggested that if the police had helped them when they had asked them to, they would not have committed the offence they committed.

> I crossed a line, I should have been wiser, but I had already asked the police to help me and they didn't. If the police are not willing to help ... well what other option is there?
>
> (Male offender, violent theft and threat of arson
> (respondent 24), non-participant)

Also, one of the offenders said that when he calls the police because he finds himself in a threatening situation they are not eager to intervene – they think he can solve such situations himself because he has the reputation of being a fighter ('if I get beaten up and I call the cops they're like: "you can handle this yourself"').

When criminal proceedings prevent needs from being met

Victims expressed a number of needs that the police could not meet because the nature of the criminal proceedings prevented them from doing so. For example, four victims testified about how difficult it was for them to have the police in their homes. This is of course often part of the procedure when a crime is reported, yet to victims it was difficult to deal with the police's presence in their house or at their door because they felt a need for some privacy. The two victims described above who had been reluctant to go to the police office again for a new interrogation provide another example: the criminal proceedings may have been conducted correctly, yet prevented victims' need to be left in peace from being met. Finally, those who wish to participate in the investigation or evidence-gathering come up against a brick wall as they find that there is a lack of opportunities for doing so. It seems, then, that sometimes external reasons – as opposed to police attitude or unwillingness – explain why the police did not meet certain needs.

Social standing

A category labelled 'social standing' was created as two respondents (both victims) mentioned that they feel shame and embarrassment when police officers come to their houses. They expressed concern about police cars being clearly distinguishable and nosy neighbours therefore being able to see that the police are paying them a visit.

> Each time they [the police] called me to make an appointment for an interview I always said I would come to the police office. I really didn't want the police to come by my house (...) in their uniforms, oh, no. The neighbours would see it and all that.
>
> (Mother of female victim of sexual abuse
> (respondent 23), non-participant)

Neutrality

Tyler and Lind (1992) defined the concept 'neutrality' as consisting of three subcomponents. These were: (1) absence of bias or prejudice; (2) fact-based decision-making; and (3) honesty. The analysis of the interviews conducted for the sake of the current study confirms this conceptualisation; all participants' remarks on the neutrality of the police were found to fit one of these three categories. There was no need to create new, extra categories, nor were any of the categories defined by Tyler and Lind found to be redundant, though it must be said that while ample examples were found to fit the first two categories, participants' remarks about police honesty were fewer. All three categories are discussed below.

Absence of bias or prejudice

This category groups all interview fragments that relate to (a lack of) police objectivity. 'Absence of bias' was interpreted as impartiality between victim and offender or between accomplices; 'absence of prejudice' was understood to mean absence of premature judgement about the alleged offender's guilt or about the victim's role in the offence. Starting with absence of bias, two victims accused the police of favouritism. They had the impression that the offender had contacts within the police force that were either protecting him or supplying him with information. One victim for instance was convinced that the police was providing her stalker with information on the identity of visitors to her house. She believed the police obtained this information from the car number plates of her visitors. One offender mentioned an example of the police favouring the victim(s). The police upon arresting him in the presence of his victims had told the victims that they could go to a bailiff who could then confiscate some of the offender's belongings in order for them to get monetary compensation.

This was the only offender complaining about the police favouring the victim(s). Five offenders had had the impression that the police were protecting or favouring an accomplice. For example, one offender was upset about the fact that he had been held in a police cell for a night while an accomplice, who contrary to him had a criminal record, was not. Another offender declared that the police had urged him to adapt his statement so as to absolve his accomplice of the crime; he had felt so overwhelmed that he indeed changed his statement.

R1:   It's as if someone [within the police force] is protecting him [the accomplice]. Why else would an officer ask a suspect to change his statement in favour of another suspect?

R2:   Right. Why else would it be of any interest to that officer? Why would he care? But if the other guy knows a cop … These things happen. A cop thinking to himself 'I can't let this happen because this is the son of this or that guy'.

((Mother and father of) male offender, intentional assault and battery
(respondent 26), participant)

As to absence of prejudice, two victims were surprised to learn that the police did *not* show racism in their case. For example, a person of mixed race had expected that the police upon seeing him would have assumed that he had incited the fight he had been involved in. He had been pleasantly surprised that they had not. Two victims of breaking and entering said the following:

R1: Rumour had it that gypsies were camping around here, so people said it's probably them, they must have observed your house for a while and they knew you were gone (...). But the police said, no, it's not them.

R2: People easily rely on stereotypes, but the police didn't. It was very clear that they didn't want to do that. I thought that was great. They handled the matter in a very correct manner.

(Male and female victim of burglary and theft
(respondents 51 and 52), non-participants)

Then there was the issue of prejudice about the victim's role (guilt) in the offence. One victim's mother – her daughter was the victim, her son the assailant – faulted the police for judging her; she felt that they put the blame for her son's behaviour on her and felt very irritated about this. Another victim's mother – her son was the victim, her boyfriend the offender – felt exactly the same. Her son was often unmanageable at the time, and she felt that the police judged her for not being able to handle him.

He [the intervening police officer] had already made up his mind about our case, he acted all condescendingly and, you know, policemen are supposed to be neutral, but he was not neutral at all (...). I was like, hey you, what do you know? Why don't you come live here with us and see for yourself what it's like.

(Mother of male victim of intentional assault and battery
(respondent 30), participant)

Another participant had a very different experience. She was the mother of a victim of sexual abuse; the perpetrator had had access to the child because the mother was in a relationship with him. She was very content about the police not showing any sign of disapproval towards her despite her role in the story.

What I did was not right either. (...) But they [the police] allowed me to explain myself, they listened to me and they said that they would investigate the case. I never for one moment felt like they were prejudiced or anything. That was very important to me.

(Mother of female victim of sexual abuse
(respondent 50), participant)

Offender interviews revealed several issues pertaining to prejudice. Four offenders mentioned that the police had pressured them into confessing to crimes they did not commit or at least had tried to do so because they readily assumed that the suspects were guilty. They did this for example by threatening that if the offender would not confess, they would keep him in custody for a longer time, by threatening with the time the participants would have to serve in prison if they kept denying the offence or by threatening that the offender would not get his car (which had been confiscated) back if he did not confess. Note that none of the victims reported having felt pressured to say things they did not mean to say to the police or had felt that words had been put into their mouths.

R1: I didn't realise the accusations were that serious. I thought I had been arrested for a fight, and they [the police] said: 'No, you are being accused of participating in an armed robbery at night and with conspiracy. Do you realise that you risk 20 years in prison?'.

R2: We were completely unaware of what was going on and they talked all big and tough about how many years' imprisonment we were facing and that we would be stuck in the police station for a long time.

(Male offenders, intentional assault and battery and vandalism
(respondents 9 and 10), participants)

Four offenders explained that the police had condemned them from the very start; they complained that the police would not take anything they said into account. One man said that the police had tried to provoke him into aggressive behaviour. He suggested that they were trying to create extra 'proof' that he is an aggressive person in order for that information to be used against him during the trial.

But then this one guy [a police officer] started accusing me of lying, and he said 'well I have all the time in the world, we can stay here until morning'. (...) They just push and push people until they break and they get something out of them. (...) I found it very sad that they didn't believe me.

(Male offender, theft
(respondent 40), non-participant)

Two offenders, both recidivists, reported the feeling that the police are pre-judiced on the basis of offenders' criminal records. According to these two offenders, the police do not take the effort of conducting a thorough investigation when one of those involved in an offence is a recidivist: in such case, they said, the police just assume that person's guilt. These offenders in other words linked suspects' criminal records to police willingness to conduct a good investigation. Another offender was convinced that, because he had been marked as 'aggressive' by one police officer, all police officers he would meet in future would be prejudiced towards him and treat him harshly.

In my experience, with this case and other cases too, the way they handle it ... As soon as they find a suspect with a criminal record, the case is closed. They just won't want to put any more effort in investigating it.

(Male offender, intentional assault and battery
(respondent 7), non-participant)

In my view they [the police] didn't do any effort, they just decided to believe the other guy. And the reason, I'm sure – this is my big disadvantage – the reason is that my friend and I have a criminal record. So what happened? They discovered that we were involved, they found out we had been involved in fights in the past, and they said to themselves 'those guys must have been the ones who started the fight'.

(Male offender, intentional assault and battery (respondent 8), non-participant)

An additional example of how offenders may be treated differently because of their past was raised by an offender who said that when he had called the police to report his having been assaulted, they did not respond to his call. Because he had a record of fighting with and assaulting others, they thought he could take care of himself. This example was described above.

Fact-based decision-making

The analysis of the interviews with respect to the element 'fact-based decision-making' was complicated by the confusion over the concepts 'fact-based decision-making' and 'decision accuracy'. Both have been used in justice research, and they seem to have been used interchangeably. The first concept figured in Tyler and Lind's (1992) model of procedural justice, which to these authors meant that judicial decisions should be based on facts, not opinions. The second concept was used by Lind and Tyler in their 1988 book; it was defined there as 'the frequency with which each procedure convicts the guilty and acquits the innocent' (19). Yet Tyler (1990) in order to assess the importance of the element 'accuracy of decision-making' asked his respondents whether the authorities had gathered all the information they needed in order to make a good decision and whether they had brought all this information into the open. Finally, Leventhal (1980) used the concept 'decision accuracy' to point to procedures being based 'on as much good information and informed opinion as possible (...) with a minimum of error' (41). In other words, the concepts 'decision accuracy' and 'fact-based decision-making' have been used interchangeably. They have been taken to point to three issues: (1) that the guilty are convicted and the innocent acquitted; (2) that all information that is needed to make an informed decision is gathered; and (3) that decisions are based on facts, not opinions. Any interview fragments relating to the first issue will not be considered below since these do not concern evaluations of the fairness of the actual procedure. Any remarks that participants made about the influence of authorities' personal opinions on decisions were included under the category 'absence of bias or prejudice' discussed above. This means that the category 'fact-based decision-making' was conceptualised as the authorities gathering all the information and evidence needed to make an informed decision on the case. The ensuing paragraphs describe what participants said about the importance of information-gathering.

Three victims commented on the quality of information-gathering. One victim felt that the police and the prosecutor should gather more information about the victim than they currently do. He suggested that the police pay an extra visit to victims some time after taking their witness statement in order to check if the damages that the victim described are indeed authentic or if they were exaggerated. This extra inquiry would have to result in a report that would be handed to the judge. The second victim is the one who said that if the police had treated her disrespectfully she probably would not have told them her story in full detail, which would have had a negative effect on the quality of information-gathering. The third person stated that reconstructions of offences should be organised more often.

One recurring remark in offender interviews that fits this category was the comment that the police had not investigated the case sufficiently well and had not done their best to uncover the truth about the facts. Five offenders complained about this; one of them was the mother of a young adult offender who suggested that the police when dealing with young adults should talk to the parents to get a more complete picture of the offender. Another offender, who was accused of battery of his stepson, thought it was not correct that the police had not talked to the boy's mother. He too felt that the police had not gathered sufficient information to acquire a good understanding of the situation. One offender, accused of stealing, was angry because the police had not been careful when confiscating goods at his home: they had taken several items that he had obtained in an honest manner. Finally, there's the two offenders who thought the police investigation had been superficial because they had a criminal record.

Honesty

In victim interviews, nothing was found that related to honesty on behalf of the police other than the fragments described under 'absence of bias or prejudice' (e.g. about the police supplying the suspect with information). Three offenders complained that the police had twisted their words when writing up their statement or had written falsehoods in those statements. Victims had no complaints relating to the wording or the contents of their statements.

> It's unbelievable how much power they have when writing up people's statements. Un-believable. (...) The way they write things up, they make sure it's to their own advantage. (...) They tell you 'we can write whatever we like, if you don't agree you can always defend yourself afterwards' but that's not true, people will always believe the police.
>> (Male offender, intentional assault and battery
>> (respondent 54), non-participant)

> They needed me to confess and they really pushed me, they were very tough. The words that are used in my statement are words that I never used. It says, for example, 'and then I lashed out at her'. Seriously, as if a

19-year-old girl would ever use that word. But I signed it and I can't change it anymore. That night, it was … really hectic.
(Female offender, intentional and unintentional assault and battery (respondent 46), participant)

One offender said that he had the impression that lawyers sometimes make arrangements with the police in order for cases not to be prosecuted. This is an example of perceptions of unethical behaviour.

Those lawyers, they talk to one another. Or maybe they know someone through the grapevine. They arrange things with the police so the police won't pursue the case any further.
(Male offender, intentional assault and battery (respondent 7), non-participant)

Performance

The third theme that emerged from the analysis of both the victim and the offender interviews was not advanced by Tyler and Lind (1992). It was labelled 'performance'. When talking about how they experienced the police intervention, respondents made several comments about the way the police function and about the quality of their work. Performance was included as a determinant of perceptions of procedural justice because it seems that participants' perceptions of police performance had an impact on their perceptions of standing and neutrality, which in turn determine perceptions of procedural fairness. This relationship will be discussed in detail in Chapter 6; below, the results that led to this conclusion are presented.

An important issue to seven victims was whether the police caught the offender. Some said that the fact that the offender(s) had been arrested was 'a relief' because it added to their perception of safety and thus their well-being, others said that it was 'good to know' that the offender(s) had been arrested, to others the police apprehending the offender(s) felt like a form of victim recognition. It also added considerably to victim satisfaction with the police. One participant for example to the question 'How was the contact with the police?' replied 'Very good, because they caught the offender'. Another participant indicated that if the police had not found the offenders, his opinion about the police would surely have been less favourable.

But my perceptions of the police would have been very different if they hadn't found the offenders. They did, luckily, by chance, they caught them and so I'm okay. But if they hadn't I would certainly have criticised them, you know, saying things like 'if only they had been a bit quicker, their office is just around the corner, what took them so long?'.
(Male victim of intentional assault and battery (respondent 12), non-participant)

It's a form of acknowledgement. The fact that they caught the thieves is a recognition.

(Female victim of burglary and theft
(respondent 52), non-participant)

Two victims were very disappointed about the fact that the police had not immediately apprehended the offender after they had reported the crime, even though the offender's identity was clear and the victim could provide the police with the offender's name and address. One of them said that it had given her the feeling that the police did not take the case seriously.

I don't understand that they didn't go after the offender immediately. (...) We gave them the guy's address, and still they didn't. They didn't even go to the bar where it happened to interrogate the people there or anything. (...) That gives us the impression that they don't care, that to them it's just a fight among some guys not worthy of any attention.

(Mother of male victim of intentional assault and battery
(respondent 20), non-participant)

One could argue that the issue of the police apprehending the offender is a purely outcome-related issue and therefore should not be described here. However, it clearly influenced victims' perceptions of standing: whether or not the police apprehend the offender has an influence on whether victims feel recognised and feel that their case is taken seriously. This is also evinced by the importance to victims of the police putting effort into trying to identify the offender in those cases where the offender's identity was not clear. Four victims explicitly discussed whether the police had according to them genuinely tried to identify and find the offender; some accused the police of a lack of effort. One example is that of a victim's mother who said that her husband and son (the victim) had gone to report the offence at night, as it had happened at night, and had got the impression that the police did not feel like taking much action precisely because it was night-time. This had seriously affected her trust in them.

It happened on a Friday night, a Saturday morning in fact, and they [the police] clearly didn't feel like leaving their office. My husband said that they clearly didn't want to go out, really, they just didn't feel like driving up there because it was night-time. (...) If this is the message that the police gives us – 'we don't care' – then how could I put any trust in them?

(Mother of male victim of intentional assault and battery
(respondent 20), non-participant)

A second example is that of an employer who suspected that one of his employees was stealing money from the cash register. He too had expected the police to make more effort to find out who exactly was the thief. In the end, he had successfully managed to identify the thief himself, yet, as he said, *he* had solved it, not the police. He did show some understanding of the police's lack of effort in this matter:

> I guess I thought the police would have been more active in tracking down the thief. But, well, I do understand why they weren't (...). The amount of money involved was not that big, if one would count how much it has cost us in terms of the number of hours we have spent on trying to find out who the thief was ... If the police would do that, well I understand that they can't, it wouldn't be justifiable.
>
> (Male victim of theft
> (respondent 37), non-participant)

Seven victims when discussing the police intervention brought up police response times, that is, the time it had taken the police to arrive at the crime scene. This seems to be a very sensitive issue. An important reason for this is that when it takes a long time for the police to arrive at the crime scene, this conveys a message of nonchalance and indifference. As one person said, it seems to suggest that it is 'okay to just let the offenders get away with it'. One victim took into account the distance between the police station and the crime scene; he reasoned that as the police station was 'just a few hundred meters away', it had taken the police too long to turn up. Victims when discussing the time it took for the police to arrive at the crime scene generally talked in terms of 'too slow' or 'quick'; only two of them were more specific, indicating that it took e.g. a quarter of an hour for the police to arrive.

> Q: Is there anything about the police intervention that you found remarkable – in a good or bad sense?
> R: I thought it was great that they arrived so quickly.
>
> (Male victim of intentional assault and battery
> (respondent 21), participant)

> Q: And how did the police become involved?
> R1: Well, that was quite a joke.
> R2: Only after a very long time.
>
> (Female and male victim of intentional assault and battery,
> threats and vandalism
> (respondents 44 and 45), non-participants)

Five victims made a remark about the length of the police intervention or of the interview that had taken place at the police station. To two of them, the fact that the police had taken ample time to deal with their case had been an indicator that they were taking their case seriously. The others seemingly mentioned it heedlessly, without paying further attention to it or expressing a judgement about it. Those who said that the intervention had not taken very long were not dissatisfied about this.

But apart from that ... it didn't really take long either. They wrote a short report, and they told me that they would call me again a couple of days later to talk more in detail. They only stayed here for a short time.
(Male victim of intentional assault and battery
(respondent 21), participant)

Three victims said that the police officer on duty had called a service that was actually closed or a police officer who had already left home once they understood what the case was about and that specialised help was needed. This too was perceived to be an indicator that they were taking the case seriously.

I took my eldest son to the police, and they took our story very seriously. The same night they called the Youth Service, while in fact that service is only open during the daytime.
(Father of male victims of intentional assault and battery
(respondent 6), non-participant)

Negative remarks with respect to the quality of the police's work concern, first, the police's knowledge of particular cases. Two victims complained about this. One (the mother of a victim) talked about how the police had called her partner's (the offender) cell phone and was surprised to learn that the police were not aware that her partner was in prison. The other victim said that the police had never suggested the possibility of bundling all the complaints that she had been filing against her stalker; she found out about this possibility from a victim support worker. To cap it all, when the public prosecutor asked her for the identification numbers of her evidentiary statements she was unable to comply: the police had provided her with the wrong numbers.

The police called my partner [the suspect]; I had his cell phone with me so I could keep track of his missed calls [while he was in jail] and so I noticed that the police had tried to reach him. So I called them and I said my partner is in prison – I was like, you are the police, how's it possible that you don't know about that?
(Mother of male victim of intentional assault and battery
(respondent 30), participant)

You know, I had all these statements and documents, but ... (...) It's getting better now because I got some help from the mediator and the office for victim services, but at the start it was pure chaos. Each time I went to the police to report a new offence I got a copy of the police report, and that was that. (...) I reported the offences in two different cities, you would think there is one centralised database where they keep the records. But that's not the case. This file is such a chaos, I cannot see the forest for the trees anymore. (...) The prosecutor asked me to send him the identification numbers of the police reports of my case, so I asked the police, and it turns out that they gave me the wrong numbers. The whole time things like that happen. After a while you just feel like giving up.

(Female victim of stalking
(respondent 18), non-participant)

Second, two participants (victims in the same case) complained of a lack of cooperation between the police services of two different cities. Third, three victims mentioned mistakes on behalf of the police during the investigation of the case. For example, an employer who suspected his employee of stealing money from the cash register had asked the police to come to catch the employee in the act. Yet the police had come an hour earlier than agreed and had parked their car right in front of the entrance of the shop. As the participant said, he had been very lucky that the employee had not noticed the police car. Another example is that of two victims of burglary (same case) who had suggested to the police that the police trace their stolen computers. The police told them that that would not be possible because of a lack of specialists capable of conducting such an investigation.

Turning to offenders' opinions of the performance of the police, the issues that they came up with seemed to predominantly affect their perceptions of the neutrality or objectivity of the police. First, offenders tended to come up with the number of police officers that had been sent to intervene or to arrest them. Two men talked about the 'great show of force' that had been displayed when arresting them and that in their opinion was disproportional to the offence. One said that such a great show of police force is like a red rag to a bull: it elicits aggressive behaviour from offenders.

It was just too much. Too much. Two police cars and a bunch of cops, it's not as if they killed someone or anything. Absolutely exaggerated.

((Mother of) male offender, burglary and theft
(respondent 43), participant)

Staying with the topic of the police and use of power, two offenders accused the police of using their power to keep them in detention for as long as legally possible.[1]

They put me in custody and they kept me there for a long time. They kept me there for two days, the maximum that is allowed, until they had no choice but to let me go. And then they took me to see the investigating judge. They could have done that at 9 in the morning but they only did so at 4 in the afternoon.

(Male offender, partner violence (respondent 17), participant)

Q: Were you in jail?
R: Yes. For 24 hours. They kept me there for as long as possible. They wanted to screw with me and they did.

(Male offender, intentional assault and battery
(respondent 54), non-participant)

Another issue that was discussed by offenders was the police's methods of interrogation. Two offenders expressed disdain about the so-called 'good cop, bad cop' tactic, indicating that it did not work on them at all. This finding is in line with the finding reported above that people are more willing to cooperate with the police when the police treat them respectfully. Another offender recalled that the police officer interrogating him had asked him to choose between two methods of reporting about the interrogation: one option was that they would write everything down very elaborately, the other that they would only write down the essentials of what would be said. Yet they immediately added that if he opted for the first method, 'he would be stuck in there for several hours'.

> And as for the interrogation the day after, I don't know what to think about that. There were two of them, one that I could talk to and another one who was rude and stupid. That's a trick they say, to have a good cop and a bad cop.
>
> (Male offender, violent theft and threat of arson
> (respondent 24), non-participant)

Another offender had a problem with the two-way mirror in the interrogation room; the awareness that people were watching him had made him feel restless. He also mentioned the technique of the interrogators leaving the interrogation room for half an hour, then coming back, leaving again, and so on. He said that all this had been 'a bit too much' for him. A fifth offender remembered that the police had asked him every question 'in five different manners', as if to set a trap.

Finally, offenders also talked about police response times. Two of them mentioned that months passed between the offence and the police contacting them. Another indicated that an hour and a half had passed between the moment the police had called him to ask where he was – in order to be able to arrest him – and the moment they actually arrived at that place, and made fun of that because they had actually given him ample time to flee.

> They called me and said 'where are you?'. I said 'I'm in [town], why?' They said I would be extradited to [country], and I said 'okay, come pick me up then'. They arrived an hour and a half later. No chance for me to flee, if you see what I mean.
>
> (Male offender, robbery
> (respondent 27), non-participant)

Note

1 In Belgium, in line with art. 5.3 of the European Convention on Human Rights, the police cannot detain a suspect for more than 24 hours; after 24 hours an

investigating judge needs to decide whether the suspect should be released or should be held in custody (for a maximum of five days). Before the end of the five-day term an investigating court should decide whether the suspect should remain in preliminary custody.

References

Edwards, I. (2004). "An ambiguous participant. The crime victim and criminal justice decision-making." *British Journal of Criminology,* 44 (6): 967–82.

Leventhal, G.S. (1980). "What should be done with equity theory? New approaches to the study of fairness in social relationships." In Gergen, K.J., Greenberg, M.S. and Willis, R.H. (eds), *Social Exchange. Advances in Theory and Research* (27–55). London: Plenum Press.

Lind, E.A. and Tyler, T.R. (1988). *The Social Psychology of Procedural Justice.* New York: Plenum Press.

Malsch, M. (2009). *Democracy in the Courts. Lay Participation in European Criminal Justice Systems.* Aldershot: Ashgate.

Tversky, A. and Kahneman, D. (1979). "Prospect theory: an analysis of decision under risk." *Econometrica,* 47 (2): 263–92.

——(1984). "Choices, values, and frames." *American Psychologist,* 39 (4): 341–50.

Tyler, T.R. (1990). *Why People Obey the Law.* Princeton, NJ: Princeton University Press.

Tyler, T.R. and Lind, E.A. (1992). "A relational model of authority in groups." In Zanna, M.P. (ed.), *Advances in Experimental Social Psychology vol. 25* (115–91). London: Academic Press.

Weitzer, R. and Tuch, S.A. (2004). "Race and perceptions of police misconduct." *Social Problems,* 51 (3): 305–25.

4   Perceptions of procedural justice in pre-trial encounters with the judiciary

During the pre-trial interviews respondents were asked not only about their experience of the police but also of the judiciary, that is, those magistrates that had been appointed to lead the investigation of their case. In Belgium, criminal investigations are typically led by the public prosecutor; an investigating judge is appointed in case the investigation requires actions that might infringe individuals' freedom, such as when a decision needs to be taken on whether a suspect should be placed in preliminary custody or in case DNA tests or house searches need to be performed. Note that whereas each participant had had contact with the police, the majority of the participants had not actually met the public prosecutor or investigating judge that led the investigation of their case. This is customary; litigants do not usually meet any of these magistrates unless, in suspects' cases, a decision needs to be taken on whether to keep/place a suspect in preliminary custody. In such cases, the suspect is interrogated by the investigating judge. Therefore, only the offenders who had been brought before an investigating judge had actually met a magistrate at the time of the pre-trial interview. Still despite this general lack of personal contact between the participants and the judiciary in this phase of the criminal proceedings, the study revealed some noteworthy observations concerning the way litigants assess these magistrates and their work. The factors that were found to influence perceptions of procedural fairness again relate to issues of standing, neutrality and performance.

Standing

Perceptions of the degree to which the judiciary had made participants feel respected were determined by: (1) perceptions of respect for dignity; and (2) perceptions of the degree to which the judiciary showed concern for participants' needs.

Respect for dignity

As said, most victims never meet a magistrate in person during the pre-trial phase. Not surprisingly, then, two victims complained about impersonal treatment by the criminal justice system. One of them said that he felt like a number because during the criminal proceedings, so he said, virtually no attention is paid to victims. He felt completely neglected. The other victim compared the contact she had had with 'the criminal justice system' with the contact she had had with the police, rating the second as much more personal. Whereas the police, so she said, had always come by personally to hand over letters or to invite her for an extra interview, the prosecutor contacted her through letters sent by mail. The reason why she felt dissatisfied about this was that when police officers came by, they had always immediately explained to her why a (new) interview was necessary. Quite to the contrary, the letters from the prosecutor's office asking her to come by for an interview did not explain why, nor was there anyone to advise her. This had caused distress. Information, then, again appears to be an important factor for preventing victim distress.

> At some point we received an invitation for an interview at the Youth Prosecutor's office. (...) all the other invitations we had received for interviews had been brought to us in person: someone would come by and give us a letter or personally say 'could you please come by our office again, we have another couple of questions, don't worry'. But this was an invitation through mail (...) inviting us both [the respondent and her husband] for an interview, and we were asked to come at different times, so we were worried about what was going on.
> (Mother of female victim of sexual abuse
> (respondent 50), participant)

Even though victims had had no personal contact with the prosecutor, the prosecutors dealing with their case did influence their perceptions of standing. The lack of personal contact did not seem to prevent the communication of information relevant to standing. Prosecutors through their actions conveyed messages that victims felt confirmed or rather lacked acknowledgement of victim status. For example, a victim of stalking said that the fact that all her complaints had been dismissed by the public prosecutor made her feel like she was on her own and that they did not take the facts seriously. Another victim explained that the language and terminology used by the prosecutor in letters confirmed her victim status.

> Every letter I got from the prosecutor said 'You are receiving this letter because of these facts and since you were threatened with a weapon we take this case very seriously ... ' That made me feel listened to.
> (Female victim of robbery
> (respondent 47), participant)

References to magistrates' actual attitude were only found in interviews with offenders who had been interrogated by an investigating judge, since only these participants had had face-to-face contact with the judiciary. Three of the four offenders talking about their encounter with the investigating judge described this judge as strict, firm, angry, brutish and rude. One of these offenders said that if investigating judges want people to cooperate they should not behave like this, as such attitudes do not compel respect.

> The moment I came in he started scolding me saying 'you're a coward' and stuff like that. And I didn't really get a chance to tell my story. I couldn't get a word in edgewise. I mean, I was allowed to tell my story but (...) he said 'doesn't matter, you're a coward'. I asked him what would happen to me and he said 'you and your friends you'll get thrown in the can' and he yelled at me the whole time.
>
> (Male offender, violent robbery
> (respondent 48), participant)

An often mentioned consequence of the investigating judge's tough and severe attitude was that the offenders did not dare to speak much during the encounter, afraid as they were that anything they would say would increase the chance that the investigating judge would decide to keep them in custody. One person made a similar remark with respect to the judge that he had encountered in the investigating court:

> I came in and the judge was really rude, yelling 'why did you do this and why did you do that, you have committed theft before, why would I allow you to go free' (...). Of course I didn't dare to say anything anymore; I wanted him to release me from custody so I didn't dare go against him.
>
> (Male offender, theft
> (respondent 40), non-participant)

Two respondents perceived a relation between the judge's attitude and the criminal history of the suspect. Both expected that the judge would be unfriendly towards the suspect because of his criminal history. Another respondent said that judges do not realise the impact that their words have on those they speak to. He said that judges do not understand how it feels to be on trial and how important it is to be treated decently.

> You know, it would be good if judges would experience for themselves what it is like to be standing in front of them. (...) It would make them understand what it's like when you're standing there. (...) I don't think they know what it feels like to be on trial. They just do their jobs and they have no clue.
>
> (Male offender, theft
> (respondent 40), non-participant)

In general, the respondents perceived magistrates as cold and stiff people. Also, magistrates are perceived as being distant from 'ordinary people' through clothing and use of jargon.

These people, they dress in a certain manner, and the whole atmosphere in court is aimed at maintaining their job, their status, and their power.
(Male offender, intentional assault and battery
(respondent 36), participant)

During the interviews, as explained in Chapter 2, the participants were asked to comment on a number of statements asking them about the importance of the different subcomponents of procedural justice. Four statements gauged the importance of being treated with respect by judges. These were: (1) 'it is important that the judge will treat me with respect, friendlily and politely'; (2) 'it is important that the judge will respect my dignity and will not say hurtful things'; (3) 'it is important that the judge will give me the feeling that he is taking me seriously'; and (4) 'it is important that the judge will not behave pretentiously or give me a feeling of inferiority'. One victim on the first of these statements commented that judges should never be impolite. Nevertheless, she said, they ought to clearly reprimand offenders using a firm voice, whereas they should show understanding to victims so as to confirm that what the victim has been through was hurtful and difficult. In other words, she differentiated between victims and offenders; this recalls what was reported in the previous chapter about some people being more deserving of respectful treatment by police officers than others. Overall, participants thought it is self-evident that judges treat litigants with respect. Three participants with previous experience of the courts, one as a victim and two as offenders, with respect to the second statement ('it is important that the judge will respect my dignity and will not say hurtful things') said that they had experienced judges being tactless during their previous court experience and that this had impacted upon their self-esteem.

Really, the things these people say ... Sometimes I feel like asking them if it's even worth investing any time in me, because, the way they talk about me, it's like I'm no good for nothing.
(Male offender, sexual abuse
(respondent 53), participant)

Upon leaving the courtroom all I feel like is going to a bar and getting a drink. In court people are given the feeling that they don't count, that they have failed, that they have done things that are not right. That makes it all the more hard to get back on one's feet. Ever since all that happened I have a lot of trouble going to work and doing my job decently.
(Female offender, burglary and theft
(respondent 4), non-participant)

In relation to the third statement ('it is important that the judge will give me the feeling that he is taking me seriously') one offender replied that if this requirement is not satisfied, he would not dare say anything. Another one said

that judges can easily give people the *feeling* that they are taking them seriously but said that he does not believe that they actually do. The fourth
statement ('it is important that the judge will not behave pretentiously or give
me a feeling of inferiority') elicited comments from victims especially; they
said that judges are people like anyone else and therefore have no right to act
in a superior way. They should be 'people of flesh and blood'; one participant
said: 'it would be a literal sign of coming closer to people if they would not be
sitting on a raised bench'. However, the same participant thought that if
courts would eliminate all physical signs of their superiority, such as the robes,
they would lose their value. These signs according to this person are necessary
in order to illustrate that a courtroom is not a place for chitchat but for serious
matters. This specific issue will be further discussed in the next chapter.

Concern for needs

The interviewees expressed two types of needs to be met by the judicial
authorities: (1) the need for involvement in the criminal procedure and (2) the
need for authorities being available when needed.

The need for involvement in the criminal procedure

As described above, victim and offender involvement in the criminal procedure
can take one of two forms. Litigants may either become actively involved in the
procedure – in such case they are said to be participating in the procedure – or
they may be kept informed about the procedure, which was defined as a passive
form of involvement. Starting with the need for information, six offenders and
eight victims charged the authorities responsible for the investigation of their
case with failing to properly inform them about how the criminal proceedings
would develop, about the progress being made in the investigation or the actions
being taken by the authorities and about how much more time it would take for
the case to go to trial. Offenders also expressed a need for being informed about
what exactly they are being accused of and about the punishment they risk.

> I'm anxiously waiting for information (...). I lie awake at night some-
> times, thinking about this, wondering what will happen, what punishment
> do I risk, how much will I need to pay, things like that (...). If they
> would just give me a little more information at least I would know where
> I stand. (...) This is the reason I don't feel treated right.
>
> (Male offender, theft
> (respondent 40), non-participant)

Victims want answers to such questions as 'who will pay for my surgery?' or
'what will my role in the trial be?', and two victims were astonished to find
out, during the pre-trial interview, that they would not be informed of the
date of the trial unless they were registered as injured persons. As for information

on how much time it will take for the case to go to trial, one of the victims said that it is understandable that the criminal justice system cannot process all cases within a short time-span, but that victims should at least be informed about the progress of the case and about whether the suspect will be brought to court. Someone said that receiving a letter saying that it will still take a while before the case will go to court is preferable to not being informed at all.

The analysis suggests a link between receiving information and participation in the criminal proceedings, in that a lack of information about one's rights and the criminal proceedings inhibits active involvement in the trial. One victim referred to the fact that the letter that victims receive to inform them of the day of the trial does not explain in detail how exactly a trial works. There was also an offender who commented on the letters that litigants receive from the court in anticipation of the trial. He especially stressed their old-fashioned nature and their incomprehensibility to ordinary people, and said that these factors have a major influence on offenders' capacities to attend the trial. He said that it should be no surprise that many, especially those from lower social classes, are convicted in absentia. In fact, he claimed, only highly skilled citizens are able to understand the possibilities for participation in the trial.

> In fact I'm absolutely sure that a lot of people just stare at the document and don't have a clue as to what it's saying. (...) But it's important to understand it in order to be able to defend one's interests or to have one's interests defended; it's essential to understand that letter and its purpose and one's options.
>
> (Male victim of theft
> (respondent 37), non-participant)

The criminal justice system is also perceived to be highly complex; it is not sufficiently transparent for litigants to be able to participate in the criminal proceedings and thus to properly defend their interests. One victim, herself a social worker and thus possessing some knowledge of the criminal justice system, said that even to her the system is not transparent.

> I got documents informing me about the possibility of registering as an 'injured person'. And somewhere in those documents it said: 'if you want to get compensation, you might want to get a lawyer because the system is very complex'. That's so ... That's what I think is wrong about the criminal justice system: it's too complex, it's not workable.
>
> (Male victim of violent robbery
> (respondent 49), participant)

> As a victim, without a lawyer, one feels like a small fish in a very big pond. Because of my job I know a thing or two about the system, and even for me, it's really ... (*sighs*).
>
> (Female victim of stalking
> (respondent 18), non-participant)

One should of course, before accusing the criminal justice system of making it too difficult for victims and offenders to participate in the trial, first ask the question whether people actually *want* to participate. Each of the victims participating in the study was asked whether they planned to attend the trial and whether they wished to speak in court. Some victims had not taken a decision on this issue yet. Eight victims mentioned one or more reasons for attending the trial; eighteen mentioned one or more reasons for not doing so. Eleven victims mentioned one or more reasons for speaking in court; thirteen victims mentioned one or more reasons for not doing so. The reasons that victims gave for their decision not to attend the trial were the following:

- It would require too much of my time. (N = 3)
- I'm afraid that if I go, the offender will take revenge (case of neighbours' quarrel). (N = 3)
- I participated in mediation and we reached an agreement on compensation; the case is now closed for me. (N = 3)
- I participated in mediation; on a psychological level the case is now closed for me. (N = 2)
- Attending the trial would require me to relive the experience; I find that too hard. (N = 2)
- The case is clear, all information is in the file, so there is no need for me to go. (N = 2)
- From now on it's not up to me anymore, it's up to the judge. (N = 2)
- I'm afraid of the courtroom context. (N = 2)
- I'm afraid to see the offender. (N = 2)
- I want the offender to remain anonymous to me. (N = 1)
- I leave everything to my lawyer. (N = 1)
- I would only feel sufficiently confident to attend the trial if I had a lawyer, but a lawyer is too expensive. (N = 1)
- I don't feel like going. (N = 1)
- My attendance will have no impact on the outcome anyway. (N = 1)
- The offender's family will be there and I don't want to meet them. (N = 1)
- I do not see how attending the trial would be beneficial for me. (N = 1)
- Why should I go? I've done nothing wrong. (N = 1)
- If I would go, I would reward the offender (a stalker) with attention. (N = 1)
- The only reason to go would be to learn the sentence. I can learn about the sentence afterwards. (N = 1)

Reasons for victims to attend the trial were:

- I've never attended a trial; I'm curious to see what it's like. (N = 3)
- Because it's necessary in order to receive financial compensation. (N = 2)
- To hear what is said. (N = 1)
- To see the offender. (N = 1)

- To find out what the offender has to say, what his arguments are. (N = 1)
- To receive information about where I stand and how the case will proceed. (N = 1)
- To communicate to the offender that what he did was wrong, just by my presence. (N = 1)
- Because it puts an end to the case; I want to attend that moment. (N = 1)
- To find out whether the fact that we participated in mediation has an impact on the sentence. (N = 1)
- To learn the verdict. (N = 1)

The reasons that were mentioned for not speaking in court were categorised in two categories. A first category of reasons are those that pertain to the specific situation in the particular case. A second category of reasons are those that relate to the victims' characteristics: they are individual character-istics that would prevent the victim from speaking in court no matter the specific case. Starting with the reasons victims said they would not speak in court in the particular case they were involved in, these were:

- The case is clear, I have nothing to add. There is no need for me to speak in court. (N = 4)
- I have been able to tell my story to a victim support worker (N = 1)/I have been able to tell my story during mediation/to the mediator (N = 2); I am fine now.
- I fear revenge by the offender if I would speak my mind in court (case of neighbours' quarrel). (N = 1)
- The crime was not very serious. (N = 1)
- The offender has learned his lesson by now; there is no need for me to address him again. (N = 1)
- I'm satisfied with the way the case has been dealt with (trust in the authorities). (N = 1)
- I would not want the things I say to have an effect on the sentence; I don't want to be the one responsible for a harsh sentence. (N = 1)
- It would be too difficult for me to answer questions about the offence in the presence of the offender. (N = 1)

Reasons of a general nature for not speaking in court – that is, reasons that would prevent the victim from speaking in court no matter the specific circumstances – were the following:

- It's not up to victims to judge their offender(s). (N = 3)
- I'm not the type of person that wants to get the most out of such a case (financially). (N = 3)
- I'm afraid that the offender's lawyer will ask me questions. (N = 2).
- It's not something I would ever do/I wouldn't dare to. (N = 2)
- I'm too afraid of the whole setting. (N = 2)

- Talking to a judge is dangerous; there is a big chance of misinterpretation of one's words. I would be too afraid to say something that could be misinterpreted. (N = 1)
- I leave it to my lawyer; she has studied the law and knows exactly what to say. (N = 1)
- I would not be able to control myself if the judge behaved arrogantly towards me. (N = 1)

Those victims who said that they would like the chance to speak their mind during the trial advanced the following reasons:

- I would like to express my opinion on punishment to the judge. (N = 5; note that each of these five victims said they would like to request the judge to be *lenient*).
- I would speak if the defence starts telling lies and falsehoods. (N = 2)
- I would do it to make sure that the judge imposes a contact-ban on the offender. (N = 1)
- I would like to say that I hope the offender gets punished for his acts. (N = 1)
- I want to confront the offenders so that I'm not just an anonymous person anymore for them. (N = 1)

In discussing offenders' wishes for active involvement, attention should go not only to their plans for participating to the trial but also to the degree to which they feel that they had a chance to voice their opinion during the interrogation by the investigating judge. Two of the four offenders who encountered an investigating judge reproached this judge for not having taken the time to listen to their story; moreover, as reported above, the manner in which they were treated prevented three of them from really having their say.

Q: So all four of you were sent to jail for ten days? (...) In your view, was that a correct decision?
R: No, it wasn't. Not at all in fact. I haven't had the chance to ... Well they should have at least taken more effort to listen to my story, the investigating judge too.

(Male offender, violent robbery
(respondent 48), participant)

Turning to offenders' plans to attend the trial and speak in court and their reasons for (not) doing so, none of the offenders participating in this study had any doubt about whether to attend the trial; it was quite obvious to them that they would. Probably for this reason, only three offenders expressed a specific reason to attend the trial. These were:

- To show that I care about my future. (N = 1)
- To see the people who will decide about my future. (N = 1)

- To ask the judge whether he would allow a payment plan so that I can pay compensation to the victims in instalments. (N = 1)

There were only three offenders who said that they would refrain from voicing their opinion in court. The topic of having one's say during the trial too was a self-evident one for offenders; offenders as opposed to victims know for sure that they will be given the chance to address the judge. Most of them plan to make use of this opportunity. The three offenders who said that they would not speak, gave the following reasons for their decision:

- Lawyers are better trained to speak in court; they know exactly what to say. (N = 1)
- One should be very careful about what one says in court (risk of mis-interpretation). (N = 1)
- I told my story to the investigating judge; there's no need to repeat it to the trial judge. (N = 1)

Six offenders said that they did not believe that speaking in court would change anything about the outcome. As this concerns an important debate in the procedural justice literature (i.e. about the instrumental versus the value-expressive value of voice, see Chapter 1), it merits some highlighting. One of these offenders said that the only reason that offenders are offered a chance to speak in court is to make them feel good; another one added that what happens in court is 'only show'. Only one offender made an allusion to the fact that voicing one's opinion in court may be fulfilling for oneself – the other ones regarded speaking in court solely in instrumental terms, that is, with a reference to whether it would potentially influence the outcome. Offenders who had previous experience of the courts were not generally impressed by the degree to which judges had listened to their stories on those previous occasions. Some blamed judges for this, others said that there is simply not sufficient time for judges to do so – which some said they understand.

> I think it's all about keeping up appearances, just to make sure that people don't get the feeling that they didn't get a chance to say something and everything was decided over their heads.
>
> (Male offender, theft
> (respondent 39), non-participant)

Two final remarks on active participation are the following. First, when people say that they will not attend the trial or speak in court this does not mean that they do not value voice or opportunities for participation. Active participation in the trial is sometimes avoided for reasons such as being afraid of the offender or of the court context, as explained above; however, that does not mean that the opportunity for voice is not valued. People do attach great importance to the possibility that a lawyer or another person (someone suggested their therapist) represents them in court and conveys their story to those present there in the event that they do not feel up to it themselves. Voice, then, as in having one's side of the story told in court, is important to nearly everyone, but not all are comfortable about voicing their story themselves. The second remark relates to this first one: it seems that what is important to people is to know that if one would like to participate in the trial, it is possible to do so. People should be able to freely choose if and how they would like to be represented in court. Freedom of choice, then, is paramount:

> I do think it's important to feel like one at least has the chance to have a say. And that everybody can decide for themselves, knowing that if they want to have a say, they can. That's very different from going to court and knowing beforehand that you won't have an opportunity to have a say.
>
> (Mother of female victim of sexual abuse
> (respondent 50), participant)

Respondents' need for participation in the criminal proceedings was not only gauged through open questions; respondents were also asked to judge a number of statements relating to participation. Three statements asked respondents for their need for process control, which was interpreted in a strict sense as having control over the procedures used in court. Court procedures are strict; all roles are defined as well as when certain people are allowed to speak and when they are not. The three statements on process control were constructed so as to find out whether people agree with these procedures or would like to have more of a say on them. The three statements were: (1) 'it is important that I will be able to exert some control over the proceedings'; (2) 'it is important that I will have a say on the court proceedings' and (3) 'it is important that I will be able to intervene if I believe the procedures are not being applied correctly'. In general, those respondents who were familiar with how trials work thought that trial practices are correct; they did not indicate a need to change these. The main reason for their approval of court procedures was that in their view the procedure allows all the parties to speak. Everybody is allowed a moment to voice his/her opinion, several participants said, and therefore the procedures are correct. This is important information with a view to the significance of voice, but the participants did seem to overrate the chances that victims get for speaking in court. In reality, those victims who did not register as a civil party are seated on the public benches and are not involved in the trial in any way. Only civil parties are physically seated in the area where the judge, lawyers and defendant(s) are seated and are questioned by the judge. Yet that does not mean that they actually get time to tell their story. Some judges will allow victims a couple of minutes to tell their story, but other judges limit their conversation with the victim to some brief and factual questions about the amount of compensation the victim is seeking. Belgium does not have a system of victim impact statements; therefore, the time that is given to an individual victim to tell his/her story during the trial very much depends on the judge presiding at the trial.

In the end, the current system allows all parties to have a say. That's good. At the end of the day everybody is interviewed and everybody has a say.
(Mother of male victim of intentional assault and battery (respondent 30), participant)

As for the need for actual control over the procedure, the respondents felt that the course of the proceedings should remain in the hands of the judiciary. One person said that if litigants were to have a say on the court procedures the system would become unfair. Still, it was considered important that one is allowed to intervene when one remarks that the procedures are not applied correctly. One participant did say that in order to be able to do so, litigants need to *know* the procedures, which is where the shoe often pinches.

I think the parties should be informed of everything so they can keep track but they shouldn't be the ones in control of the procedure; things wouldn't be fair anymore if they were.
(Female offender, intentional and unintentional assault and battery (respondent 46), participant)

I think it's highly unlikely that I would notice when procedures are not being applied correctly.
(Male victim of intentional assault and battery, threats and vandalism (respondent 45), non-participant)

Another five statements gauged people's need for voice. These statements were: (1) 'it is important that I will have ample opportunity to state my position and clarify my wishes'; (2) 'it is important that the judge will give me feedback after I have spoken'; (3) 'it is important that I will be able to speak to the judge in person if I wish to do so'; (4) 'it is important that I will be allowed to spontaneously address the judge if I have a question' and (5) 'it is important that the judge will allow me to speak on my request'. The first two statements did not elicit many comments, but the other three statements did give rise to a great deal of discussion. The third statement, for example, gauged the extent to which respondents would like to be able to talk to the judge who would decide on their case in private. At present this is not possible in Belgium, but respondents were asked whether they would choose to do it if it were an option. Answers were divided; many had doubts. Two offenders and one victim liked the idea of speaking to the judge in private because it would give them a chance to tell their story without being watched by an audience. One offender said that talking to the judge in private would be good because it would allow the judge to personally get to know the offender instead of having to rely on documents describing the offender. One victim said that he would like to speak to the judge in order to ask the judge not to be too harsh on the offender when deciding on the sentence. This was the only victim who explicitly mentioned an instrumental reason for talking to the judge in private; yet note that the instrumental reason in this case was to influence the sentence so that it would be *mild*. None of the offenders explicitly mentioned an instrumental reason for speaking to the judge; those who explained their reasons were more concerned with being able to tell their story in private and in a quiet environment. One offender said that he would not want to speak to the judge because of the way judges act (i.e. being rude) and two others said that personal contact with the judge cannot be combined with judges' neutrality. Finally, two offenders said that all would depend on whether the case was clear.

> But, well, this leads us back to a former question, would he be impartial? I don't think he could be impartial if that was allowed.
>
> > (Male offender, intentional assault and battery
> > (respondent 31), participant)

> It would allow me to say things that I don't dare to say in public. Personal things.
>
> > (Male offender, fraud
> > (respondent 33), participant)

> That's a difficult question – it depends on the case. In my case it's important, but if I had just stolen something, what would there be to say? In such case it wouldn't be that important. It's important to me in this case because my case is very complex. But it wouldn't be necessary in each and every case.
>
> > (Male offender, intentional assault and battery
> > (respondent 8), non-participant)

The participants also took the practical side of litigants having private meetings with judges into account, saying that it is simply not feasible for judges to talk to every single victim and offender in person because of a lack of time.

> R1: Poor judge. Imagine what would happen if everyone would ask for that …
> R2: They would never finish their work, it would be even worse than it is today.
>
> > (Male offenders, intentional assault and battery and vandalism
> > (respondents 9 and 10), participants)

The fourth and fifth statement (about being allowed to spontaneously address the judge if one has a question and to be allowed to speak when one requests it) elicited similar comments. Many said that if everyone were allowed to spontaneously talk in court, chaos would be the consequence, but some added that it should be possible to raise one's hand for permission to say something or make a comment, although this opportunity should be used sparingly. The participants clearly felt that it is important that everybody respects the rules and waits for one's turn to speak.

> I think the trial would descend into chaos. If you really feel like there is something you want to say, then just write a note for yourself and wait until the time is right. (...) It's only normal, there's procedures everywhere. I mean, in the doctor's waiting room people await their turn too, right?
>
> (Female victim of intentional assault and battery
> (respondent 32), participant)

The need for the authorities to be available

During the interviews, two persons talked about how the judicial authorities had not been there when they had needed their help. One offender explained that the courts had refused to help his family by putting his stepson in a juvenile institution, which had led to an escalation of the situation and as such to him committing an offence against his stepson. The father of two child victims expressed a need for magistrates to protect child victims to a greater degree. His children were living with their mother – he had divorced her – but were repeatedly beaten by their mother. Still the judge did not take any measures to take the children away from their mother pending the trial.

Neutrality

Absence of bias or prejudice

Few references to the judiciary being biased or prejudiced were found throughout the pre-trial interviews. The absence of references to this issue could be due to the lack of personal contact between respondents and the judiciary, which would prevent litigants from noticing where those responsible for the investigation of their case were being biased or prejudiced in doing so. Alternatively, the participants just did not have any remarks relating to this matter. Only one person, an offender who had encountered an investigating judge, mentioned the issue of the judiciary being biased. According to this participant, (investigating) judges are harsher towards young men such as him than they are to 'older people with good jobs', which he considered unfair.

> He [the investigating judge] was just rude (...). His attitude was like 'you're young, you're gonna pay for this'. (...) They wouldn't be like that with an older suspect. An older man with a good job will get less of a punishment than a young guy. That's not correct. That's totally wrong.
>
> (Male offender, theft
> (respondent 40), non-participant)

During the interviews, participants commented on three statements about the need for judges to be impartial. The first statement was 'it is important that the judge will be impartial and will favour neither party', the second was 'it is important that the judge will treat all parties alike, that he will not discriminate', the third was 'it is important that the judge will apply methods that treat all parties equally'. These statements led respondents to discuss whether it is justifiable for judges to be harsher on offenders than on victims; as with the police, opinions were mixed.

> He should be more sympathetic to victims than to offenders. To offenders he should be more resolute; offenders must be pointed at their mistakes. An offender should be treated more firm than a victim.
>
> (Female victim of intentional assault and battery (respondent 32), participant)

> He must be fair, that means he must treat everybody the same way. (...) No matter who the victim is, I am human too.
>
> (Male offender, sexual abuse (respondent 53), participant)

Fact-based decision-making

The element 'fact-based decision-making', that is, the degree to which the authorities have done their best to gather all relevant information on the case, was by far the most alluded to element of 'neutrality'. During the interviews, respondents mainly uttered negative remarks about the thoroughness of the investigation that had been performed in their case. For example, an offender complained that the authorities do not make the effort of making sure that the judge possesses recent and up-to-date information. He referred to the use of reports about his personality which according to him are outdated, because they date back to the time he first entered prison. After a few years in prison, so he said, his personality had changed, but no new psychological report was composed for the sake of his new trial. The judge therefore would need to take a decision on the basis of outdated reports. One victim had found that the police sometimes insinuate or misunderstand certain things and then pass this incorrect information onto the legal authorities. She said that even though she had been able to prove the police's information to be wrong, the judiciary had kept on using the information. Another victim said that the authorities should make more effort in trying to find out what kind of person the victim is. The reason for this, he explained, is that judges are forced to take on the role of psychiatrist, something they have no training in. It would be better, this person said, if judges received reports not only about the offender but also about the victim in order to make a proper judgment.

I think that'd be really useful for him [the judge], for someone to interview the victim. (...) I think reports should be made about all the people that come to court, because the judge has to decide cases in a very short time. They're like 'okay this one looks like a serious guy and this one doesn't'; they're expected to do what a psychiatrist should actually do. It shouldn't be like that.

(Male victim of intentional assault and battery
(respondent 11), participant)

In a similar vein, one offender stated that those investigating the case should gather more background information about offenders (such as their family and financial situation and their place of residence) so judges can take an informed decision on how to sanction any particular offender. Arguing that psychiatrists have had more than ten years of training, he said that it is impossible for judges to properly assess the people they are confronted with, especially given the limited amount of time that is available in court.

It cannot be that hard to fill out a short survey about people so they [judges] at least get an idea of people's social backgrounds. (...) If you tell me which street someone lives in I can tell you: okay, that is an upmarket residential neighbourhood so this person has a good home. Basic facts like is a particular person married or divorced or do they have kids, seven or eight indicators should suffice for the judge to get a better idea of the woman or man standing in front of him, to get an idea of people's background.

(Male offender, intentional assault and battery
(respondent 36), participant)

The offender who had participated in penal mediation said that she had the impression that to the authorities it was more important that one of the parties confess than to uncover the actual truth. Another offender felt that the authorities had made absolutely no effort to investigate his case; in his opinion, it had been 'guesswork'.

It took two years for the case to get to trial, and still they didn't conduct a proper investigation. This was just guesswork.

(Male offender, intentional assault and battery
(respondent 8), non-participant)

Some people did express satisfaction about the quality of the investigation. An offender who was satisfied about the thoroughness with which the case had been investigated referred to the fact that there had been a mediation process, that a justice assistant had come to his home in person to observe the situation and that reports had been written of all these actions. Importantly, he said that all this had raised his confidence that the trial would be conducted fairly. In other words, a fair trial for this respondent is based on a thorough investigation of the case, with all the relevant information being gathered, to enable the judge to make an accurate decision.

Four statements explored respondents' expectations about the judge's investigation of their case. The statements were: (1) 'it is important that the judge will carefully examine the evidence', (2) 'it is important that the judge will carefully explain the reasons for his decision', (3) 'it is important that the judge is very well acquainted with the case file and is thoroughly prepared' and (4) 'it is important that the judge will examine the case carefully and will take the time to do so'. The common denominator marking the comments on these statements was that they are important yet unfeasible because of judges' heavy case loads and because files often run to hundreds of pages. The participants attached great importance to the judge being well prepared, but some added that one cannot expect judges to know the smallest details of every case. One offender and one victim said that it is not *desirable* that judges know the case in great detail in advance because if they do, they might be less open to new information adduced in court. As for the statement that sufficient time should be taken for dealing with cases in court, again people thought that it is important that their case is not dealt with in a hurry but some respondents replied that it is not feasible to take much time for every case in court because of the high case loads. Some added that the time that should be spent on a case in court depends on the complexity of the case.

> Well it's a bit utopian to expect that, I mean, some case files consist of ten thousands of pages. It's not possible for a judge to know all the details of such cases. And in my case, I guess the file will not be very extensive but still …
> (…) Judges can't be expected to know all files in detail. That's impossible.
>
> (Male victim of theft
> (respondent 37), non-participant)

> You know I actually think it's better if the judge hears the story for the first time in court. (…) It's important for him to be aware of what the case is about, of course, but he should still be open to things that are not included in the file, things that are brought out in court which are new.
>
> (Female offender, intentional and unintentional assault and battery
> (respondent 46), participant)

> Judges can't spend endless time on cases, right, they have to make progress, they need to take decisions. They can't keep delving into files endlessly and get down to the last detail.
>
> (Male victim of intentional assault and battery
> (respondent 12), non-participant)

One last word about the category 'fact-finding', which evinces its importance, is that some respondents' main reason for participating in mediation was that doing so allows them to convey extra information about the crime and its consequences to the judge (i.e. by means of the mediation agreement that is sent to the judge). Two victims and one offender mentioned this as their main motivation for participating in mediation.

Honesty

Statements pertaining to magistrates' (dis)honesty were found in two offender interviews. The first offender said that the investigating judge had asked him if he had ever committed a crime in the past, to which the man had replied that he had not. The judge then confronted him with a copy of his previous criminal record that showed that he had indeed committed a crime in the past. The offender explained that he had misunderstood the question – he thought he had been asked whether he had ever been in prison. He felt unfairly treated by this interrogation tactic. Another participant had in a previous trial had the impression that lawyers and magistrates had made deals about his sentence.

> My lawyer was having coffee with the investigating judge and they car-pooled. I mean, seriously? Where does that end? Where does that end?
>
> (Male offender, robbery
> (respondent 27), non-participant)

> In a previous case of mine my lawyer said 'you'll get six to eight years', and there, I got seven years. It's obvious that they discussed that beforehand. And I have more examples of such so-called coincidences.
>
> (Male offender, robbery
> (respondent 27), non-participant)

One survey statement gauged the importance of honesty; the statement was 'it is important that the judge will behave correctly, will be honest and will not lie'. The only comment that was given with respect to this statement was that it is simply unimaginable for judges to lie. The self-evident nature of the statement may explain why few people felt a need to comment on it.

Performance

A number of participants indicated that a criminal justice system is indispensable for any society to function well, yet throughout the interviews the participants did point to a number of flaws in the system. The time it takes to process a case was by far the most cited problem (twelve victims, four offenders). It was hard for the participants to understand that even when their case was clear and the offender had confessed, the criminal proceedings took several months or even years. The fact that trials are often spread out over multiple sessions was heavily criticised too.

> Like I said, this procedure has been going on for more than a year and a half and it's still not finished. I get called to court, I go there, the other

guy's lawyer says he hasn't got the complete file yet and bam, the whole thing is postponed and I'm expected to go back a couple of months later. I don't understand how that's possible.

> (Male victim of intentional assault and battery
> (respondent 21), participant)

Participants mentioned different reasons for why exactly the slowness of the criminal justice system was bothering them. First, victims' recovery process may be hampered when it takes a long time for a case to be processed and completed. If a victim recovers from the victimisation experience before the case is dealt with in court, the trial can open old wounds.

> So it's been one year and now the case is set for trial. Maybe it'd be better if things would go a bit faster. (...) Just for the sake of the victim's recovery. It's better for the trial to take place while the victim's still recovering from what happened 'cause then maybe the judge's decision can provide some comfort and helps getting over the offence. But after such a long time old wounds are ripped open again.

> (Female victim of intentional assault and battery
> (respondent 32), participant)

A second reason for the discontent about the slow pace of the criminal justice system is that offenders are not discouraged from continuing their wrong-doings and may even flee; such slowness in the system, some said, induces a breeding ground for impunity. In a similar vein, victims believe offenders learn nothing from being sentenced months or years after the fact.

R1:   [respondent's wife] If they [the offenders] would see my husband now they'd probably think nothing really happened to him, he looks fine, but if they had seen him the day after, they would have been surprised.

R2:   That's right. I was all black and blue and I couldn't see. But if they'd see me now they'd probably be like: 'what's the big deal?'.

> (Male victim of intentional assault and battery
> (respondent 12), non-participant)

> After a while I started thinking 'Really, they're just gonna get away with it? How's that possible?'

> (Male victim of intentional assault and battery
> (respondent 12), non-participant)

They [the criminal justice system] should react much more quickly. Whenever something happens they should do something about it as soon as possible. When people commit a crime, arrest them, try them immediately and give them a punishment of some kind so they realise their mistake right there and then. If they [the authorities] wait too long, like they did with me, sentences have no effect, people won't learn from them.

> (Male offender, intentional assault and battery
> (respondent 8), non-participant)

A third reason for criticism of the slow pace of justice delivery is financial: one victim said that his company risked going bankrupt because he could not recover the money that had been stolen by an employee without a court order. Fourth, victims have many questions but no one to answer them until the case goes to trial. Fifth, it was considered unfair towards offenders to punish them months or even years after the fact, because in those months or years they may have got themselves together, changed their lifestyle and found a job, and suddenly all that is taken from them. This may very well lead them astray again, victims said.

> This may sound strange, but in fact it's not fair to the offenders either. (...) Maybe they already got themselves together or are really trying to make something of their lives when suddenly they are confronted again with what they did in the past. It'd be better if they would pronounce a sentence right after the facts.
>
> ((Wife of) male victim of intentional assault and battery
> (respondent 12), non-participant)

This concern was also voiced by offenders:

> There came a point where I turned my life around, I realised I had to change and grow up. I quit the business, I found a job (...) and then all of a sudden it all starts again.
>
> (Male offender, intentional assault and battery
> (respondent 8), non-participant)

> Like I said, I'm in prison now doing time for things I did 19 years ago. That's something I think is very wrong about the system. In the meantime I made something of my life again and they just took all that away from me.
>
> (Male offender, intentional assault and battery
> (respondent 31), participant)

Finally, according to one offender and one victim, the problem with the criminal proceedings taking a long time is that one forgets the details about the crime; it becomes hard to recall the exact circumstances.

Despite the criticism, a few participants expressed understanding for the slow pace of the criminal justice system. These people realised that theirs is not the only case to be dealt with and that crime rates are too high for the system to keep up. Yet this does not mean that the slow pace of the system does not bother them.

> There's a flood of criminals swarming the streets. I know that; I realise that it's not easy to deal with each of them swiftly. But it really frustrates people.
>
> (Male victim of intentional assault and battery (respondent 12), non-participant)

Two participants said that it is a good thing that the trial does not follow the offence immediately, because the time in between offers one the chance to participate in mediation and to prepare oneself for the trial. A victim said that it would be too difficult for victims to face their offender(s) too soon.

> One must be able to prepare for the case, right. And get some time to calm down. Also, that's the time period in which people can go through mediation.
>
> (Male offender, fraud (respondent 33), participant)

> I liked the timing in my case. You see, if they had tried the case, say, two weeks after the facts, I wouldn't have been up for it. If they had done it two weeks after the facts, I wouldn't have had the courage to face them [the offenders] yet.
>
> (Female victim of robbery (respondent 47), participant)

A second main theme in the performance category was responsibility: four victims talked about whether or not the judicial authorities in their view had taken their responsibility seriously. One of the victims said that because all members of the criminal justice system chain had taken their responsibility seriously she felt recognised as a victim and did not have any urge to take part in the criminal proceedings. From the quote below a link between being recognised as a victim and the need for participation can be detected, and also a relief on behalf of the victim that she did not *need* to take part in the criminal proceedings.

> In my view everything has always been very clear and everyone involved has taken their responsibility to heart; everybody did what they had to do in order for the offenders to be punished or at least confronted with what they did. And since they did, there's no need for me to do so. All I have to do is tell my story about the consequences of what they did since I happen to be the only one who knows what the consequences were. But I don't feel like I am the one who has to make sure they get tried.
>
> (Female victim of robbery (respondent 47), participant)

Two victims said that the judicial authorities had not taken their responsibilities seriously. They were disappointed over the strict separation of powers among different services (e.g. court clerks, justice assistants, social workers) and the limited knowledge of the people working at each service. They had expected that the people working at the different services would have a broader knowledge of the system as a whole. Moreover, they said, all had shuffled responsibility to other services when concrete decisions had to be taken.

> But then again, each of them has their own limited field of authority, and that's that. I did think that people's field of authority would be broader or that they would possess more knowledge about each other's competences. But they can't do anything beyond their limited authority.
>
> (Father of male victims of intentional assault and battery (respondent 6), non-participant)

> As soon as they are expected to take a decision, they delegate responsibility and pass the problem on to someone else. It takes for ever for a final decision to be taken.
>
> (Father of male victims of intentional assault and battery (respondent 6), non-participant)

> It's not about the way they treated us or if they listened to us or whether or not they showed understanding, they did fine on those things and they really seemed to be the right people in the right place. But the result is just superficial and disappointing. They gave us the feeling that they understood our problem (...) so we had high hopes, but when we got their report we were just so disappointed; they didn't help us at all.
>
> (Father of male victims of intentional assault and battery (respondent 6), non-participant)

Related to this, no fewer than ten victims believed that the different services making up the criminal justice system lacked cooperation. First, the information flow between different services was considered deficient. A prime example is that of an offender who while in prison received a letter from the public prosecutor informing him of the possibility of mediation at home. Second, victims in each step of the proceedings meet new people to whom they have to tell their story all over again. Not only is this last aspect difficult for victims, the strict separation of powers and the lack of cooperation between services also makes victims lose oversight.

> These services, they all operate on their own, it's so hard to get them to cooperate. (...) The prosecutor's office is following up on my case, there's someone at victim support that I'm in touch with, there's a lawyer working on my case and there's a mediator working on my case. All these different people at different locations ... There's no structure and also each time I've had to tell my story all over again.
>
> (Female victim of stalking (respondent 18), non-participant)

Third, even though victims reported a crime to the police, they had to go to yet another service (i.e. the prosecutor's office) to register as an injured person (which is the status they need to take in order to be informed about the main decisions made during the criminal proceedings). In the meantime, the legal provisions concerning registration as an injured person have been adapted to make the procedure less complex, but at the time of the study, victims had to go through the procedure as outlined above. It was considered absurd that the prosecutor's office was not informed automatically about who had reported a crime; instead victims had to inform the authorities about their victimisation twice.

> At the police station, where I just officially reported that I was the victim of a crime, they gave me a flyer saying if you want to register as an injured person you should go to this other office where you have to officially state 'I was victimised'. Again. As if they don't know that yet.
>
> (Male victim of violent robbery
> (respondent 49), participant)

5 Perceptions of procedural justice in encounters with the courts

This chapter describes how the participants assessed the fairness of the trial and how they experienced the aftermath of the criminal proceedings. Five elements were found to determine people's assessments about the fairness of the trial. These were perceptions of standing, perceptions of neutrality and perceptions of performance, but also the court setting/trial practices and the behaviour of the opposing party. Each of these elements will be dealt with in this chapter. Note that, in Belgium, trials take place anywhere from a couple of months to two or more years after the offence. This very much depends on the judicial district where the offence happened and the type of crime. Also, most of the participants' cases were tried in one session, but in some cases there had been multiple sessions due to continuances. Furthermore, in Belgium, court hearings involving adult defendants are, as a rule, open to the public. There are exceptions to this rule – the court may for example order hearings or a certain part of them to take place behind closed doors in the interest of public order or to protect the privacy of (one of) the parties (e.g. cases involving a minor or sexual offences). This exception applied in one participant's case; all the others had been involved in a public trial.

Standing

Participants' post-trial references to perceptions of standing related to: (1) respect for dignity; (2) respect for rights; (3) concern for needs; and (4) social standing.

Respect for dignity

This first subcategory concerns elements mentioned by the respondents that related to respect for them as a person, to respect for their dignity, or to the attitude of officials. An element mentioned by one victim was recognition of victim status. In her case, recognition of victim status had resulted from the judge conveying a message of understanding of what she had been through and confirming the seriousness of the facts. The respondent attested that she had more self-confidence now that she had finally met a judge who did not blame her for what happened but to the contrary expressed understanding for her position. She had met several judges on other occasions and each time had felt that the judge blamed her for what happened in her family.

> The other judges I met clearly felt that we as parents were the evil ones and that we failed to decently educate our kids (...). Time and time again that's what they said and now it was very different, it was a completely different feeling.
>
> (Mother of female victim of sexual abuse (respondent 23), non-participant)

Two elements infringing offenders' feelings of standing were the use of handcuffs and the fact that judges are seated on a raised bench. As to the first aspect, two offenders declared that being handcuffed in court brought them down to the level of cattle. The second aspect according to one respondent makes one feel inferior to the judge. Yet other respondents talking about judges' physical position vis-à-vis litigants did not experience it as problematic. They did say that for judges to be seated on raised benches is an old-fashioned custom, but did not express the feeling that it made them feel inferior to the judge. This particular aspect of trials will be discussed in more detail in the section on court setting and organisation.

> [on being brought into the courtroom handcuffed] That's what frustrates me most of all, and you know why, because the message to the people in court is: 'look at him, a true bandit, a villain'. They're gonna judge me as a person but they treat me like an animal.
>
> (Male offender, sexual abuse (respondent 53), participant)

The respondents were asked to describe the judge and the public prosecutor that dealt with their case in their own words. As for judges, offenders described them in terms of whether they had been neutral on the one hand and in terms of whether they had been understanding, offensive, respectful, correct, patronising or friendly on the other hand, which are all issues related to judges' respect for the dignity of the offenders. Overall, offenders were satisfied with the behaviour of the judge that had tried their case. Two offenders were truly dissatisfied about the judge; they said that the judge was a cold-hearted person who had never tried to understand their position and had been prejudiced. Victims too when evaluating judges talked about understanding and friendliness and thus about issues pertaining to receiving respect for one's dignity, but they added firmness towards the offender and likewise attached considerable importance to the judge reprimanding the offender publicly. In other words, victims spontaneously brought up how the judge had behaved towards the offender, whereas offenders only considered the judge's behaviour towards themselves. The majority of victims were content about the judge, those who were not were so particularly because the judge had not been listening carefully during the trial or had not reprimanded the offender.

She [the judge] really hammered it into him that what he did was wrong and that it wasn't the first time ... Well, she really stressed that he made a big mistake.

(Female victim of rape
(respondent 38), participant)

When asked what they thought about the prosecutor, both victims and offenders talked as much about the prosecutor's sentence demand as about his/her attitude towards them. Victims also took into account whether the prosecutor had reprimanded the offender.

During the first hearing I thought she [the prosecutor] was very firm. You see the lawyer asked for a conditional sentence but she demanded a prison sentence.

(Father of male victims of intentional assault and battery
(respondent 6), non-participant)

Two additional observations on respectful treatment are the following. First, one offender said that people who come before a judge several times for committing crimes lose the right to be treated with respect. This reflects what respondents said with respect to the right to be treated respectfully by the police – here too, some said conditions apply. Second, defendants were not offended by judges reprimanding them as long as the disapproval of their behaviour was expressed in respectful terms. This is interesting because some victims said that they were not sure whether it is possible for a judge to express censure and behave respectfully to defendants at the same time.

He [the judge] said, 'Well, Mr [respondent's surname], don't let it happen again, okay? I don't ever want to see you here again'. Well, something like that. He was really okay.

(Male offender, fraud
(respondent 33), participant)

In seven interviews evidence was found that litigants build expectations about the judgment on the basis of the judge's attitude towards the offender. When the judge treats the offender very unkindly in court, litigants expect the sentence to be very severe. Also, people feel somewhat frustrated where the judge's behaviour does not allow them to predict the judgment.

When she [the judge] interrupted him [the defendant] saying 'I've had enough!' I was like, wow, she's gonna be tough on him, he's gonna get a real harsh sentence.

(Female victim of rape
(respondent 38), participant)

> She [the judge] insisted that it was her courtroom and that she was the one in charge. She gave people a chance to take the floor but she made it clear that there were lines that weren't to be crossed. At the end of the hearing she changed; she became more accommodating. It left me feeling confused: it's impossible to know what to expect from someone like that.
>
> (Male offender, intentional assault and battery (respondent 31), participant)

A last finding concerns the degree to which one can tolerate lack of respect in court. A victim had been told by her lawyer that chances were high that the judge would treat her harshly because of the fact that she was partly responsible for what had happened. But she kept in mind that none of the friends or family members who knew what had happened had failed her. She said that she would hold on to their support in case the judge treated her badly.

> I've told my story to a couple of people and they haven't ... I mean, those people are close friends of mine and they didn't drop me. So I don't care what the judge says about me.
>
> (Mother of female victim of sexual abuse (respondent 50), participant)

The four statements that were presented to the participants about the importance of being treated with respect by judges elicited some – but not many – comments. The statements were: (1) 'it is important that the judge will treat me with respect, friendlily and politely'; (2) 'it is important that the judge will respect my dignity and will not say hurtful things'; (3) 'it is important that the judge will give me the feeling that he is taking me seriously'; and (4) 'it is important that the judge will not behave pretentiously or give me a feeling of inferiority'. Someone replied to the second statement that it all depends on the gravity of the offence, another one pointed to the difficulty of striking a balance between reprimanding the offender and being polite. As to the fourth statement, one offender referred to the fact that judges are seated on raised benches; another felt that as judges are highly educated it is impossible not to feel inferior.

Respect for rights

In Chapter 3, the category 'respect for rights' was defined as having two components: (1) references to actual breaches of the law by the authorities or to those instances where a right had been respected; and (2) references pertaining to perceived breaches of rights. Complaints about actual breaches of rights were only found in offender interviews. One complaint was that the subpoena deadline had not been respected. The Belgian Code of Criminal Procedure prescribes that offenders should be informed of the date of the trial at least ten days in advance (three days when they are being held in preliminary custody); in one offender's case, this deadline had not been respected.

So then I got this letter saying you'll have to appear in court, the trial date being the week after. (...) all of a sudden I get this letter, I didn't have time to arrange for anything! So I called my lawyer and I asked him: 'what on earth should I do?'.

(Female offender, intentional and unintentional assault and battery (respondent 46), participant)

As for breaches of rights during the actual trial, one offender had arrived in court without a lawyer but had been prohibited from defending himself. This is a violation of art. 6(3)c of the European Convention on Human Rights, which declares that everyone charged with a criminal offence has the right to defend himself, whether in person or through a representative.

Last week on Friday they [the prison authorities] suddenly informed me that I was expected in court that day concerning the appeal of my insurance company, but I hadn't been informed and neither had my lawyer and all of a sudden I was expected to go to court. So I went there and they said: 'Don't you have a lawyer?' I said 'No, but that's fine, I'll just defend myself'. They said I couldn't. I was like: 'That's nonsense'. 'No', they said, 'we don't work that way'.

(Male offender, robbery (respondent 27), non-participant)

The interviews showed a number of references to a perceived lack of respect for rights. One offender claimed that he had been handcuffed in a non-legal way, in that he had been handcuffed at the back instead of at the front upon being taken to and into the courtroom. Though the Belgian law specifies *when* the police may proceed to handcuff a citizen, it does not provide information on *how* that should be done. Training handbooks spell out that people are preferably handcuffed at the back (Bruggeman, 2006). This respondent was wrong, then, in thinking this handcuffing was not legal. One victim complained that she had only been informed about the date of the trial two days in advance, yet there are no legal provisions as to the time within which victims should be informed of the trial date. Likewise, two offenders complained that they had not been informed about the date of the trial in time, yet in their cases the subpoena deadline had been respected. The reason for their frustration was that in their view there was not enough time between them receiving notice of the date of the trial and the actual trial for them to decently prepare their defence. One should keep in mind that one of these two offenders had already been informed by the mediator that he would be summoned and thus was prepared to an extent.[1] He was already aware that he would be summoned; he just had not received the letter yet. Frustration about the short time range between receipt of summons and trial date may therefore be even greater for offenders who do not participate in mediation, as they only know about their being summoned when they actually receive the summons.

Concern for needs

The needs that came to the fore during the post-trial interviews were: (1) emotional needs; (2) practical needs; and (3) the need for involvement in the criminal procedure. References to the first two types of needs were only found in victim interviews.

Emotional needs

A number of victims expressed a need for more support before, during and after trial. For example, three victims suggested that more should be done to inform victims of the victim services available to them. Two victims said that victims should be accompanied to court by professionals where they do not have anyone else to do so. In Belgium, victim support workers are available to accompany victims to trial, but the two victims cited here apparently were not aware of this. Moreover, there seems to be a need for aftercare, that is, the opportunity to be able to talk about one's experience to someone after the trial. In fact, two victims said that they were particularly happy about having participated in the current study exactly because it had felt like a kind of aftercare: it had allowed them to talk about their experience and vent their feelings. Also, there is a need for a service that victims can go to post-trial; this would also be useful where someone required having the judge's decision explained to them in clear terms.

> The same with the judgment. Suppose I would receive it – there would be no one to explain it to me, no one who could tell me what it actually says. (...) all these articles of the law and the sentences they use, I don't understand them.
>
> (Mother of female victim of sexual abuse
> (respondent 23), non-participant)

Practical needs

One need was coded under the category 'practical needs', i.e. the need for an interpreter to be present when the trial is not conducted in one's mother tongue. One participant had been faced with this problem and was very satisfied that an interpreter was called on to assist him during the trial.

The need for involvement in the criminal procedure

The need for active participation was a more dominant topic during the post-trial interviews than during the pre-trial interviews. While during the pre-trial interviews, participants were much more concerned about issues relating to receiving information, during the post-trial interviews they spent quite some time discussing their opportunities for active participation during the trial. The participants were not in general dissatisfied about the possibilities for participation in the trial, but they did mention a number of conditions and circumstances that impeded them from using these opportunities fully. Indeed, a number of concerns seem to inhibit litigants from speaking in court, or at least make it difficult for them to do so. First, five offenders feared that expressing their opinion in court would have a negative effect on the outcome. Two offenders who had previous experience of the criminal courts argued that they had previously found that both verdict and sentence depend not only on suspects' nonverbal behaviour in court but also on their eagerness to defend themselves. They therefore argued that sometimes it is better not to talk in court. One said: 'The more you argue, the more resistant the judge will become'. Therefore it was said that with a view to the sentence it is sometimes better to remain silent.

> My lawyer told me: be as friendly as possible, and by all means don't get angry. (...) It would be stupid to see my time in prison extended with six months just because I can't keep my mouth shut. So ...
>
> (Male offender, intentional assault and battery
> (respondent 31), participant)

Second, three victims and an offender mentioned that emotions make it difficult to speak in court.

> I don't know if they realise that there's people who are really not up for that.
>
> (Female victim of rape (respondent 38), participant)

> In court one is so emotionally charged (...). I mean, court is about punishment and stuff, that's a really sensitive issue and so sometimes you just don't succeed in saying the things you have in mind.
>
> (Male offender, intentional assault and battery
> (respondent 8), non-participant)

A third category of reasons for not actively participating in the trial pertains to the organisation of the criminal justice system and the courts. Some people mentioned that: (a) the criminal justice system is overly complex, making it nearly impossible to participate:

> It seems to me that it's so inaccessible that one shouldn't even consider or try to take things in one's own hands and defend one's case.
>
> (Male victim of theft
> (respondent 37), non-participant)

The presence of an audience in court (b) too made litigants more reluctant to tell their story. People feel that their case is not these other people's business. After one of the participants had said that he would prefer trials to be organised without an audience present this suggestion was verified during interviews with subsequent respondents, who without exception embraced the idea. People would feel more comfortable about trials if these would take place without members of the general public being present.

> It's also very hard to show certain emotions because the room is filled with people who have nothing to do with the whole thing, so that makes it difficult to express certain thoughts or emotions. If those trials took place behind closed doors and one could talk to the judge face to face, that would make things a little easier.
>
> (Male offender, intentional assault and battery
> (respondent 8), non-participant)

Next is the fact that victims are not fully aware of their rights and the possibilities for participation (c). This prevents them from actively participating in the trial *and* from participation in the criminal proceedings before and after the trial (e.g. they don't know where to go to get a copy of the judgment).

> As for the information aspect, information on how the courts work, we have always been very well informed but I can imagine that in some people's cases that was very different. (...) And if they haven't been informed of what to expect and what the procedure will be like, it becomes really, really difficult for them.
>
> (Mother of female victim of sexual abuse
> (respondent 50), participant)

Another element is the court setting (d), both in terms of architecture and in terms of procedures. Starting with the first, courtrooms in general were perceived as impressive, overwhelming rooms. This particular courtroom architecture added to the nervousness of several victims. Some said that for this particular reason they did not dare to speak in court. Two respondents (one victim and one offender) came up with an alternative, i.e. to keep trials in everyday office-like rooms, where all parties and the judge sit at a table. This proposal was verified with subsequent respondents, who had mixed feelings about the idea: they generally said that it would be good for victims but not for offenders. It was considered a good thing that the formality of a courtroom intimidates offenders.

> You know, I would feel much more at ease if we would just be sitting in a small room with the judge. Just not a courtroom, whatever it looks like.
>
> (Female victim of stalking
> (respondent 2), non-participant)

> Authority has a lot to do with perception. So I can imagine that maybe in some cases it wouldn't be a good thing for everyone to be seated on the same level.
>
> (Male victim of theft
> (respondent 37), non-participant)

As for courtroom procedures, the fact that there is no time in court to tell one's story in detail (e) was criticised. One victim mentioned that while in court he had been very much aware of the fact that the longer he spoke, the longer others would have to wait for the court to start with their case. Another one had felt like he had to hurry because the judge would interrupt him at any given moment.

> The feeling I got was: 'hurry up and say what it is you have to say so we can move on'. (...) I got the feeling that at any moment the judge would interrupt me and say 'okay, next'.
>
> (Male offender, intentional assault and battery (respondent 8), non-participant)

> I don't feel like I could take a lot of time to do my thing (...). The letter said that the trial would take place between 9 and 12, and at noon it was finally my turn, but so many people were still waiting for their turn, I mean, that doesn't encourage people to take their time to tell their story when it's their turn.
>
> (Male victim of theft (respondent 37), non-participant)

In summary, factors that may impede people from actively participating in trials are: fear of harsher sentences, emotions, the complexity of the criminal justice system, the presence of an audience in court, a lack of knowledge about one's rights and opportunities for participation, the court setting and courtroom procedures.

The participants that *had* taken the floor in court were asked whether they felt that they had been given sufficient opportunity to give their account of the facts. Most of them were content about their opportunity to speak. Four respondents had after the trial been wondering whether they should have taken another lawyer or whether they should have said different things in court than they had. One offender and one victim were manifestly discontent about the opportunity they had had to speak. The victim complained that her lawyer had not been given the time to state her point of view because the judge had become tired of the opponent party's lawyer acting irritating and had abruptly ended the trial before her lawyer got a chance to speak. The offender complained that the judge had constantly interrupted her. But people differ; another offender who had been faced with a judge who constantly interrupted him believed that to be a sign that the judge was well prepared and had a thorough knowledge of the file, which he very much appreciated. The fact that she had often interrupted him indicated to him that she already knew what he was saying from reading the file. Also, one participant had not had much time to have a say in court but added: 'But, well, the result is good'. He was satisfied with the outcome so he did not want to complain about a lack of time for speaking in court.

And this judge, she reacted in a way like (*in a very sarcastic voice*) 'alright miss, that'll suffice', you know, so rude (...). It would be nice to at least get the feeling that you matter, it would be nice if someone would take some time to listen, instead of brushing people off like that.

(Female offender, intentional and unintentional assault and battery (respondent 46), participant)

In order to find out whether having had the chance to speak in court (voice) has an effect on perceptions of fairness irrespective of whether it has an influence on the outcome, respondents were asked whether they believed that what they had said had influenced the judge's decision in any way. The results are mixed: some indicated that it is good to be able to speak one's mind no matter whether it influences the outcome of the trial, whereas others said that it had been completely useless to attend the trial as, in their opinion, nothing they had said had had an influence. Three offenders said that they were not sure that they would attend trial again, were they ever to be involved in a criminal procedure again, as they didn't think that in the current case their presence had made any difference. The general feeling emerging from the interviews is that people do want what they have said to be taken into account by the judge.

So you're allowed to take the floor, to say what's on your mind, but ... It's as if they don't really do anything with that information, as if it's all just pretence. (...) So I'm left with this very bitter taste in my mouth.

(Father of male victims of intentional assault and battery (respondent 6), non-participant)

People should be heard. They should be allowed to tell their story (...). And something should be done with this information. They [the courts] can't just be like 'okay so say what you have to say and that's it'. People need to have the feeling that what they said is actually taken into account.

(Male victim of theft (respondent 37), non-participant)

Two offenders explained how the fact that the judge had not given them a decent chance to tell their side of the story had given them the feeling that the judge was prejudiced.

The last judge I met (...) actually gave me the chance to discuss a couple of things, she didn't interrupt me as soon as I started talking, but the first judge did. The first judge I think was prejudiced towards me.

(Male offender, intentional assault and battery (respondent 8), non-participant)

The results furthermore suggest that victims who take the floor in court especially wish to address the judge, not so much the offender. Obviously, when victims address the judge, the offender automatically hears what is said, but only one of the victims explicitly said that she wanted to address the offenders in person in court. She wanted to tell them how much harm they had caused her in order to make them realise what they had done. In general, then, it is important to victims that the judge reprimands the offender, but victims seem to have little need to speak directly to the perpetrator in court themselves. Furthermore, those victims who participated in mediation showed less need to attend the trial and speak in court than those who did not. This is understandable given the fact that they had already been able to convey messages to the court (through the mediation agreement) and the offender (either in person or through the mediator) and had already had an opportunity to vent their feelings. But the fact that the financial aspect of the matter had been taken care of already – the offender had agreed to pay a certain amount of compensation as part of the mediation agreement – too played a role in their decision not to take any part in the trial. The list of reasons victims gave for not attending the trial (see Chapter 4) shows this tendency too.

As part of the questions on the need to be involved in the criminal proceedings, the respondents were asked to judge three statements about the importance of having process control. These were: (1) 'it is important that I will be able to exert some control over the proceedings'; (2) 'it is important that I will have a say on the court proceedings'; and (3) 'it is important that I will be able to intervene if I believe the procedures are not being applied correctly'. Respondents in general said that they are okay with how trials proceed and with the fact that it is the judge who decides who is allowed to speak and who is not, but one participant did say that he would like to bring a change to all the odds and ends that come with a trial (he called it 'a big posh affair', referring to the robes, the raised benches and the need to rise when the judge enters or leaves the courtroom).

> No, that's not something important, you know I wouldn't like other people interfering with my job either. Right? The judge knows best how to do his job.
>
> (Female victim of intentional assault and battery
> (respondent 32), participant)

Still, it was considered important to be able to intervene when one feels that rules are violated. However, some participants said that ordinary citizens do not possess the knowledge necessary to recognise those situations in which procedures are not being respected.

> One should be able to protest or to say that one doesn't agree (...). But in a polite manner, saying 'Your Honour please may I add something or explain something because I don't think this is correct for this or this reason'. One must always respect the other person of course.
>
> (Mother of female victim of sexual abuse
> (respondent 23), non-participant)

The statements on need for voice and participation in the trial were: (1) 'it is important that I will have ample opportunity to state my position and clarify my wishes'; (2) 'it is important that the judge will give me feedback after I have spoken'; (3) 'it is important that I will be able to speak to the judge in person if I wish to do so'; (4) 'it is important that I will be allowed to spontaneously address the judge if I have a question' and (5) 'it is important that the judge will allow me to speak on my request'. The first statement was considered very important; one victim explained that it is good that judges hear the individuals involved in person because there is a difference between how one is portrayed in documents and how one comes across in person.

> There's a difference between how one comes across in person and how one comes across on the basis of police documents. (…) If people can communicate to the judge in person I'm sure the judge will have a different opinion of them than he would have on the basis of documents that are written by the police.
>
> (Male victim of theft
> (respondent 29), non-participant)

The statement on feedback elicited comments that refer to acknowledgement: the judge confirming that the victim has been through a lot, or simply confirming that (s)he is listening, is highly valued.

> That's important too of course, for the judge to say 'I understand, you have been through quite a lot indeed'. Yes.
>
> (Female victim of intentional assault and battery
> (respondent 32), participant)

Opinions on the statement asking whether one would like to be able to speak to the judge in private again were mixed. Also, whereas some considered speaking to the judge before the trial, others considered opportunities for talking to the judge after the sentence has been pronounced. Reasons people gave for feeling *no* need to talk to the judge after the trial were: (1) the feeling that nothing can be achieved by talking to the judge after the trial: it will not affect the outcome anymore ($N = 3$); (2) that one is fed up with everything that comes with a trial and does not want to spend any more time or energy on it ($N = 2$); and (3) that the judge probably has good reasons for the judgment ($N = 1$). Reasons for not speaking to the judge before the trial were (1) that everything there is to know about the case is included in the file ($N = 1$) and (2) that judges' neutrality would be affected ($N = 3$).

> No, that's not fair. It's very dangerous too. Even if both parties could talk to him. No, it's out of the question.
>
> (Male victim of intentional assault and battery
> (respondent 3), participant)

Those who said that they would want to talk to the judge if that were possible said that they would do so before the trial: (1) in order to explain to the judge what exactly has happened, so (s)he would be fully informed, and this in a quiet, private setting (N = 3); and (2) because they would feel more comfortable about going to court if they had become acquainted with the judge before the trial (N = 1). Those who were in favour of allowing litigants to talk to the judge after the trial were so because: (1) it would allow them to do away with lies told by the other party (N = 1); (2) one often leaves the courtroom with questions or remarks on what happened (N = 1); and (3) it would allow asking questions about how the investigation was conducted, how the authorities discovered who committed the offence, what life in prison will be like for the offenders, and so on (N = 1).

> I'd be curious about how they investigated the case, what happens in prison, how they found out who did it, what the procedure was like, how they connected the dots.
>
> (Female victim of burglary and theft
> (respondent 52), non-participant)

The last two statements gauged the extent to which litigants feel that they should be allowed to spontaneously address the judge and to speak on their own account. The majority of the participants said that it is neither feasible nor desirable that litigants are allowed to intervene whenever they feel like doing so, though four participants did say that there had been moments during the trial at which they would have liked to intervene. But in general people said that the courtroom would turn into – in participants' own words – a marketplace, a circus or a rat's nest. Also, several people said, time to tell one's story is provided to every participant anyway, so there is no need to interrupt others. The respondents did say that litigants should be granted the opportunity to respectfully ask the judge if they can add something at a later moment. The judge can then decide about the exact time that the litigant is allowed to speak.

> I understand, of course people should not start shouting and interrupting each other. When another person's talking and I have a question about what they're saying I shouldn't interrupt them either. But I do feel it's important that I get a chance to ask my question at some point.
>
> (Male offender, intentional assault and battery
> (respondent 34), participant)

Turning to the results concerning what has been defined as passive involvement, i.e. the importance of receiving information about the criminal procedure and about the judgment, victims especially said that they had not received sufficient information for them to be able to stay up to date with the proceedings or to be sufficiently prepared for what would happen in court, which in some cases was the cause of their not participating more actively in the proceedings.

Offenders did not complain about lack of information at this stage of the proceedings.

> Well I think ... the police pay a lot of attention to the victim, but the courts do not. For example, thanks to you [the interviewer] we registered as a civil party. Thanks to you and the mediator. So if we hadn't had the chance to participate in a mediation procedure we would never have known about this possibility and we would never have been informed of the fact that the offenders had to stand trial. That's ... it's disgraceful.
>
> (Male victim of burglary and theft
> (respondent 51), non-participant)

Some participants pointed the finger at the criminal justice system for not automatically informing them about the outcome of the trial. In Belgium, victims who are not a civil party in the proceedings are not automatically informed of the outcome of the trial; they need to go to the registry of the court to be informed of the judge's decision. Six victims and one offender mentioned that it is not right that litigants do not automatically receive the judgment. They said it should be sent to them by default, through mail, for example, and for free. Also, receiving a copy of the judgment involves a lot of paperwork and costs money, people said, and two victims said that the language used in judgments prevents them from fully understanding the judgment and its concrete implications.

> I feel very let down. We only heard about the offender's sentence from our lawyer; we didn't have any information sent to our own place and there was nowhere we could go.
>
> (Female victim of rape
> (respondent 38), participant)

A further note on receiving information about the progress of the case is the following: victims said that the fact that one does not hear from the authorities about the case conveys the impression that nobody is working on it. When nothing is *seen* to be done, people think that nothing is indeed being done. For example, those victims who do not register as an injured person or a civil party are not informed when the case is brought to court. These people believe impunity reigns, whereas it could be that the offenders *have* been summoned.

> If you'd hear from them you'd get the feeling that they are working on it and doing something about it. But if nothing is heard from them, of course it's like they're not doing anything about it and the offenders just go unpunished.
>
> (Female victim of burglary and theft
> (respondent 52), non-participant)

Social standing

The post-trial interviews just like the pre-trial interviews gave rise to the creation of a subcategory of standing comprising those interview fragments in which people said that they suffered a loss of social status as a consequence of their involvement in the criminal proceedings. The majority of these fragments relate to the presence of an audience in court. Both victims and offenders talked about how the presence of other citizens in court infringed their privacy and hence their social status. As outlined earlier, the presence of an audience in court is seen as an aspect of trials that makes some people hesitant to speak in court. But the presence of an audience in court was experienced as disturbing for other reasons too. One reason is the fact that complete strangers hear details about one's life. Three victims and six offenders said that strangers have no business with their lives or that of the other party. It is painful when details about one's life are brought into the open in a court for strangers to hear, and people added that there is always a risk that someone one is acquainted with (e.g. a colleague) is present in court. Especially members of the public who are not awaiting their own case but just come to watch a trial are resented. Furthermore, two victims said that the fact that the audience was constantly talking and sometimes even laughing gave them the impression that their case was not being taken seriously. Some said that the audience causes a lot of noise, which causes distraction and makes it hard to understand what is said by the parties, the court officials and the lawyers. There were also three people, two of whom were offenders, who felt distressed by the condemning looks of the spectators.

> It's distressing to have all those people around. I would prefer if the trial took place in private, with only the judges and the lawyers being there. You know, it's very possible that someone in the audience knows you but didn't know you're involved in a trial and then they're like 'oh look this person's on trial!'. While it's a private matter in fact.
>
> (Male offender, fraud
> (respondent 33), participant)

> Everyone's just staring at you thinking 'oh my God what kind of a person is that?'.
>
> (Female offender, intentional and unintentional assault and battery
> (respondent 46), participant)

Feelings that social standing is being compromised do not only result from the trial itself. Two respondents were very anxious about their colleagues at work finding out why they were absent from work for a couple of hours on the day of the trial. One respondent referred to the fact that the letters that she had received from the prosecutor's office had been sealed with tape, not glue, which gave her the uncomfortable feeling that anyone who got the letters would have been able to read them had they wanted to.

> And another thing that I really don't like is that they don't close the letters they send, the envelopes are basically open, there's just a little piece of tape on top to close them. Anyone can open them and close them again. (...) It's just a silly little piece of tape. As if the envelope contains just any random advertisement. It's a detail, but it matters. What if the postman's like 'oh a letter from the court let's see what she's done'?
>
> (Mother of female victim of sexual abuse
> (respondent 50), participant)

Finally, one of the offenders who had participated in mediation said that one of the good things about mediation is that it allows repairing the emotional damage done to one's family and partner. His offence had not been directed towards his family, but he felt that he had caused them a great deal of pain by engaging in a criminal activity. Showing responsibility for his actions by participating in mediation, he said, had allowed him to make amends with his family and partner. This observation too indicates that people care about how they are perceived by others – either those to whom they are close, or any random citizen – when involved in a criminal procedure.

Neutrality

In the previous chapters, three subcategories of neutrality were discerned, based on Tyler and Lind (1992). These were: (1) absence of bias or prejudice; (2) fact-based decision-making; and (3) honesty. These categories also proved useful during the analysis of the post-trial interviews, thus confirming Tyler and Lind's conceptualisation of neutrality.

Absence of bias or prejudice

As explained above, absence of bias was understood as impartiality between victim and offender or between accomplices. Absence of prejudice was understood as absence of premature judgement about the alleged offender's guilt or about the victim's role in the offence. In all, remarks about favouritism were few; also, none of the respondents accused the judge of being biased in favour of the other party. Their allegations were directed at the criminal justice system as a whole or at administrative and supportive staff. One victim for example complained that while the offender had received a copy of the judgment she had not. Another victim had the impression that the offender had received more psychological support and information than herself, and yet another victim said that too much attention is paid to offenders' objections to certain steps of the procedure or investigatory measures and that criminal authorities are too benevolent towards offenders. The single offender who had the impression that the authorities were in favour of the victim got this feeling as she was waiting in the waiting area for the trial to start and she observed the clerk informing the victim about how much longer she would have to wait for the trial to start, whereas he did not inform her.

> But then when I went to collect the judgment (...) that was a dis-appointment. I am the victim and the offender can collect the judgment but I'm not allowed to know which sentence he received.
> (Female victim of intentional assault and battery
> (respondent 32), participant)

> And I also feel like offenders are pampered too much. They can ask for trials to be postponed and all that, and a lot of attention is paid to their objections. Compared to what is done for victims they're too benevolent toward offenders.
> (Male victim of burglary and theft
> (respondent 51), non-participant)

As for perceptions of prejudice, two offenders had had the feeling that their judges had been convinced of their guilt in advance and had not been receptive to new information. One of the two offenders had put a lot of effort into pro-viding evidence about the case himself, but in the end he had the feeling that the judge had not taken this evidence into account at all. He was very fru-strated that all his efforts had been in vain. The other offender said that the judge had constructed her own version of what had happened and had refused to revise that version in light of the information provided during the trial.

> He was very reserved and he was prejudiced. He had made up his mind beforehand.
> (Male offender, intentional assault and battery
> (respondent 8), non-participant)

> At one point the judge was arguing that what I was saying couldn't be true, and that it made no sense. (...) And then she just made her own story out of it, making all kinds of claims about what I did and what had happened and saying that her story was the most plausible.
> (Female offender, intentional and unintentional assault and battery
> (respondent 46), participant)

One additional aspect that fits the prejudice category is a gender issue. Six respondents (three victims and three offenders) mentioned the sex of the judge that had judged their case; four of them added that judges' gender potentially has an influence on case outcomes. In particular, female judges are perceived to be more severe than male judges, especially when the offence involves children.

And I also believe that the judge and those other people that were sitting next to the judge ... – I also told my husband this: they were all women. There wasn't a single man. And I think that makes a difference in a case like this.
(Mother of female victim of sexual abuse
(respondent 50), participant)

The statements about bias and prejudice that were presented to the participants were: (1) 'it is important that the judge will be impartial and will favour neither party'; (2) 'it is important that the judge will treat all parties alike, that he will not discriminate'; and (3) 'it is important that the judge will apply methods that treat all parties equally'. A number of remarks on these statements concerned the difference between victims and offenders: some participants argued that offenders should be approached in a more severe manner than victims. Two respondents mentioned that neutrality has to do with respect, and one linked it to voice. The first two implied that being treated with respect is a precondition for perceptions of neutrality to arise. The second said that judges who do not allow offenders opportunities for voicing their opinion are perceived as biased.

The judge is usually neutral; judges don't generally go around and scold people saying they're the biggest scumbags they've ever seen.
(Male offender, intentional assault and battery
(respondent 31), participant)

Of course he [the judge] must be as neutral as possible. He must show respect for me.
(Male victim of intentional assault and battery
(respondent 3), participant)

If you're faced with a biased judge you really get the feeling that you have nothing to say in the matter.
(Female offender, intentional and unintentional assault and battery
(respondent 46), participant)

Fact-based decision-making

Several issues relating to whether the judge had carefully considered the case evidence and had made an effort to take an informed decision were discussed during the post-trial interviews. Respondents talked about such issues as whether the judge was well prepared and had taken the time to study the case. For instance, three victims and one offender had the impression that cases are pushed through court as if on an assembly line. The victims argued for example that the judge had made no effort to check their financial claims – he had simply agreed the amount that they had asked for. The offender said that he had provided plenty of evidence to the judge invalidating the victims' financial claims, but that nothing had been done with this evidence. All these people said that their judges had simply opted for a solution of convenience, unwilling to spend time on investigating the truth value of the financial claims. Finally, an offender said that judges are not professional, i.e. that they treat cases in a superficial manner and do not truly make the effort to come to a well thought-out decision.

> To me it seems that this court runs like an assembly line. They don't take a lot of time to judge cases, they need to deal with loads of cases every single day so they're like: 'okay, so what shall we sentence this guy to?'. I really feel like things are being discussed behind people's backs, that they just decide on these things over a beer and without giving them much thought.
>
> (Male offender, intentional assault and battery (respondent 8), non-participant)

> It's as if these people [the judiciary] have forgotten that they're dealing with people. With people's lives, in fact. (...) These are people who have been granted a very high position in society, they owe it to us to perform their duties in a decent manner. And I don't feel like they do.
>
> (Male offender, intentional assault and battery (respondent 8), non-participant)

Contrary to the participants who said that courts provide assembly-line justice, four victims indicated that they believe that judges do look at the specifics of each case and each offender in order to pronounce a sentence tailored to the specific offender. Different offenders are not, so they said, tarred with the same brush. This individualised approach is highly valued.

> So first of all there's the mediation service, then for offenders there's the investigation of their background and stuff, yes, I do believe they're taking pains to reach a fair sentence.
>
> (Male victim of theft (respondent 37), non-participant)

One victim suggested that judges should spend more time on investigating the case themselves instead of relying on police records. The specific respondent referred to a Dutch reality TV show called 'De Rijdende Rechter' (free translation: 'The Travelling Judge') in which judges perform visits to crime scenes even when deciding on cases as small as neighbour disputes and talk to all parties involved in person.

> R1: It's more easy to come to terms with the situation when these people take the case seriously. If they wouldn't care about the case ... there's more than enough examples of court cases where things just don't move.
> R2: It's a sort of recognition.
>
> (Male and female victims of burglary and theft (respondents 51 and 52), non-participants)

Six participants throughout the interview talked about whether the judge and prosecutor had in their opinion sufficiently studied the file and were well prepared for the trial. Except for one, all were satisfied with the judge's and prosecutor's efforts to prepare for the trial. People find signs of thorough preparation in the specificity of judges' and prosecutors' questions or remarks (e.g. the prosecutor remarking that the victim has no financial claims, thus showing that he has read the mediation agreement). Interestingly, the fact that the prosecutor started the trial by giving an overview of the accusations and the facts – which is normal procedure – led one victim to conclude that the judge had not prepared the case well. Not being aware that trials always start out that way, she thought this meant that the judge did not know what the case was about at all. Also, there was a respondent who thought that it would have been better in her case had the judge not prepared the case as well as she did, because she felt that the judge had not been open to any new information that was not included in the file.

> [respondent's wife] You [to her husband] told me that the judge asked specific questions, which to you meant that she had read the file. You told me that you were surprised about some of the questions she asked, that she didn't simply pluck questions out of the air.
>
> (Stepmother of male victims of intentional assault and battery
> (wife of respondent 6), non-participant)

The parents of a young adult offender addressed the issue of what happens where an adult and a minor commit an offence together. Their son indeed had an underage accomplice, and they thought it was incorrect for their son's case to be dealt with in the absence of the accomplice. As different tribunals are competent for juvenile offenders and for adult offenders, they would be tried by different courts. The fact that the accomplice would not be there at the time their son would get tried to them was not right as that would prevent the judge from getting a good understanding of the facts.

One final aspect of fact-based decision-making is whether the judge allocated sufficient time to try the case. The majority of the participants were satisfied about the time allocated to try their case, with most saying that there was not much to be said because the case was clear, the judge was well prepared, and there was simply nothing further to add to what had already been said. One exception was the following:

> She [the judge] had her own opinion and she was constructing her own story, she just wanted it out of the way as quickly as possible.
>
> (Female offender, intentional and unintentional assault and battery
> (respondent 46), participant)

The statements on fact-based decision-making that respondents were asked to judge were: (1) 'it is important that the judge will carefully examine the evidence'; (2) 'it is important that the judge will carefully explain the reasons for his decision'; (3) 'it is important that the judge is very well acquainted with the case file and is thoroughly prepared'; and (4) 'it is important that the judge will examine the case carefully and will take the time to do so'. Remarkable comments came from the person who said that judges should not be acquainted with the file to the degree that they are no longer then open to new elements that are raised at trial; and the person who said that currently too much time is devoted to try cases – as there is a case file containing a large number of documents on the case, he reasoned, there is no need to spend much time on cases in court.

> I think they actually spend too much time on these cases (. ...) I mean, there's been an investigation, there's been multiple interrogations, there's a lot of reports available, expert reports, lab reports and the like. So why spend all this money and time and have all these people in a courtroom waiting, listening, chattering? It never stops.
>
> (Male offender, sexual abuse
> (respondent 53), participant)

Honesty

References to the honesty of the court officials were few. A remark uttered by two respondents concerned the professionalism of the administrative staff of the court responsible for helping people who come to fetch (a copy of) the judgment. In both cases, the clerks had been indiscrete, breaching their professional secrecy by informing the respondent of the judgment in a way that was not allowed (e.g. by telephone).

Performance

Just as in the pre-trial interviews, during the post-trial interviews people discussed several issues pertaining to the way they feel the criminal justice system functions, or, to be more precise, to what they perceive to be dysfunctions of the criminal justice system. The most often mentioned critique was that the criminal justice system is too slow. Eleven respondents (eight victims, three offenders) brought this up. Most of them talked about the time that passes between the crime and the trial. A number of them mentioned the fact that trials are often postponed to a later date for all kinds of reasons, and a few brought up the time elapsed between trial and judgment being passed. The reasons why people are irritated by the slow pace at which cases are disposed of by the courts are several; some of these were addressed in the previous chapter. Additional reasons mentioned throughout the post-trial interviews were the fact that the costs of compensation rise as interest is added (one offender's trial took place more than four years after the offence; she had to pay more than four years' interest on top of compensation), the fact that the other party's lawyer has ample time to build a defence based on lies to make things appear worse than they are, and

the fact that one needs to spend time waiting for the trial in preliminary custody. The most often cited reason was the uncertainty with which people live
while awaiting trial. This was mentioned by both victims and offenders.
People have no idea what is happening while they are waiting. Yet one victim
said that it might be a good thing that offenders have to wait a long time
before knowing what will happen to them, because the uncertainty that comes
with it is a kind of punishment in itself. Three offenders confirmed that the
time spent waiting for trial had felt like a punishment to them.

> The three years before the trial were kind of a punishment in itself cause
> it's three years of living in uncertainty and not knowing what's gonna
> happen.
>
> (Male offender, intentional assault and battery
> (respondent 8), non-participant)

Another important remark is that the time that passes before a case is
brought to court may be perceived to be longer than it actually is; the subjective experience of time may therefore be more important than the actual
time elapsed. One participant overestimated the duration of the criminal
proceedings and was surprised to find out during the interview that in fact,
'only' one year and a half had passed (she said: 'Oh okay, that's not that long
after all. I had the impression that it had taken longer'). Another participant
said that the one year that had passed since he had been victim of an offence
had felt like two or three years.

In a similar vein, the fact that trials are often postponed to later dates is
much disapproved of. Also, the time in between two court sessions (in cases of
continuances) is perceived as too long. One respondent explained that the
problem is not only that one has to wait oneself, which gives rise to the
uncertainty and concerns discussed above, but also that the judge must each
time start from scratch again and study the file again. Then there was a
respondent who said that too much time passes between the trial and the day
the judgment is pronounced. In Belgium, the judgment is usually pronounced
between two and four weeks after the trial. The particular respondent was
especially upset about this because the judgment in the end contained no
specifics about the case; it did not state any reasons for the decision. Why,
then, did they need so much time, the man asked himself.

> For example, almost four weeks passed between the trial and the day
> they pronounced their decision. I really wonder what they did in that
> month? (...) In the end what we got was the most default judgment anyone
> can get, a copy paste, and the agreement we came to with the other party
> was not even mentioned in it. So to me that's ... Please don't tell me you'll
> take the time to pass a proper judgment and then deliver a copy paste.
>
> (Father of male victims of intentional assault and battery
> (respondent 6), non-participant)

The fact that it takes much time for the criminal justice system to process cases led some respondents (especially but not exclusively offenders) to remark that the criminal justice system's main goal is not to fight crime but to maintain itself. The complexity of the procedures, the perception that people who instruct a lawyer receive milder punishments than others and the many continuances all contribute to the perception that the criminal justice system is mainly preoccupied with keeping itself in business.

> I have the feeling that the courts just deliver their sentences and think: if you don't like it, appeal it. That's how they make sure the system can keep going.
>
> (Male offender, intentional assault and battery (respondent 8), non-participant)

> It's just this impression that I have ... what I'm irritated about is that the criminal justice system's main goal is to sustain itself, rather than to combat crime. (...) They're always postponing cases, again and again and again, the procedures are so very cumbersome, lawyers appeal cases arguing there's been procedural irregularities and so on. So it's like they need to keep themselves busy, as if they need to make sure that they can apply their system.
>
> (Male victim of burglary and theft (respondent 51), non-participant)

> I know I shouldn't be this strict with the kids, but I don't want them to make the same mistakes as I did. (...) And to me what the judge said came across as: 'if you're gonna educate your children in such a way that they won't commit any mischief we will be out of work soon'. That may sound banal, but that's the way it sounded. (...) As if she was worried that she will be out of work one day.
>
> (Male offender, intentional assault and battery (respondent 31), participant)

By way of a first exception to the rule, one respondent explained that the trial had actually taken place very soon after she had reported the offence, which had given her the impression that the authorities wanted to quickly get the case over with without properly informing or involving the victims. By way of a second exception to the rule, one respondent, an offender, said that the choice between waiting for the trial a little longer to allow the authorities to investigate the case well or receiving a sentence that does not at all fit the offence is not a difficult one to make.

A number of respondents advanced alternatives that, in their view, would allow speeding up the criminal procedures and making them less costly – the cost of the administration of justice to society was addressed by many respondents. One suggestion was to shorten the procedures when suspects are conclusively proven guilty by DNA material or when suspects were caught in the act. Another suggestion was to make an arrangement with offenders at the very start of the procedure and drop the charges if they agree to pay compensation – which resembles the Belgian practice of penal mediation – or to drop the charges when the parties to the crime come to an agreement through mediation. Someone proposed that trials could take place in an office, with just the conflict parties, their lawyers and the judge being present, which would save both staff and time.

> I paid these lawyers – I had two – an awful lot of money. (...) If they [the judiciary dealing with the case] had just made an arrangement with me at the very start the case wouldn't have come to this [a trial]. It would have cost the system much less time.
>
> (Male offender, theft
> (respondent 14), participant)

Finally, two victims remarked that the criminal justice system is very bureaucratic, involving a lot of paperwork.

Courtroom design and trial practices

When discussing their experience of the court, participants made several remarks relating to trial practices. Hence this fourth category was created. To begin with, four victims and two offenders commented on the way time is used in court. Letters inviting victims and offenders to the trial in general state that the trial starts at 9 o'clock in the morning. Since all those whose trials are scheduled on the same day receive a letter saying the trial starts at 9, in reality, litigants often need to wait for more than one or two hours before it is actually their turn. This custom does not meet with approval – far from it. Not only does waiting in court for one's own case to start cause stress, people without any experience of the criminal justice system sincerely expect their case to start at 9 and feel confused when this expectation is not met. It was suggested several times that time management in court should be improved. One proposal was to set a specific time for every case and to mention this exact time in letters sent to parties when citing them to attend trial.

> So I got the letter informing me about the trial, but everyone receives the same letter saying they're expected at 9 in the morning. So some people need to wait until lunchtime for their turn. Why don't they just plan ahead, why don't they just schedule thirty minutes per case and send people letters saying at what time exactly their case will be up. It's no use having people sit there and wait for three hours.
>
> (Male offender, intentional assault and battery
> (respondent 31), participant)

I had to wait forever. I was told to be present at 9 and I only left at 12. Well. (...) It was only three hours but to me it felt like three months. It was very unpleasant.

(Male offender, theft
(respondent 14), participant)

Notwithstanding these complaints about the way time is organised before the trial actually starts, the respondents were satisfied with the organisation of the trial itself, that is, about the fact that there is a procedure that prescribes when each participant is allowed to speak. Respondents said that this procedure is good because it allows each of those present some time to speak (even though there is a feeling that more time should be available to do so) and because it gives structure and certainty.

I thought it was good, it gives some certainty and structure and I think it went very well. I have no issues with that. And the defendant was given a lot of time to defend himself. It's okay like that.

(Male victim of burglary and theft
(respondent 51), non-participant)

Three victims commented on their position vis-à-vis the offender in court: one said that it is difficult to feel at ease in court because the victim and offender sit on the same (public) benches while awaiting the trial, and two others mentioned that it is desirable that the victim and the offender are seated in a position that allows avoiding eye contact. One offender had felt uncomfortable because she and the victim had to await the start of the trial in the same waiting room. A related remark is that of an offender who said that the holding cells for detained offenders in the courthouse are 'nineteenth century, freezing cold and utterly small'.

People were asked during the interview to describe the courtroom in order to find out how they had felt about the courtroom itself and about the customs and habits governing courtroom procedures. Elements included in the answers were that courthouses are much like labyrinths, that the judge is seated on a raised bench, that everyone is required to rise when the judge enters or leaves the room, that not just one single magistrate but five magistrates are present (a three-judge panel, a clerk and the public prosecutor), that there is a lack of security (i.e. that anyone can enter a courtroom – there is no security control), that magistrates wear gowns, that the interior of courtrooms is quite special, and that acoustics are bad and it is therefore difficult to understand what is said. As for the bad acoustics, victims sitting on the public benches often have a lot of trouble understanding what is said by the judge, the prosecutor, the lawyers and the defendant. Someone said that for this reason, victims do not actually leave the courtroom any wiser than they entered it, which provides food for thought with a view to their involvement in the trial.

It's all these … the building itself is ugly, if they forget to use the micro-
phones no one understands a thing, these people are sitting on a platform …
I don't like it, nor do I like the lawyers' costumes and stuff.

(Male victim of theft
(respondent 37), non-participant)

What annoyed me the most was that I hardly understood what was said.
(…) So the whole thing is just a ritual that doesn't really tell you anything. (…) I didn't understand a thing. My presence there didn't make
me any wiser.

(Male victim of burglary and theft
(respondent 51), non-participant)

The customs whereby judges are seated on raised benches and that it is obli-
gatory to stand up when they enter or leave the courtroom are commonly
regarded as outdated and somewhat ridiculous, but only one person expressed
having problems with these habits. Courtroom interiors similarly were regarded as old-fashioned,[2] but those discussing the interior of the courtroom
they had visited in general said that the rooms are nice. Nevertheless, these
customs, habits and interiors contribute to courtrooms being perceived as
intimidating. The impression that is conveyed is that what happens in the
room is serious. The participants who discussed this aspect were generally of
the opinion that it is good that courtrooms make that impression because
as such they command respect from offenders. One respondent did say
that one should see through this display of power: the criminal justice
system may display its power with all the customs and habits, as recounted,
but, in the end, he said, many of those sentenced to prison are quickly
released from prison or never even imprisoned in the first place because
of prison overcrowding, which then undoes the intimidating effect of
courtrooms.

Maybe it's okay to display power but … well, it's empty power because …
I'm not sure to what extent what they say is true but when I watch the
evening news it tells me that people are released from prison very soon
after beginning their sentences because the prisons are overcrowded and
stuff … . Well, yeah, this shows that the system is in fact very weak.

(Male victim of violent robbery
(respondent 49), participant)

Behaviour of the opposing party

A topic that several respondents spontaneously came up with when discussing
their experience in court was the behaviour of the opposing party; therefore
this fifth category was created. For instance, two offenders and three victims
mentioned that the other party had been lying in court.

I was blamed for a great many things in court, she [the presumed victim] also told a great deal of lies (...). Really, I was just speechless.
(Female offender, intentional and unintentional assault and battery (respondent 46), participant)

Victims' remarks about the behaviour of the opposing party went beyond what the defendant said by way of defence. In fact, nine victims addressed such issues as whether the offender expressed remorse in court or showed some expression of emotion. Victims feel distressed if the offender does not evince a single sign of emotion in court. For example, one victim felt very bitter about the fact that the first thing the offender had done in court when he was asked whether he wished to say anything was not to apologise but to hand the judge documents proving that he was taking therapy. The offender was perceived as thinking only about himself and about saving his own skin. Those victims who did receive apologies from the offender in court expressed great satisfaction about this. To victims, then, whether or not the offender shows remorse is an important issue, one that co-determines how they experience the trial.

I watched him [the defendant] the whole time because I wanted to see how he'd react. But he didn't show any reaction. He just stood there like a pillar of salt. I really thought he would at least look at me at some point – that's what I focused on.
(Mother of female victim of sexual abuse (respondent 50), participant)

He looked completely indifferent. That was so ... Well, yeah, I guess I expected to see some sign of emotion, but there was none. So it really seemed like he just didn't care at all.
(Male victim of theft (respondent 37), non-participant)

Instead of apologising for what he did – I mean, he did apologise at some point, but the very first thing he said was 'here's a document proving that I'm taking therapy'.
(Mother of female victim of sexual abuse (respondent 50), participant)

Five victims discussed the behaviour of the offender's lawyer; each and every one of these five participants was dismayed about the defence lawyer. Two had felt personally attacked by the defence lawyer because he had given them the feeling that they were in fact the guilty parties. One victim said that the fact that the defence lawyer spoke about her using her family name but never prefacing it with 'Ms.' came across as extremely disrespectful, and one was appalled by the way in which the defence lawyer had tried to disparage an expert as biased.[3] Interestingly, one victim attached considerable importance to the fact that the offender's lawyer was a completely incapable man who had made no effort at all to prepare the case (she knew this for a fact because the lawyer had said this to her own lawyer in her presence). She considered it unfair that the offender had not received an adequate defence.

> He [the defendant's lawyer] just plainly said that he wasn't planning on doing much about it. So I thought, well, in fact that's not fair either.
>
> (Mother of female victim of sexual abuse
> (respondent 50), participant)

Notes

1 In most respondents' cases, the mediator had been the one who had informed them of the fact that the offender would be summoned. Usually the mediator was the first person to contact victims and offenders about their case after they had been interviewed by the police (and, in some cases, an investigating judge); this contact generally took place a couple of months after the aforementioned interviews. For this reason, and since mediation usually takes place a number of months before the trial, it was the mediator who brought most participants the news that the case would go to trial. Participants had not yet received the actual letter announcing that the case would go to trial when the mediation process started.

2 It must be said that the courthouses that the respondents were confronted with were primarily old buildings, built between the first half of the 12th century and the first half of the 20th century. Obviously, the fact that these are all old buildings has influenced the findings; one might expect for example that acoustics are better in modern courtrooms.

3 Lawyers in general had a bad name among the participants but were nevertheless hired by many because they believed that they would *need* a lawyer to make it through the criminal proceedings.

References

Bruggeman, W. (2006). *De aanhouding*. Antwerp: Maklu.

Tyler, T.R. and Lind, E.A. (1992). "A relational model of authority in groups." In Zanna, M.P. (ed.), *Advances in Experimental Social Psychology vol. 25* (115–91). London: Academic Press.

Part III

Conclusion: The meaning of procedural justice

6 New perspectives on the antecedents of perceptions of procedural justice

This chapter is concerned with a discussion of the findings resulting from the study. Chapters 3 to 5 provided a detailed and in-depth description of the elements that determined the participants' evaluation of their experience of the police and the judiciary. This chapter summarises these findings and explains how the study improves our understanding of some of the key concepts of procedural justice theory. The main goal of the study, as set out in the introduction, was to gain insight into what these key concepts mean exactly to lay people who become involved in a criminal procedure. So far, our understanding of these concepts has been based mainly on researchers' conceptualisations. This chapter compares the literature's understanding of the key concepts to actual litigants' understanding of these concepts.

The chapter also addresses the underlying reasons for the importance of each of the key concepts to people's fairness judgements. Procedural justice theory argues that people are concerned about procedural information because of social identity reasons; the current study suggests that two additional motivations explain people's attentiveness to issues of procedural fairness. Another issue that will be addressed is the conditionality of respectful treatment – as the previous chapters show, respondents seemed to think that some people are less entitled to respectful treatment by the police and the legal authorities than others. This chapter also explains the reason why trust was not retained as an antecedent of procedural justice, arguing that trust in authorities in fact follows from positive perceptions of procedural justice. It furthermore includes a discussion of the findings that relate to the determinant 'voice/participation', addressing among other things the value-expressive and instrumental value of voice and the impediments to active involvement that were found throughout the interviews.

The chapter then goes on to elaborate on the antecedents of perceptions of procedural justice that have not figured in previous research. These are police and judiciary performance, peers, and courtroom design and trial practices. The chapter explains how these have an impact on perceptions of procedural fairness and what these 'new' determinants can contribute to procedural justice research. This chapter also addresses the role of formal sources of justice. Whereas procedural justice theory was developed on the assumption that personal contact takes place between authorities and subordinates, this study shows that in the context of criminal justice such personal contact is often limited. Attention should therefore be on how 'the system', as opposed to the actors (police officers and judges) that people deal with, affects perceptions of procedural justice. The chapter furthermore includes a discussion of the importance of decision control – a factor that was advanced by Thibaut and Walker but abandoned by subsequent research – to perceptions of procedural fairness. Finally, a number of relationships and incompatibilities between the antecedents of perceptions of procedural justice are outlined. The chapter closes with a number of reflections on the future of procedural justice research.

The interpretation of the traditional concepts: standing and neutrality

Concretisation of the concepts standing and neutrality

The interview data allow specifying and concretising the procedural justice elements of standing and neutrality. The descriptions presented throughout the previous chapters provide for insight into which issues people consider exactly when answering typical survey questions such as 'People's basic rights are well protected by the police in your neighborhood' (example from Sunshine and Tyler, 2003) or 'Was the judge neutral in the process of the trial?' (example from Ohbuchi *et al.*, 2005). The data, then, render both concepts more concrete, suggesting in fact that they have been interpreted in too narrow a sense. Both elements and their subcomponents are discussed below.

Standing

Four subcategories of standing were found to be important to the participants' procedural fairness judgements. These were: (a) respect for dignity; (b) respect for rights; (c) concern for needs; and (d) social standing.

RESPECT FOR DIGNITY

Quantitative studies aiming to examine whether people feel that they were treated with respect for dignity by the authorities typically ask participants whether they feel that they were treated in a polite and courteous manner. The interview data show that police officers' and judges' attitudes towards the participants were indeed crucial to their sense of how fairly they had been treated. Yet perceptions of respect for one's dignity result not only from being treated in a friendly and polite manner by the police or from magistrates using respectful language and being friendly towards litigants. In fact, the concept is much broader. Throughout the interviews, a number of elements came to the fore that have not previously appeared in procedural justice literature. Specifically, the interviews show that perceptions of respect for one's dignity also depend on such things as the police providing people with a drink during the interrogations and the degree to which the police put trust in the victims and alleged offenders they are confronted with. These were things mentioned by both victims and defendants. Victims in particular also mentioned the importance of the police believing their story and taking the case seriously; the language used in letters sent by the public prosecutor; the degree to which the judge had expressed understanding for their situation and whether the judge had reprimanded the offender. As for offenders' perceptions of respect for their dignity, the use of handcuffs came to the fore as an issue of major importance clearly affecting their sense of identity. These additional elements go beyond politeness and friendliness. The police and the courts, then, communicate about the degree to which they value litigants as a person in more ways than prior research suggests. The implication for quantitative studies is that questions asking litigants if they felt treated in a polite manner do not suffice for measuring whether people felt that their dignity was respected by the criminal authorities.

RESPECT FOR RIGHTS

From the very start, procedural justice researchers have drawn attention to the fact that litigants interpret procedural justice very differently from criminal authorities. The latter base their evaluation of whether procedures were fair on whether all applicable procedural rules and regulations have been respected, whereas the former look for signs of respect for them as a person. Perhaps because of this contrast, procedural justice research has so far not done justice to the concept of respect for rights. Studies investigating the importance of standing tend to focus on litigants receiving respect and being treated in a polite manner, i.e. on the first subcategory of standing. The aspect 'respect for rights' seems to have been largely neglected in the face of constant attention to aspects relating to dignity and politeness. The present study shows that procedural justice research would benefit from re-evaluating the significance of the element 'respect for rights'. In fact, it shows, first, that perceptions of breaches of rights mark people's experience of the criminal justice system to a larger degree than previously thought and, second, that the concept of respect for rights, just like the concept of respect for dignity, has suffered from an overly narrow interpretation.

This argument is rooted in the observation that participants on several occasions throughout the interviews said that one of their rights had been breached by the criminal authorities when in fact this had not been the case. Lay people often mistakenly believe that they have a right to something (e.g. information, a phone call). When answering questions asking whether their rights have been respected throughout the criminal procedure, then, people are more likely to report perceived breaches of rights than actual breaches of rights, all the more because actual breaches of rights are not typically recognised as such. Multiple respondents said that ordinary citizens are not sufficiently knowledgeable about their rights to actually notice when a right is not respected. All this has consequences for procedural justice research. The fact that people are more likely to report perceived breaches of rights than actual breaches of rights is in itself not problematic since subjective interpretations of situations are at the heart of procedural justice theory. When people do not realise that a right has not been respected, the breach of their right will not affect their perception of procedural justice. Hence, a breach of rights not being reported does not get in the way of correctly measuring perceptions of procedural fairness. Yet it is important that justice researchers understand what people's answers to questions about respect for rights are based on, i.e. that *perceived* breaches of rights will determine their answers to a large extent.

CONCERN FOR NEEDS

The participants in this study displayed a variety of needs, as such confirming that being involved in a criminal procedure is a multifaceted and often difficult experience. The needs reported included emotional needs and practical needs: participants discussed whether the authorities had helped them on an emotional and/or practical level. These two types of needs are the needs that are traditionally considered in questionnaires gauging if people feel the authorities paid heed to their needs. The current study draws attention to a number of additional needs. First, the participants showed a great need for information about the criminal procedures, about their rights and about the progress being made in their case. This observation is not new in that prior research into litigants' needs has pointed out this need for information repeatedly – though its focus lay on victims, not offenders (e.g. Wemmers, 1995, 1999; Carr *et al.*, 2003). Yet none of the models of procedural justice outlined in Chapter 1 has paid much attention to litigants' need for information. The need for active involvement in the procedures (voice or process control) has dominated the procedural justice literature, whereas participants in this study actually exhibited a greater need for information (passive involvement) than for active participation to the criminal proceedings.

Second, participants attached great importance to the criminal authorities being available to citizens. A number of participants reported an example of a time where the police had not been willing to assist them or intervene at a time they had needed them – someone reported that the police would not see her anymore ten minutes before the police station was due to close; another participant said that the police would not help him when he needed their help, because they believed he could handle the situation and take care of himself. Another participant blamed the judiciary for not acting quickly enough to remove abused children from their abusing parent. This particular need for the authorities being available to citizens has not received a lot of attention so far, though the item does figure in the London Metropolitan Police Service's Public Attitude Survey (Stanko and Bradford, 2009), which asks citizens 'Do you agree that the police in this area can be relied to be there when you need them?'. The item is one of four items measuring the latent variable 'police commitment to and engagement in the community', which in turn has a significant effect on public confidence in the police. Concluding, then, while procedural justice theory has stressed and empirically validated the importance of authorities meeting litigants' needs during times of personal contact, such as on arrest, during an interrogation or in court, the application of the model to the specific context of criminal lawsuits suggests that the importance of showing concern for litigants' needs reaches beyond the realm of personal contact.

SOCIAL STANDING

When evaluating their experience of criminal justice, a number of participants took into account whether their involvement had an impact on their reputation, that is, on how they are perceived by fellow citizens. They worried about what their neighbours (where police visited them at home) or colleagues (who inquired why they were absent from work in the morning) would think, or showed unease about random citizens being present in court on the day of trial. Someone even pointed out that the letters from the public prosecutor were not properly sealed so strangers could potentially have read them. This is a category that has not featured in procedural justice literature before. It shows that the fact that people feel their sense of self-esteem is being compromised does not only result from contact with group authorities – which procedural justice has always focused on – but may also result from concern for the relationship with – in procedural justice terms – fellow group members.

Neutrality

Participants' perceptions of the neutrality of decision-making were based on: (a) their perceptions concerning the presence or absence of bias and prejudice on behalf of the authorities; (b) their perceptions of the quality of the information used to take decisions (fact-based decision-making); and (c) their perceptions of authorities' honesty.

ABSENCE OF BIAS AND PREJUDICE

A good number of interview fragments concerned participants discussing whether the police and the courts had favoured one of the parties or had operated on the basis of premature judgement about the suspect's guilt or the victim's role in the offence, thus confirming the importance of the element of absence of bias or prejudice to perceptions of procedural justice. Yet the interview data again call for a broader interpretation of the concept, as victims and offenders mentioned much more diverse examples of how they experienced bias or prejudice than was expected on the basis of the literature. For example, offenders' strong feelings about accomplices having been favoured were not expected. The literature tends to focus on the authorities favouring one conflict party over the other, which in criminal lawsuits means favouring the victim over the offender or the other way around. Such situations were discussed by the participants, but offenders in fact focused much more on issues that did not involve a comparison between how they were treated and how the victims were treated. They instead focused on the way their accomplices had been treated and whether the latter had been favoured. One person for example compared the police cell where he had stayed the night to the cell in which his accomplices had been detained, concluding that he had been clearly disadvantaged.

As for issues of bias, participants with a criminal record strongly felt that the authorities were biased because of their past. Procedural justice literature has always stressed that litigants attach great importance to authorities being open to each person's story, but in the context of criminal lawsuits this element seems to gain extra meaning. It also potentially conflicts with the wish that all information relevant to a criminal case is gathered before deciding on the case (fact-based decision-making): recidivist offenders feel that when all information about their past is out in the open, authorities are unlikely to judge their case objectively. A final issue relating to bias that was not anticipated concerns judges' gender. A number of respondents clearly thought that female judges are more likely to pronounce harsh sentences than male judges.

FACT-BASED DECISION-MAKING

As explained, fact-based decision-making has in the past been confused with decision accuracy and has been taken to mean different things. This study suggests that issues relating to decision-making being based on opinions instead of facts and to whether or not people think the judicial decision respects the principle that the guilty should be convicted and the innocent acquitted do not belong to this category. Fact-based decision-making refers to the quality of the investigation and information-gathering by the authorities, which was indeed found to have a major influence on participants' perceptions of fairness. Participants discussed such issues as whether the police investigated the case well enough; whether the judge actually went to the trouble of ascertaining victims' claims for compensation, or simply relied on a solution of convenience; whether the judge gave time to their case, or saw it as one of many; and whether the judge had adequately studied the file.

HONESTY

Few references to lack of honesty were found in the interviews. The examples mentioned concern, first, the specific wording of offenders' words in the minutes of interrogations (and, related to that, the police's interrogation tactics);

and, second, the belief that deals are made between the criminal authorities and lawyers. The first example has distinctive relevance to civil law countries such as Belgium, where this study took place, because these countries' court procedures are based almost exclusively on police records and documents (Merryman and Pérez-Perdomo, 2007). Victims', offenders' and witnesses' statements are not usually reproduced in court, and experts are only invited to deliver an oral statement on rare occasions. The judge's decision relative to the offender's alleged guilt and related sentence is based on documents produced by police and experts. As such great importance is attached to these documents produced by the police, it is essential that the documents reflect the truth accurately (Malsch *et al.*, 2010). As one participant said: 'no matter what I say, they'll always believe what the police wrote down'. Given the essential role of police reports in the trial, this issue may have special relevance to the study of procedural justice in civil law countries.

By way of a general conclusion, then, the results of this study suggest that the concepts of standing and neutrality have both been interpreted too narrowly. The antecedents of procedural justice that have been identified by previous research all proved relevant to the analysis of the interview data, but this study suggests that they are in need of a broader conceptualisation. The only exception is the category fact-based decision-making, which would in fact benefit from being more clearly delineated.

The rationale for the importance of standing and neutrality

The procedural justice model is based on the assumption that people care about procedural fairness because their sense of identity and self-worth is linked to the way they are treated by the authorities of the groups to which they belong. In other words, procedural fairness matters because of the impact that being treated in an unfair manner by group authorities has on the development and maintenance of a favourable identity and as such on people's evaluations of self-worth (Lind and Tyler, 1988; Tyler and Blader, 2003a, 2003b). Specifically, the degree to which people feel that they are a respected group member and the degree to which they feel that they can take pride in their group membership are at stake (Tyler *et al.*, 1996; Tyler, 1999; Tyler and Blader, 2003a). Procedural fairness information allows people to assess the nature of their relationship with and status in the groups to which they belong, and matters especially when the nature of one's place within a group is changing – e.g. in response to a promotion in the workplace or when entering a group (Gonzalez and Tyler, 2007). It is not hard to imagine that becoming involved in a criminal procedure also triggers re-evaluation of one's relationship to and status in a group, i.e. society, and several interview fragments confirm this assertion. Yet the interview data suggest that the significance of fair treatment stretches beyond its impact on social identity. In fact, procedurally fair treatment was also found to convey messages about the likelihood of obtaining certain outcomes and to have an impact on participants' well-being. The overview below describes which function was accorded to each of the subcomponents of standing and neutrality.

Standing

RESPECT FOR DIGNITY

As was to be expected on the basis of procedural justice theory, the degree to which authorities respected the participants' dignity affected participants' sense of identity. Obvious examples of this are found in the offenders' stories about being handcuffed and about being treated in a brutal manner by the police or (investigating) judges. Those who had had this experience explicitly said that this treatment had left them with a reduced sense of identity and a feeling of worthlessness (feeling like a nobody). The same process was at work for victims, yet their contact with the police had usually strengthened their identity. Victims said that the police or judge expressing respect for them had made them feel acknowledged; some even said that they had only realised that they were actually 'a victim' after talking to the police for the first time.

Yet other mechanisms were at work too. Victims' stories show that the degree to which victims experienced dignified treatment (including police officers believing their story and taking the case seriously) had an impact on their well-being and recovery. Feeling acknowledged by the authorities facilitated their recovery from what had happened, while bad treatment (e.g. the police openly doubting the victim's story) led to feeling victimised twice: once by the perpetrator and once by the police. As such, undignified treatment exacerbated victim distress. Furthermore, outcome concerns were at work. Those offenders who said that they had experienced impolite treatment by a judge reported that they had refrained from voicing their opinion to the judge out of fear that if they were to try to defend themselves, the judge's decision on whether to keep them in preliminary custody would be unfavourable. Litigants were also found to derive outcome expectations from the judge's attitude towards the offender: if the judge treated the offender rudely, they expected (s)he would pronounce a harsh sentence. This particular finding corroborates Heuer *et al.*'s research (2002); these authors indeed found that information about standing informs people not only about group status and self-worth but also about the chance of obtaining a preferred outcome. The reason people derive these outcome expectations, however, does not just have to do with the prospect of obtaining a favourable or unfavourable outcome. In fact, the information that is derived from the judge's attitude matters especially because it reduces the uncertainty that people have faced for a long time. Before the trial, people experienced a long period of uncertainty about what would happen to them or to the offender; the trial can finally provide an indication of what to expect in terms of outcome. In all, then, victims and offenders alike base predictions about the outcome of the trial on the way the judge treats the latter in court.

RESPECT FOR RIGHTS

Close inspection of the reasons for people's concern about breaches of rights reveals that both outcome concerns and concerns about social identity played a role. A number of participants' complaints related to not having sufficient time to read one's statement before signing it, or to police officers pressuring them to change their statement in favour of an accomplice. Both point to outcome concerns: people worry because they know that their statement will be crucial to the judge's decision. Another remark was that one had been handcuffed in an unauthorised manner – this aspect of criminal procedure was repeatedly found to affect the offenders' sense of identity. The same goes for offenders' concern about the police not respecting their duty of professional secrecy – offenders feared a decrease in social status – and the complaints about physical force used by the police; about the police's entering a suspect's home without permission; and about the police not informing young suspects' parents of their arrest. Each of these examples points to a lack of respect for the citizens involved, which confirms procedural justice theory's argument about procedurally fair treatment communicating social identity-relevant information.

CONCERN FOR NEEDS

Concern for victims' and offenders' needs was found to matter for different reasons, depending on the exact need that had been taken care of. The police and the judiciary paying heed to participants' emotional and practical needs and need for information was found to be important with a view to participants' well-being. For example, victims were better able to cope with the victimisation experience and felt more secure where they received information about the progress of the case and about the decisions that were taken about the offender after arrest. Offenders mentioned emotional and practical needs less frequently than victims but those that were mentioned (e.g. when a police officer stood by an offender after the latter had become upset following interrogation) also showed the impact of concern for needs upon well-being.

The criminal authorities' concern for people's need for active involvement in the criminal proceedings seems to matter for social identity reasons, outcome-related reasons and reasons of well-being. Those participants that planned on voicing their opinion in court often gave reasons that related to influencing the outcome; furthermore, opportunities for participation in the trial seemed to be valued especially where people believed that their input had been taken into account by the judge. A number of participants said that voicing one's opinion in court has a value in and of itself, regardless of whether it influences the outcome, which reminds us of procedural justice theory's stance that procedurally fair treatment conveys a message of respect for the people involved and as such affects their sense of identity. Finally, it seems that as far as victims are concerned, being able to voice one's opinion in court or to tell one's story to the police, the judge or a mediator is especially valuable because being able to do so provides relief, thereby aiding victims' recovery and enhancing their well-being.

SOCIAL STANDING

The finding that people involved in a criminal procedure care greatly about what this involvement will do to their reputation vis-à-vis neighbours, colleagues, family members or citizens in general is a prime example of how procedural fairness information matters because of concern for social identity: people worry about how their involvement in criminal proceedings will affect how they are perceived by other people.

Neutrality

ABSENCE OF BIAS AND PREJUDICE

The participants who indicated that the police had been biased or prejudiced were concerned with several things. First, being treated in a biased or prejudiced manner had an impact on their sense of self and identity. Some offenders for example said that they had been approached as if they were a seasoned criminal; or had been called a liar, which did not match their sense of self at all; and one of the offenders who thought that the judge had been prejudiced said that she had felt like 'a nobody'. Victims' concerns about neutrality, also, were to a large degree related to maintaining self-esteem. For example they referred to being treated like anyone else despite their race and about not being blamed for the offence when the police would actually have had reason to be suspicious about their role in the offence. The second concern, found exclusively among offenders, was the impact of authorities' (lack of) neutrality on short-term outcomes (such as being held in custody) and/or the outcome of the trial (for example, the police's lack of neutrality had made them confess to crimes they did not commit). The third concern, found exclusively among victims, relates to the impact of objective and neutral treatment on feelings of safety and well-being. Victims who had the impression that the police were protecting offenders or felt they were being blamed by the police or the judge for what had happened clearly experienced distress – the fact that the authorities questioned their 'right to victim status' made it more difficult for them to deal with what was happening.

FACT-BASED DECISION-MAKING

The thoroughness of the investigation and the quality of information-gathering by the criminal authorities was found to matter to participants out of a concern for the outcome of the trial: they feared that the judge would reach an unfavourable or unfair decision if the police and the judiciary failed to gather all the relevant evidence and information. Yet it is worth probing this issue in more detail, because participants' concern about the outcome was in fact motivated in large part by a concern for social status. The interview data suggest that the reason why litigants are anxious about the judge having all the necessary information at his/her disposal is that they feel that sentences should be fine-tuned to each and every specific offender's situation. This is considered important in order to make the offender less likely to commit further crimes. Victims would for example say that the only way in which their particular offender could be made to realise his mistake would be to impose a fine or that the worst punishment for their offender would be to take him away from his family. Offenders when asked which sentence would be the most appropriate also referred to their specific situation, reasoning for example that because of their precarious financial situation it would make no sense to impose a fine on them. The participants' opinions about the most appropriate sentence were tailored to the specific situation of the offender as much as possible because of the importance of such tailored sentences to the prevention of future wrongdoing by a particular offender. This, then, is an important reason why people want the judge to have as much information about the offence and the offender available as possible. Furthermore, some of the participants who had been victimised by a family member said that the sentence would also affect their and their children's status. Another indication of the importance of high-quality fact-finding to perceptions of status and identity is the fact that part of the reason why victims cared about good information-gathering and the judge studying the file well had to do with acknowledgement: authorities taking the time and effort to adequately investigate the case conveys the message that they are taking the case seriously and as such affirms victim status. To sum up, then, the data suggest that although at first sight outcome concerns drove the participants' need for high-quality fact-finding, social identity concerns played a role too.

HONESTY

Problems with police officers acting in a dishonest way mattered to participants out of concern for the impact of this behaviour on the outcome of the trial, for example because it created disparity between offenders and inequality before the law.

In conclusion, while procedural justice theory insists that procedurally fair treatment matters because people's sense of self and self-worth are closely tied up with how they and their case are treated by the legal authorities, this study points to additional reasons for the importance of procedural fairness. In particular, procedurally fair treatment was also found to affect participants' level of well-being and was sometimes perceived as a prerequisite for outcome fairness. The latter observation is in line with the conclusions of Heuer *et al.* (2002), who argued that litigants care about standing, trust and neutrality in part because the degree to which the authorities respect these key elements of procedural fairness conveys a message about the likelihood that they will obtain preferred outcomes. When people are confronted with a lack of neutrality on behalf of the authorities, for example, they deduce from that that their chances of receiving a desirable outcome are low. Heuer *et al.* (2002), then, argue that procedural justice theorists have underestimated the significance of other than social standing concerns in explaining the importance of standing, trust and neutrality. This study confirms this stance, especially since a third factor was found to be important in explaining the significance of procedural fairness. In particular, the results suggest that procedural fairness is also important to litigant well-being. This conclusion can be related to the literature on the impact of perceived (in)justice on emotions and affect. Several studies have related experiences of (in)justice to a host of emotions, such as anger, frustration, guilt, sadness, disgust, anxiety and happiness (e.g. Mikula *et al.*, 1998; Weiss *et al.*, 1999; Krehbiel and Cropanzano, 2000; Murphy and Tyler, 2008; for an extensive review of models integrating the justice and emotions literature see Cropanzano *et al.*, 2011). Experiences of procedural unfairness have also been associated with higher levels of depression and poor emotional well-being (Tatar II *et al.*, 2012), while fair treatment has been found to lead to decreases in stress levels (Vermunt, 2002; Vermunt and Steensma, 2003) and to facilitate reductions of the negative psychological consequences of crime by giving victims a sense of closure and empowerment (Elliott et al., 2013). The research cited and the current study, then, support a conclusion that the psychological effects of perceived procedural injustice extend well beyond identity concerns: experiences of procedural injustice also influence people's affect and emotional well-being.

The conditional nature of respect for dignity

One particular finding about the first subcomponent of standing – i.e. respect for dignity – concerns the observation that some circumstances warrant deviations from the general principle that the police should be respectful to litigants. Even though all respondents without exception attached great importance to police officers treating citizens politely and with respect, some did say that there are degrees to which the police can and should be expected to behave respectfully towards citizens. Some respondents said that it makes a difference whether the police are dealing with a victim or with a defendant – according to some respondents, victims are more worthy of respectful treatment than offenders. The seriousness of the offence too was advanced as a criterion: those who committed the most serious crimes according to some respondents are less deserving of dignified treatment than those who committed minor crimes. The attitude of the victim or defendant that the police are dealing with matters too: the police were said to have the right to treat those victims and offenders who behave disrespectfully towards them more harshly. Finally, one person argued that the police officer's job description should determine how he is expected to behave: those investigating crimes, this respondent said, are entitled to be a little more rude than those undertaking daily community-policing functions. Though these feelings were not expressed by all respondents and some explicitly said that victims and offenders should be treated in the same manner, a substantial number of people seem to hold the opinion that the 'right' to be treated with respect by the police is conditional. Another interesting finding in this respect is that participants felt the urge to give meaning to inconsiderate and impolite treatment by police officers. Those participants who had experienced the police crossing boundaries – the police using physical force, for example, or rude language – after sharing their story often added that they thought there was a reason for the police officers' behaviour. They would say 'I think they acted like this because … ', saying that they understood why the police acted the way they did. Most of them referred to their own behaviour or the suspects' behaviour to explain the police using force or being unfriendly.

It seems, then, that the characteristics of the person the police are dealing with and/or that person's behaviour determine the acceptability of improper or disrespectful police behaviour to a large extent. Heuer *et al.* (1999) and Sunshine and Heuer (2002) have reported similar findings indicating that when assessing the way they or someone else was treated, people attach great importance to notions of deservingness and entitlement. Heuer *et al.* (1999) found respondents to consider both the value of their own behaviour and their responsibility for that behaviour when judging the fairness of the (respectful or disrespectful) treatment they received from a professor; likewise, observers considered disrespectful treatment of an individual by a supervisor more fair than respectful treatment when the individual had displayed negatively valued behaviour him/herself in the first place. Sunshine and Heuer (2002) found that perceptions of procedural fairness are enhanced when people believe that the treatment they received from the police matches the treatment that they feel they deserved and that people who feel that they are entitled to favourable treatment experience a greater positive effect of favourable treatment on their perceptions of procedural fairness than those who do not experience such sense of entitlement. Both studies then demonstrate that injustice is perceived when the kind of treatment that people receive does not match the kind of treatment that they (believe they) deserve. The relationship between respect and procedural fairness, then, is mediated by perceptions of entitlement and deservingness. As Sunshine and Heuer (2002) point out, traditional models of procedural justice have not examined this deservingness effect. The present study supports Heuer *et al.*'s (1999) and Sunshine and Heuer's (2002) findings, providing concrete examples of the factors that determine people's assessments of entitlement and deservingness.

As Sunshine and Heuer (2002) rightly observe, the findings on the deservingness of fair treatment call to mind Lerner's just world theory (see Lerner, 1980; Lerner and Montada, 1998), which states that people hold firmly to the belief that in life, everyone gets what they deserve. By rationalising the unfair treatment that they received from the police, people indeed seem to try to restore their confidence in the police, which they risk losing when witnessing the police's poor behaviour. Only by rationalising and explaining this behaviour can they sustain their confidence in a just world and thus in the fact that should they become involved with the police again one day they will be treated well. This argument is supported by the fact that the participants in this study ascribed the police's use of force or unfriendly attitude not to individual officers' inherent characteristics but to situational variables (i.e. their own behaviour, the behaviour of the suspect, or the type of crime). Whereas common psychological knowledge suggests that people have a tendency to overestimate the importance of dispositional qualities and underestimate the importance of situational qualities when trying to understand the causes of other people's behaviour (Zimbardo, 2007), the participants in this study sought the cause for police officers' behaviour in situational circumstances. This too may be a tactic for preserving the idea that if they should one day approach the police again, they would be treated well.

Studies show that police officers too often operate on the basis of the principle that some people are more deserving of special attention than others. Aertsen *et al.* (2002), for example, found police officers saying that they only give certain kinds of victims special attention, or only under certain conditions. Examples are where the victim is a child, or where the victim is cooperative. It seems that citizens share this notion of deservingness; also, the criteria they use to determine whether someone is entitled to respectful treatment are quite diverse. Police officers' specific function, litigants' own behaviour and the seriousness of the crime are all considered important. It should be recalled that the participants in this study explicitly rejected discrimination based on other facts, such as race or age. Also, only one participant said that neutrality is conditional. It seems, then, that being treated with respect for dignity may be conditional, or something the right to which can be lost, whereas one's case being handled in a neutral manner is more generally regarded as a principle that cannot be infringed.

The interpretation of the traditional concepts: trust

The results of this study give rise to a re-evaluation of the status of trust in procedural justice theory in that they suggest that trust in authorities results from perceptions of procedural justice instead of being an antecedent of procedural justice. The findings that led to this conclusion are discussed below. Two additional findings concerning trust in the authorities that are discussed below are, first, the fact that participants' level of trust in the criminal authorities influenced their need for voice and participation in the criminal proceedings, and, second, the observation that (an increase in) trust in the pre-trial authorities enhances trust in the courts.

Procedural fairness increases trust in the authorities

One of the most notable evolutions that come to light when one compares Lind and Tyler's early model of procedural justice (Lind and Tyler, 1988; Tyler and Lind, 1992) with the more recent models (i.e. the group engagement model of procedural justice and the process based model of regulation; see Chapter 1) is that while the conceptualisation of standing and neutrality has never really changed, the meaning of the element of trust has been under constant revision. While Lind and Tyler advanced trust as an antecedent of perceptions of procedural justice, Tyler and Huo's (2002) process-based model of regulation conceives of trust as one element fostering willingness to defer to authorities independent of and next to procedural fairness. The group engagement model (Tyler and Blader, 2000, 2001, 2003a; Blader and Tyler, 2003a, 2003b) does not accord trust in the authorities a role as an antecedent of procedural fairness either, and neither does Wemmers' (1996) model of procedural justice (which focuses on victims' experiences specifically).

The exact meaning and status of the element of trust, then, have caused considerable confusion and seem undecided. This study suggests that trust is not to be regarded as an antecedent of procedural justice; it argues instead that trust in the authorities is in fact affected by perceptions of procedural justice, that is, by perceptions of neutrality and standing. Multiple findings point to this conclusion. To start with, the results concerning victims' perceptions of the attitude of police officers suggest a relationship between the police treating victims in a dignified manner and taking their case seriously and victims' level of trust in the police. One victim testified about how the fact that the police had behaved courteously towards her had raised her confidence both in the police and in the judicial authorities; another victim said that because the police had been behaving so poorly, she had lost faith in her belief that the trial would settle the conflict. Perceptions of respectful treatment, then, affect victims' level of trust in the police and the courts (see also Bradford *et al.*, 2009). Offenders' stories too revealed a relationship between procedural fairness and trust, yet in their case this did not have to do with respectful treatment but with neutrality. A number of recidivist offenders causally related 'having a criminal record' with 'a lack of effort in investigating the case'. They were convinced that the police did not/would not investigate their case properly because there was a recidivist involved on whom they could simply put all the blame. This finding suggests that a relationship exists between perceptions of police prejudice and trust in the police. On the basis of these results, the thesis is advanced that trust is not to be considered a component of procedural justice and thus not an antecedent of perceptions of procedural fairness but a consequence of perceptions of procedural fairness. Those citizens who perceive the criminal authorities to be acting in a procedurally fair manner (that is, with respect for the principles of standing and neutrality) are more likely to put trust in these authorities.

Trust in the authorities decreases the need for voice and participation

On several occasions it was observed that the more people feel that they can trust the authorities, the less they feel a need to actively participate in the investigation of the case or in the trial. In Chapter 3, a victim was cited as affirming that her confidence in the police had grown as the police had acknowledged her hurt and what had happened to her. She said that because of this experience she did not feel a need to intervene in the investigation of the case. Another victim testified that she lost all trust in the police because of the way they handled her case: she said that they did not put serious effort into investigating the case and never gave her the feeling that they were taking it seriously. For this reason, she had felt obliged to try to get things moving herself, urging the authorities to take action. She described it as a battle. Another victim said that because all police officers and magistrates had according to her done their job and taken their responsibilities seriously, she did not feel any need to keep them on their toes and see to it that they performed their tasks. In other words, the fact that the authorities put effort into the case increased her level of trust in them, which in turn decreased her need to become involved in the criminal proceedings. Each of these stories suggests that there is a relationship between level of trust in the authorities and feeling the need to participate.

Trust in authorities has traditionally been related to willingness to cooperate with authorities, the relationship being such that increased trust in authorities leads to increased willingness to cooperate with authorities (e.g. De Cremer and Tyler, 2007; Tyler, 2011). This study shows that the degree to which people put trust in the police not only affects the degree to which they are willing to cooperate with the police when asked to, but also the degree to which they feel a need – or feel that they should try – to get control of the criminal proceedings and to participate in them. Tellingly, participants' stories show that in case of low trust in the authorities the need for participation is not so much motivated by a feeling that one *wants* to participate but rather by a feeling that one *has no choice* but to intervene. It is a feeling of obligation, of having no choice but to take matters into one's own hands. This finding is in line with Murphy *et al.*'s (2008) finding that to the degree that people feel that the police are doing a good job, they report lower levels of willingness to help the police fight crime, that is, to take up an active role in crime prevention themselves, and Kautt's (2011) finding that people who take more self-protective measures (i.e. secure their homes) are more likely to say they believe the police do a poor job. Trust in the police affects the degree to which people feel compelled to take control over the situation themselves.

This is an interesting observation since procedural justice research has traditionally looked at the matter of voice and participation from the point of view that litigants *like* and really *want to* participate in the criminal procedure. This study demonstrates that sometimes they would rather not participate but feel that they have no other choice. This issue will be further elaborated upon below, when discussing how this study contributes to our understanding of litigants' need for participation in the criminal proceedings.

Fair treatment by the police increases trust in the courts

The study suggests that the degree to which people put trust in the courts depends in part on the degree to which the police treated them in a procedurally fair manner. This observation is interesting because one important recommendation that follows from research into procedural justice is that authorities can boost public confidence through the fair exercise of authority. It has been argued that by improving the way they interact with citizens, authorities can raise public confidence in their actions (e.g. Sunshine and Tyler, 2003; Tyler, 2003; Bradford *et al.*, 2009). Without denying this argument, it is important to note that there may actually be only so much the courts can do to enhance public confidence in the courts because people's level of confidence in the courts depends in part on how the pre-trial authorities treat them and handle their case. Unfair treatment by the police, prosecutor or investigating judge may negatively affect people's confidence that the court will render a fair ruling.

The interpretation of the traditional concepts: voice/participation

When Thibaut and Walker (1975, 1978) conducted their first inquiries into the psychology of procedural justice, they found that the participants to the mock trials they set up perceived decision-making procedures that allowed them to voice their opinion and to exert control over the procedure as more fair than those that did not allow them to do so. Subsequent procedural justice research has thoroughly fleshed out the significance of voice/participation, as described in Chapter 1; the main conclusion to be drawn from those studies is that litigants value voice/participation not just because of an instrumental reason (as Thibaut and Walker argued) but also because being allowed to express one's views has a value in itself. The results of the current study shed new light on this need for voice and for involvement in the criminal procedures.

The need for active participation in the police investigation

Though procedural justice theory has often been applied to citizen–police interactions (e.g. Wells, 2007; Allen and Monk-Turner, 2010; Schulhofer *et al.*, 2011; Mazerolle *et al.*, 2012; Murphy and Cherney, 2012) it has remained rather silent about litigants' need for participation in the investigation of their case. The concept participation has been studied almost exclusively in the context of trials. One exception is the study by De Mesmaecker *et al.* (2013). These authors conducted a vignette study among a sample of Dutch citizens. Participants were asked to read a vignette describing an offence and to imagine that they had been the victim in the case described in the vignette. Next, they were asked to rate the importance of five forms of involvement in the pre-trial criminal proceedings. These were: (1) to be able to tell one's story to the police and the judge; (2) to receive information on the case developments; (3) to receive information about the role and rights of victims; (4) to be able to provide evidence, such as pictures or witnesses, to the judge; and (5) to have a say on how the criminal investigations are conducted. The first four options were considered highly important; the respondents showed much less interest in having a say on how the investigation would be conducted. The results of the current study too allow for an examination of the need for participation in the criminal investigations and confirm that litigants have little need for active participation in these investigations. Few respondents said that they would have preferred to be involved in the police investigation of the case to a greater degree. Those offenders who did say that they would have liked to participate in the criminal investigations in an active manner said that the police had overlooked certain information or had neglected to gather particular evidence. They wanted to make sure that their file would contain all the evidence necessary for the judge to try their case. Their reason for participation, then, was instrumental, which is important information with a view to the debate on the value-expressive and instrumental value of voice – this issue will be discussed in more detail in the subsequent paragraphs.

The value-expressive and instrumental value of voice

Litigants' need for participation in the criminal proceedings was most manifest in the trial phase. Though respondents displayed a number of concerns about speaking up during the trial, they did want their side of the story and their arguments to be heard by the court. As said, an important issue in the literature on voice is whether litigants value voice for expressive reasons or for instrumental reasons, that is, to influence the judge's decision (see Folger, 1977; Tyler *et al.*, 1985; Tyler, 1987; Lind *et al.*, 1990). The participants in this study mentioned both value-expressive reasons and instrumental reasons for voicing their opinion in court.

Starting with the first category, a number of the reasons that participants mentioned for speaking in court suggest indeed that the opportunity for speaking in court is valued in itself, independently of its effect on the outcome of the trial (see also, e.g., Tyler, 1994). For instance, while six offenders said that they did not believe that anything they would say in court would influence the outcome of the trial, four of these six still wanted to voice their opinion in court. They wanted to defend themselves either way or said that they would do it for their own relief. Similarly, victims' stories suggest that victims have a great need for voice, that is, to tell their story, but that this does not automatically imply that they have a great need to tell their story to the judicial authorities. To some victims it does not matter to whom exactly they recount their story, as long as they are able to do so at some point in the procedure. Some cases show that when a victim has been able to tell his/her story to a victim support worker or a mediator, the need to tell it in court is low. Such stories also indicate that the opportunity to share one's point of view about the case at some point during the procedure is valued for reasons other than mere instrumental ones.

Yet other findings propose that people do want their intervention to influence the judge's decision. When discussing the opportunity to speak in court, most respondents either said that something should actually be done with the information that litigants provide in court; expressed discontentment because they had the impression that what they had said had not been taken into account; or said that they had the feeling that allowing litigants to speak in court is just a sham. While introducing opportunities for voice enhances the perceived fairness of decision-making procedures, the lack of consideration of litigants' arguments and opinions may neutralise this positive effect. The reasons victims gave for speaking in court also provide an indication of the wish to have one's voice heard in order to influence the outcome, yet it should be noted that in general victims wanted to convince the judge not to be too harsh on the offender. A final indication of the instrumental value of voice concerns the common feeling among offenders that it is often better not to take the floor in court because doing so might have a negative effect on the outcome. This observation points to an instrumental reason for the *non*-use of opportunities for voice.

This study, then, suggests, as did Folger (1977) and Lind *et al.* (1990), that voice has both a value-expressive and an instrumental function. While participation in the trial has an expressive value, as procedural justice theory predicts, outcome concerns should not be overlooked. At the same time, however, outcome concerns should not be misinterpreted. In the specific case of victims especially, one should keep in mind that they may use the opportunity to address the court in order to convince the judge not to be too *harsh* on the offender when deciding on the sentence. This is an instrumental reason for participating, yet a very different one than one would intuitively assume.

Impediments to active involvement

The procedural justice literature has convincingly demonstrated that people who have been given a chance to become involved in the trial are more satisfied about the process and more likely to accept the outcome of the trial than those who have experienced it from the sidelines. Yet little attention has been paid so far to the individual differences between people that make some more likely than others to look for opportunities for involvement, or to the structural conditions of trial settings that influence people's decisions on whether to take part in the trial. The results of this study show that the decision-making process of whether to become actively involved in the trial is more complicated than procedural justice theory in its current form suggests. In fact, both individual characteristics, such as not being the kind of person to talk in public or being a very emotional person, and structural factors inherent to the criminal justice system, such as the presence of an audience in court, lead people to refrain from exerting voice.

These kinds of impediments to participation have not been studied systematically, nor has sufficient attention been paid to identifying those circumstances in which the need for active involvement is low. Granted, procedural justice researchers have examined individual differences in justice sensitivity (see Schmitt *et al.*, 1995, 2005; Schmitt and Mohiyeddini, 1996;

Mohiyeddini and Schmitt, 1997; Fetchenhauer and Huang, 2004; Gollwitzer *et al.*, 2005; Baumert and Schmitt, 2009), have tried to define those conditions under which procedural fairness matters the most (see e.g. Gonzalez and Tyler, 2007) and have looked into individual differences in the factors that are taken into account when judging the fairness of decision-making procedures (e.g. Mikula, 1974; Lissak and Sheppard, 1983; Sweeney *et al.*, 1991; Holm-vall and Bobocel, 2008). Yet there has been little consideration of what it actually means to people to participate in the trial on an emotional and practical level. This study shows that even those with significant need for participation in the decision-making procedure sometimes refrain from doing so; it would appear there are several impediments to active participation in the trial.

First, outcome concerns were found to influence decisions on whether to try to become actively involved in the trial. Defendants refrain from voicing their opinion in court out of fear that if they defend themselves the judge may decide to be more harsh on them. Second, concern for authorities' neutrality may hinder litigant participation in the criminal proceedings (this concerns the specific example of talking to the judge in private). Third, victims and offenders alike indicated that speaking in court is difficult because they are emotionally tense at that particular moment and have trouble finding the words to say what they wish to get across. Fourth, participants indicated that the complexity of the criminal justice system makes it difficult for them as lay people to participate in criminal proceedings. Fifth, and related to the fourth, a lack of information may prevent victims and offenders from becoming involved in the criminal proceedings. The jargon used in letters and a lack of information about their rights lead to people feeling unable to make sure that their story will be heard. Sixth, trial practices may prevent those litigants who would want to have their say in court from doing so. In this respect, the presence of an audience in court and the lack of time available for being able to fully speak their mind were among factors mentioned. Impediments to participation have so far not figured prominently in the writings of procedural justice scholars; this study provides a number of clues on the aspects of trial procedures that influence people's decision as to whether to speak in court that future research may want to include in analyses.

Procedural justice theory not only seems to have underestimated the complexity of participating in criminal proceedings; it also seems to have largely neglected the possibility that people do not always *want* to participate but in some cases feel that they *need to* because of a lack of effort on behalf of the authorities to investigate cases thoroughly. This was touched upon above. In such cases, participation has undesirable effects and may cause secondary victimisation. Secondary victimisation refers to victims feeling re-victimised by negative reactions from police officers or other authorities (Winkel and Vrij, 1995); Reeves and Dunn (2010) describe it as 'the aggravation of the primary offence by the insensitive behaviour of others' (52). While secondary victimisation is traditionally explained by reference to a lack of outcome satisfaction, perceptions of procedural injustice, lengthy procedures and disrespectful behaviour by authorities (Winkel *et al.*, 1991; Orth, 2002; Cotti *et al.*, 2004; Reeves and Dunn, 2010), this study shows that feeling forced to participate in the criminal proceedings may also cause feelings of secondary victimisation.

The influence of participation in mediation on the need for participation in the trial

While the factors enumerated above were experienced as obstructions to participating in the trial, one factor was found to reduce the actual *need* for participation in the trial: a number of victims said that they felt no need to attend the court hearing in their case or to speak in court because participating in victim–offender mediation had allowed them to close the matter on an emotional and/or financial level. A satisfying mediation experience, then, has an impact on some victims' need to attend trial or to speak in court. This finding suggests that the need for participation is limited, in that being able to participate at one point during the criminal proceedings seems sufficient for many. As such, it suggests that the answer to a question posed by Pemberton *et al.* (2008: 105) – who asked whether victims 'are increasingly satisfied as they gain a higher level of participation (...) [o]r is there an optimum point along the way that is preferable to positions further up the ladder of participation?' – is that there may indeed be an 'optimum point' of participation, because participation is not without its challenges and difficulties. This goes for offenders too – a number of offenders said that they had no need to speak in court because they had told their story to the investigating judge and/or because they thought the case was sufficiently clear.

The difference between a need for voice/participation and a need for representation

An important finding of this study, which proceeds from the aforementioned difficulties that come with participating in the trial, is that the fact that some people reject the opportunity to personally voice their opinion in court does not necessarily imply that these people have no need at all for their story to be heard in court. Indeed, those respondents who did not feel comfortable about speaking in court in person actively looked for alternatives, saying for example that they would prefer another person, such as their therapist, to address the court to convey their arguments and stories. The observation that a good number of litigants waive opportunities for speaking in court should thus not lead to the conclusion that procedural justice theory has overstressed the importance of participation/voice. In fact, it seems that the need to have one's story heard by the criminal authorities is universal, but preferences for the means through which to exert voice differ. Some attend the trial in person, some rely on their lawyer, others make sure that their story is included in the

mediation agreement that the judge will read as part of the file. This observation has implications for the design of survey questions that measure the
need for participation in a trial. Victims especially should be asked both for
their need for opportunities for voicing their opinion in court in person and
for their need for opportunities for representation in court. The first question
does not in itself suffice to measure people's need for voice.

The need for information

As Tyler and Blader (2003b) point out, the focus of procedural justice
research has been and still is heavily influenced by the conception of justice
that was advanced by John Thibaut and Laurens Walker, who were the first
to carry out empirical studies on the subject of procedural justice. Thibaut
and Walker's predominant attention to issues of participation and process
control has led justice researchers to spend ample time and energy on figuring
out litigants' need for voice and participation. Many of the experimental studies that have been conducted to test the importance of procedures to fairness
judgements have manipulated voice conditions, allowing subjects to either
exert voice or not (e.g. van den Bos *et al.*, 1998; van den Bos, 2001), and quite
a number of publications have focused on the question of whether exerting
voice has an instrumental or non-instrumental value (Folger, 1977; Tyler *et al.*,
1985; Lind *et al.*, 1990). This preoccupation with issues of voice and participation has led to a lack of attention on litigants' need for information. Though
a number of researchers have drawn attention to the importance of what they
call 'informational justice' (see Bies and Moag, 1986; Bies, 1987; Greenberg,
1993; Colquitt, 2001; Colquitt *et al.*, 2001), litigants' need for information has
never received the same attention from procedural justice researchers that
issues of voice and participation have. The current study lends support to the
notion that one main justice concern of those involved in decision-making
procedures is that authorities communicate to them, explain the reasons for
certain actions, explain procedures and tailor communication to litigants'
needs (Colquitt, 2001). It is recommended that future models of procedural
justice incorporate the justice concern 'receiving information'.

The extant research on litigants' informational needs focuses mainly on
victims' need for information (see e.g. Wemmers, 1995, 1999; Carr *et al.*,
2003; Strang and Sherman, 2003; Lemonne and Vanfraechem, 2010). Studies
on offenders' need for information during the course of the criminal proceedings are rare, yet the offenders participating in this study expressed a
great need for information too. They were especially in need of information
about the course of action following arrest or interrogation. Their wish for
information was motivated by a feeling of uncertainty. When people are
arrested, they cease having control over what happens to them and thus find
themselves in a state of uncertainty – some offenders said that they experienced this uncertainty as a form of punishment. There is a specific body of
literature on the importance of procedural fairness in situations of uncertainty

(see van den Bos, 2001; van den Bos and Lind, 2002), which demonstrates that procedural fairness information is especially important to people who find themselves in situations of threat or uncertainty. It is plausible, then, that feelings of uncertainty caused offenders' great need for information. As Vermunt and Steensma (2001) explain, fair procedures help reduce the threat value of a situation. Receiving information from the police and the courts, then, may reduce the threat value of the situation.

Content-wise, offenders' needs for information focused on the same issues throughout the whole procedure. Both during the criminal investigations and during the trial phase they mainly asked for information about the way the criminal proceedings are conducted and about the punishment they risked. Victims expected different types of information from the judiciary than from the police. The information that they requested from the police focused on the offender and what happened to the offender after the arrest (i.e., was he allowed to go home or was he taken into custody?). During the trial phase, they were in need of information about the criminal investigation, the way the criminal proceedings would be conducted, and their rights as a victim. Finally, they wished for the courts to inform them of the outcome of the trial. This study, then, suggests that different types of information are needed at different times. While previous (quantitative) studies have clearly demonstrated significant need for information among victims who are involved in criminal proceedings (see above), these studies have not provided for insight into the desired timing of information provision. An interview study by Aertsen and Hutsebaut (2010) among family members of road traffic victims does show, as does this study, that the timing of providing victims with certain types of information matters. Aertsen and Hutsebaut write, for example, that the family members of road traffic victims that they interviewed were not in need of detailed information immediately after they found out about the accident that killed their child; at that time, processing such information was too confronting and too burdensome. The authors propose that it may be advisable to convey only basic information immediately after the event and to convey additional and more detailed information at a later point, when victims have had time to recover from the initial shock. The current study supports this line of reasoning. In the initial phase of the criminal proceedings, victims focus on offender-oriented information because that type of information contributes to an immediate feeling of security. The realisation that someone has intentionally hurt them leads victims to distrust others and to view their world as less safe (Greenberg and Ruback, 1992; Herman, 2010). To know more about who the offender is and whether the offender is at liberty is important with a view to safety. Information about the workings of the criminal justice system is not a priority in that initial phase; the need for this type of information comes later.

By way of a final remark on the importance of transparency and information provision to litigants, the findings suggest that providing litigants with more information about the progress of the case may be interesting for the authorities, if, for nothing else, at least to do away with the image of passivity and impunity.

Van Camp (2011) from a study conducted among crime victims also concluded that '[l]ack of information implies lack of insight, for instance in whether the case is taken seriously' (133). The criminal justice system could prevent criticism about the time it takes to deal with cases by better informing litigants about the progress that is made or about the state of affairs of their case.

Extending theories of procedural justice: the importance of police/ judiciary performance to perceptions of procedural justice

When asked, through open-ended questions, how they experienced their encounter with the criminal justice system, victims and offenders tend to share their opinions on the way the authorities performed their work. The analysis of this category of remarks, labelled 'performance', shows that perceptions of the quality of the authorities' work actually influence perceptions of standing and, to a slightly lesser degree, perceptions of neutrality. For this reason, performance is advanced as an antecedent of perceptions of procedural justice.

The performance issues enumerated by the interviewees were very diverse. Moreover, differences were found between victims' and offenders' concerns, at least as far as the police are concerned. When discussing the police's efforts, victims expressed concern about whether the police had been able to find and arrest the offender; about whether the police had been sufficiently diligent in their efforts in this; and about the time it had taken the police to arrive at the crime scene. Furthermore, they mentioned the length of interrogations and expressed satisfaction about the police on duty calling social services outside opening hours or calling specialised police officers who were not present at the police station at the time the victim reported the crime. They also talked about the police's knowledge of their cases and their ability to organise their file, about the cooperation between different police services and about mistakes that the police had made during the investigation. Offenders would focus on the number of police officers that had been sent to arrest them, the methods of interrogation, the police abusing their power to keep them in detention and the thoroughness of the police investigation. When discussing the efforts of the judiciary in the pre-trial phase, participants suggested that reconstructions of crimes should be organised on a routine basis and that more attention should go to gathering information about the victim and about the offender's family and financial situation. As for the trial phase, the dominant performance concern was that criminal procedures are slow, that it takes a long time for the system to deal with cases. Other concerns mentioned were that the criminal authorities did not take their responsibilities seriously and that the criminal justice system is utterly bureaucratic.

As said, it appears that these performance issues influence perceptions of standing (especially in victims' case) and neutrality (especially in offenders' case) and as such influence perceptions of fairness in an indirect manner. To victims, the police (not) putting enough effort into the case is indicative of standing. When the police take the case seriously, arrive at the crime scene quickly, do their best to investigate the case and identify the offender, and so on, they enhance feelings of victim acknowledgement. This finding is corroborated by other research into victims' experiences with criminal justice (e.g. Bradford *et al.*, 2009; Aertsen and Hutsebaut, 2010; Elliott *et al.*, 2012). Bradford *et al.*'s (2009) study for example demonstrates that 'waiting time' (i.e. the time it takes the police to arrive at the crime scene) is an important issue to victims precisely because it is used as a measure of police responsiveness and of the importance that the police place on demands from the community. Elliott *et al.* (2012) also reported the importance of the police taking the case seriously to victims, writing that 'the major point of dissatisfaction with the police response was not the fact that the police could not find or charge the offender, or retrieve stolen property, but occurred when participants perceived that the police were not going to do much about their cases' (442). Importantly, then, victims' concern about police performance is not motivated exclusively by a need for retribution; a significant part of the reason that victims care about the police doing a good job is that the police doing so tells them that their case is taken seriously. This in turn communicates victim acknowledgement and as such affects perceptions of standing. Offenders' main performance concerns were with the methods of interrogation that were used by the police, with the unnecessary, disproportionate show of force by the police when arresting them, with the thoroughness of the investigation and with the police using their power to keep them in detention for as long as was legally possible. Each of these concerns relates to one of the subcategories of neutrality. The improper use of power during interrogations, upon arrest and during detention points to the police behaving in a biased and dishonest way; the police (not) investigating the case fully is associated with prejudice and, of course, fact-finding. This means that perceptions of police performance affect offenders' procedural fairness judgements through their impact on offenders' perceptions of neutrality.

While the performance of the legal authorities has so far not been included in models of procedural justice, performance is often included in victimisation surveys (e.g. the International Crime Victim Survey (ICVS); see van Dijk *et al.*, 2007) and surveys on citizen perceptions of the police (e.g. the London Metropolitan Police Service's Public Attitude Survey; see Stanko and Bradford, 2009). Questions measuring citizen perceptions of police performance usually focus on how effective people think the police are at fighting crime. The ICVS, for example, asks respondents 'How good a job do you think the police do in your area in controlling crime?'. The London Metropolitan Police Service's Public Attitude Survey asks people how well they think the police do at preventing terrorism, policing major events, and tackling gun crime, drug use, drug dealing and dangerous driving, but also includes questions on how well the police do at responding to emergencies promptly, providing a visible patrolling presence and supporting victims and witnesses. In fact, the latter items – those that are not directly related to crime prevention – prove more important to perceptions of police performance than those on crime control (Stanko and Bradford, 2009). The current study supports this way of measuring police performance: items used to measure perceptions of police (and court) performance should not focus exclusively on how good these authorities are at controlling crime and catching offenders but also on such things as response times and the time it takes to process cases, the use and abuse of power and cooperation between different police departments and between courts.

Extending theories of procedural justice: the importance of peers to perceptions of procedural justice

Procedural justice theory has traditionally studied the manner in which authorities' behaviour affects litigants' experience of decision-making processes and their resulting perceptions of procedural justice. This study suggests that procedural justice theory, despite its stress on group status and social identity as an explanation for the importance of procedural fairness, has overlooked the role of actual peers – those group members that have a similar hierarchical status. Three particular findings demonstrate that the degree to which people feel that their involvement in a criminal procedure – either as a victim or as an offender – negatively affects their reputation vis-à-vis fellow group members (that is, other citizens) impacts upon perceptions of self-regard and as such upon perceptions of standing. First, when considering their court experience, victims took into account the behaviour of the offender and the offender's lawyer in court. Victims were found to be attentive to whether the offender showed visible signs of remorse during the trial and to the manner in which the offender's lawyer portrayed or addressed them. Second, a number of participants felt very anxious about other people finding out about their contact with the police and their involvement in a criminal procedure. They asked the police not to come to their door in uniform and not to park the police car in front of their door, preferring to attend the police station for interrogation. Third, participants really disliked the principle of open justice – the prying eyes of other citizens judging them lowered their self-esteem, and they felt that their privacy had been invaded.

Given that procedural justice theory is based on the premise that fair procedures matter because they convey information about group status, it is not in itself surprising that concerns about standing vis-à-vis group members play a role when victims and defendants evaluate their experiences with the police and the courts. Yet no systematic investigation of peers as a source of perceptions of procedural (in)justice has taken place so far. Though Gonzalez and Tyler (2007) have spelled out the importance of procedural fairness to 'membership monitoring', which they described as 'a person's interest in the presence, duration, stability, or quality of their connection to an in-group, and/or to other in-group members' (95), research into the psychological motives underlying people's desire for procedural fairness has predominantly focused on authority relationships and the importance of fair treatment by authorities. This study suggests that other in-group members too affect perceptions of procedural justice. Moreover, in the context of criminal justice, these in-group members seem to be more likely to affect perceptions of procedural justice in a negative manner than to contribute to perceptions of procedural justice. The two issues that stand out are the importance of the offender showing remorse and people's concern about the presence of an audience in court. These merit further discussion.

First, victims who attended the trial and found that their offender showed no visible signs of remorse or repentance were upset about the offender's seemingly indifferent attitude. It seems that offenders are expected to show signs of sorrow and regret during trial. Similar findings were reported by Szmania and Mangis (2005) and Weisman (2009); these authors also wrote that victims, but also jurors and the general public, expect offenders to show remorse in court. Weisman (2009) advanced three signs of remorse. The first is the full admission of responsibility by the offender. The second is gestural expressions (e.g. crying, visible distress); the third is the personal transformation of the offender (e.g. taking therapy). While the victims participating in this study expected each of these three from their offender, it is the second category that figured most prominently in the minds of the victims, criticising the lack of signs of remorse or emotion on behalf of their offender in court. Szmania and Mangis however suggest that the legalistic setting of courtrooms, in particular 'the way that the courtroom communication environment is set up' (341), impedes expressions of remorse. The courtroom, the authors write, 'does not lend itself to direct expression from any one party' (341; see also De Mesmaecker, 2012). That would mean that courtroom design can be responsible for perceived procedural injustice. This hypothesis is confirmed by the current study – the interview data indeed show that courtroom design and trial practices have the potential of (negatively) affecting perceptions of procedural justice. This is another aspect of court experiences that has not been considered by procedural justice researchers so far; it will be discussed in detail below.

Second, many respondents, both victims and offenders, when asked about their court experience spontaneously singled out the audience present in court, i.e. litigants awaiting trial, members of the public who attend trials as a form of 'pastime' and the press. These respondents were in favour of abolishing the principle that trials are conducted in public. The principle of open justice is considered by Malsch (2009) as 'one of the most important requirements with which contemporary legal systems should comply' (15). The principle of open justice allows for democratic control of the judiciary; moreover, the public denunciation of crimes and the imposition of sentences are said to have a general preventive effect. Furthermore, it has been argued that public confidence in the courts benefits from public access to the courts (Hoekstra and Malsch, 2003; Malsch and Nijboer, 2005). Yet considering the

principle from a procedural justice point of view, it appears that the participation of the general public in trials is detrimental to litigants participating in
'their' trial.

The fact that peer group members' attitudes affect perceptions of procedural justice has important consequences for those seeking to enhance confidence in the courts. As said above, the criminal authorities have repeatedly
been encouraged by procedural justice researchers to consider how they might
adapt their conduct so litigants experience procedural fairness; yet the results
reported here suggest, again, that litigants' experience is partly beyond the
control of the criminal authorities. The criminal authorities can try to show
more respect for litigants and give litigants opportunities for speaking in
court, but when assessing their experience of the court and the police, people
apparently also take into account elements over which these authorities have
no control. While it has been argued above that there may be only so much
the courts can do to improve levels of trust because trust in the courts is
influenced to a certain degree by the way the police treat citizens, the results
reported here suggest a second influence beyond the control of the courts.

Summarising, then, it appears that justice researchers should take into
account that litigants' perceptions of fair treatment depend not only on
authorities' behaviour but also on the behaviour of the other party. The exclu-
sive focus on group authorities has obstructed the field from learning about the
importance of peer group members to perceptions of procedural fairness. While
the participants undeniably focused most of their attention on the criminal
authorities, an interesting avenue for research lies in examining how and to
what degree other group members affect litigants' perceptions of fairness.

Extending theories of procedural justice: the importance of courtroom design and trial practices to perceptions of procedural justice

As briefly mentioned above, participants assessed their court experience partly
in terms of courtroom design and trial practices. They reflected on how time
is managed in court, expressing distress about the time they spent waiting for
their turn, discussed the layout of the waiting areas and the physical position
of victims and offenders vis-à-vis one other, and considered the customs and
habits governing trials, such as the use of raised benches and gowns and the
fact that one needs to rise when the judge does.

Since these aspects of trial practice are unrelated to the actions of the
criminal authorities, procedural justice theory in its current form does not
touch upon these issues. Yet what was observed is that such issues as trial
customs, time management and court layout affect litigants' perceptions of
standing. For example, the raised position of the bench was said to lead to
perceptions that litigants are inferior to the judiciary. Poor courtroom acoustics are problematic with a view to active participation and passive involvement. Furthermore, such issues as victims having no choice but to share a
waiting room with the defendant and the nature of the holding cells where

prisoners await their court appearance have an impact on litigants' well-being. Procedural justice research would benefit from including these aspects of court experience in future analyses, building on the body of literature on how procedural rules and courtroom design define each participant's role (e.g. Thibaut and Walker, 1978; Rock, 1993; Maxwell and Morris, 2002; Peak, 2004) and on how trial procedures and the physical organisation of courtrooms limit the space for communication in court (e.g. Arrigo and Williams, 2003; Kool and Moerings, 2004; Aertsen and Beyens, 2005; Mulcahy, 2007).

As for the layout of courtrooms, what is interesting is that participants did not, in general, say that courtrooms are distasteful or ugly – many said courtrooms are actually quite nice from an aesthetic point of view, though old-fashioned – yet they did find them intimidating and pointed to courtroom layout as a source of distress. The latter finding is not surprising; Wright (2002) is not the only one to have written about the 'formal, procedurally strict and often intimidating atmosphere of the courtroom' (663). What is puzzling is that the participants found courtrooms intimidating and aesthetically nice at the same time. This apparent inconsistency can be explained on the basis of Maass *et al.*'s (2000) study on courtroom architecture, which demonstrates that one should distinguish between the aesthetic value of the courtroom and its psychological meaning. The participants to Maass *et al.*'s study also experienced the courthouse that they had visited as 'highly oppressive, threatening and hostile', but, much like the participants in this study, they 'did not generally dislike the building' (681). Maass *et al.* were not able to draw conclusions about the specific architectural features that were responsible for the psychological meaning of courtrooms but hypothesised that the size, shape and colours of the building or the nature of the building materials matter the most. The results of this study suggest that the physical organisation of the courtroom is what matters. The raised bench of the judge, the lack of separate waiting rooms for victims and defendants and the position of victims and offenders vis-à-vis each other seem to determine the degree to which courtrooms are experienced as threatening and oppressive. As such, it is possible indeed that people experience these rooms as aesthetically nice and intimidating at the same time. Bear in mind that these are facets of trial practice that, in Paul Rock's words, 'confirm identities, segregate groups, and manage relations' (1993: 197); in that sense, it is not hard to understand that these have a considerable impact on litigants' perceptions of standing and as such on their perceptions of procedural justice.

Extending theories of procedural justice: the importance of the formal sources of justice

In its current state of development, procedural justice theory holds that there are two sources of perceptions of justice (Tyler and Blader, 2000, 2003b; Blader and Tyler, 2003a, 2003b). The first source consists of formal group rules. Rules pertaining to official procedures are structural in nature, codified and fairly constant across time, situations and people. The second source consists of the actions of the actual supervisor or authority one is dealing with, and is therefore informal and dynamic. As Tyler (2009) writes, procedural justice can thus be considered 'either in terms of those authorities with whom people have personal contact, or an overall institutional issue' (323). While the earliest model of procedural justice (Thibaut and Walker, 1975, 1978) focused mainly on formal rules (i.e. the allocation of control between the litigants and the decision-maker), subsequent models such as the group-value model of procedural justice and the relational model of procedural justice (Lind and Tyler, 1988; Tyler and Lind, 1992) directed attention to the importance of people's personal contact with authorities. Tyler and Blader's group engagement model of procedural justice (Tyler and Blader, 2000, 2001, 2003a; Blader and Tyler, 2003a, 2003b), the most recent fully elaborated model of procedural justice, integrated both sources into one model. The current study provides support for procedural justice researchers focusing attention on the formal sources of justice.

In fact, since the participants in this study had had little personal contact with the judiciary that was dealing with their case, these formal sources of justice became very important determinants of their perceptions of the procedural fairness of the judiciary. When participants discussed their court experience, they referred as much to courtroom procedures and trial practices as to the behaviour or actions of the judiciary involved. When discussing the performance of the judiciary, they talked about 'the system' being slow, bureaucratic or not allowing enough time for cases in court. There has been little study of the factors that are indicative of procedural fairness in an impersonal setting such as the one experienced by many victims and defendants involved in a trial. This study lends support to Blader and Tyler's argument that the formal rules governing institutions have a more important role to play in the justice debate than previously assumed (see also Murphy *et al.*, 2009; Murphy and Cherney, 2012).

Extending theories of procedural justice: a new interpretation of decision control

The results on the need for participation in the criminal proceedings reveal that victims have several concerns when it comes to attending the trial or participating in the trial in an active manner – many of them do not dare do so, some do not feel the need to do so. Those who do decide to get involved sometimes only do so because they feel that they have no other choice, which is a distressing experience. These findings confirm what one of the victims said explicitly about the importance to victims of being able to choose freely whether they want to participate in the criminal proceedings by attending the trial, speaking in court or participating in mediation. In fact, they urge a re-examination of the importance of decision control, which was advanced as an element of importance to perceptions of procedural justice by Thibaut and

Walker, who presented the first fully-fledged model of procedural justice (1975), but has throughout the years been abandoned as a factor of importance to litigants. Several studies indeed showed that those involved in legal procedures wish for some degree of involvement in the criminal procedures but do not want to decide on the outcome of the trial (Wemmers, 1996; Tyler and Blader, 2000; Wemmers and Cyr, 2004). Yet it seems that decision control in fact matters a great deal to victims. It is crucial that victims can decide for themselves if, when, how and to what degree they want to be involved in the criminal proceedings and that opportunities exist for those who wish to participate. Decision control, in other words, is important; the reason this has escaped the attention of previous researchers is that decision control has so far solely been considered in relation to punishment. It is true that victims do not wish to decide on their offender's sentence – as the studies cited above show – but decision control is important when it relates to the decision to participate in criminal proceedings in some way. Perceptions of procedural fairness, then, benefit from people getting a range of options for participation and being able to choose freely whether they want to make use of these options. Where they have no options, or feel that they have no choice but to make use of them because the authorities are not taking their responsibilities seriously, perceptions of procedural justice are negatively impacted upon. It is important that future procedural justice research rethinks the role of decision control in bringing about perceptions of procedural justice, releasing the term from its association with control over decisions relating to sentencing.

Relationships between the different antecedents of procedural justice

The results of this study indicate that there are relationships between the different antecedents of procedural justice. Given that this study did not use a quantitative methodology these relationships cannot be substantiated with statistical data, yet the goal of the subsequent paragraphs is not to present decisive conclusions about causal relationships between the antecedents. They describe some interesting observations that clarify the results of prior research or point at previously unnoticed potential relationships between the antecedents of procedural justice that future research may want to examine more closely.

The relationship between respect for dignity and perceptions of neutrality

A number of victims and offenders doubted that judges who behave disrespectfully towards the defendant in court will judge the defendant's case in a neutral manner. Respectful treatment, then, influences the degree to which people expect that the judge will be unbiased and unprejudiced. When judges behave disrespectfully, people have trouble believing that when deciding on the case they will be neutral. Judges' behaviour, in other words, not only influences perceptions of standing but also influences perceptions of neutrality. The relationship holds true in the other direction as well. The participants' stories demonstrate that perceptions of neutrality influence perceptions of standing too. Specifically, the degree to which the police and the criminal authorities are perceived to do their utmost to investigate the case properly helps victims feel acknowledged, as mentioned above.

The observation that the antecedents of procedural fairness are related is not new. Tyler (1990), for example, found a positive correlation between 'politeness' and 'impartiality', though from the description in Tyler (1990) one cannot establish the exact correlation between the two. Wemmers' (1996) models of procedural justice for victims reveal a correlation of .71 to .87 between respect and neutrality. This means that respondents scoring high on 'respect' score high on 'neutrality', and vice versa. The present study confirms this relationship and provides concrete examples of how this relationship materialises.

The relationship between respect for dignity and participation/voice

An extremely important finding in view of the crucial nature of the participation/voice concept to the study of procedural justice is that the quality of interpersonal treatment affects the degree to which people feel comfortable about voicing their own opinion throughout the procedure. Several examples illustrate this relationship. The offenders who had felt treated brutally by an investigating judge said that they refrained from raising arguments in their defence because they feared that if they did, the judge – who was to decide whether to keep them in preliminary custody after the interrogation – would make an unfavourable decision (i.e. decide against release). There is also the example of the offender who could not muster up the courage to go back to the police station to change his statement because the police had treated him badly the first time. This is a telling example because the man truly had had no criminal intent, but the statement suggested otherwise. Therefore it was most important that he contact the police to change his statement. Another offender, when discussing whether it would be a good idea for litigants to speak to judges in private, said that he would never do so because in his opinion judges never behave respectfully towards alleged offenders.

These examples show that people may prefer not to participate in the criminal proceedings when they do not feel respected because they are afraid of the consequences of doing so. While procedural justice research has demonstrated that people become less cooperative to the degree that they find themselves disrespected by authorities, the findings reported here suggest that there is not only a relationship between the quality of interpersonal treatment and willingness to participate in information-gathering but also between the quality of interpersonal relationship and feeling comfortable about participating, or having the courage to defend oneself. In order not to risk an unfavourable outcome, people refrain from voicing their opinion, though in some cases the feeling of disrespect has such a powerful impact on people that the outcome of the case becomes a secondary concern – this is evinced by the example of the offender who did not dare return to the police station to amend his statement because of the way the police had treated him before. This observation is fully in line with procedural justice theory's main hypothesis, i.e. that the fairness of procedures has a stronger impact on people's evaluations of their experience of authorities than the favourability of outcomes. Still, the other examples show that in other cases, outcome concerns are the main reason for people refraining from speaking up. In any case, this study suggests that when people feel that they are treated disrespectfully they become less likely to voice their opinion.

Combining this finding with the finding that low levels of trust in authorities – resulting from perceptions of unfair treatment – lead to people feeling that they should more actively intervene and participate in criminal proceedings (see above), it seems that the experience of unfair treatment actually leads people to a confusing situation in which on the one hand they feel that they should get actively involved in the criminal proceedings and raise their voice but on the other hand feel that they should not do so because it may have negative consequences on the outcome, or do not do so simply because they have become afraid of the authorities.

The relationship between respect for dignity and expectations on performance

The data suggest that litigants have higher performance expectations from authorities who have treated them with respect than from authorities who have not. Litigants are more likely to believe that authorities will take their responsibilities seriously and perform their tasks well when they feel that they were treated in a respectful manner by those authorities. For example, the parents of two child victims had built high hopes on the criminal authorities; their considerate manners had made the parents hopeful that they would bring an end to their struggle. As the story of these parents shows, the danger of the existence of a relationship between being treated with respect and expectations on performance is that expectations are dashed when the authorities do not deliver the result that people had hoped for. In the end, the parents mentioned were indeed extremely disappointed about the manner in which the case had been dealt with by the criminal authorities and about the judicial decision. They felt very let down. The positive effect of respect for dignity on perceptions of procedural justice, then, was neutralised by the negative perceptions of performance.

This problem of heightened expectations has been encountered in other areas of study too, and in particular in the field of victimology. Englebrecht (2011), for example, from a study among victims who participated in a trial by means of a victim impact statement concluded that victims who had been invited to court to deliver a victim impact statement truly believed that their interests would be considered. Also, they wanted not just to voice their opinion but to have their voice recognised and heard. Yet Englebrecht also found that criminal justice workers think that the role of the victim needs to be a restricted one and that victim participation is in fact largely symbolic. As criminal justice actors and victims have different expectations and different views on the purpose of participation, victims' expectations risk being dashed. Erez and Tontodonato (1992) and Erez *et al.* (1994) in this respect found that victims who had been offered an opportunity for input in the criminal proceedings by means of a victim impact statement and thought that their input was ignored were less satisfied with the criminal justice system than those who had never had the expectation that their input would be validated. Strang's (2002) research on victim participation in restorative justice conferences led to a similar conclusion: Strang's study shows that victims who were promised that they would be able to participate in a conference but did not receive one were more dissatisfied with the way their cases had been dealt with than those who were never promised a conference at all. While these situations differ from those reported on in this study in that the latter did not relate to expectations on opportunities for participation, they are indicative of the problem. And while in the cases reported by Englebrecht, Erez, Tontodonato and Strang solutions can be thought of (e.g. explicitly warning victims that the victim impact statement is not meant to be a tool for influencing the judge and that they should not expect that it will do so), the solution for the problem at hand (i.e. expectations being raised because of respectful treatment) is far from obvious. The reason for the high expectations – respectful treatment – is a given and the authorities cannot promise to deliver certain outcomes.

The relationship between participation/voice and neutrality

It seems that there is a relationship between 'concern for the need for participation' and neutrality, yet the evidence found points in different directions. On the one hand, participants said that certain forms of participation in the trial affect judges' neutrality. When asked whether they would value the opportunity to talk to the judge in person at a given point in the procedure, for example, participants said that judges would probably not be able to be neutral anymore after having talked to litigants in private. On the other hand, some participants reported that having the feeling that one did not receive sufficient opportunities to voice one's opinion in court leads to perceptions of bias. Several offenders said that judges who do not allow an offender time to voice his/her opinion and story give the impression that they are biased. It should be noted that participants who discussed this issue did not compare the amount of time they had received to voice their opinion to the amount of time that the victim had received. The fact in itself that they had hardly been allowed an opportunity to speak their mind was sufficient for them to get the perception that the judge was not neutral. Perceptions of receiving too little or too many opportunities for participation, then, may influence perceptions of neutrality. The solution does not lie in simply allowing both parties to a conflict an equal amount of opportunities for voice, since respondents felt that even if the judge would talk to both parties in private the principle of neutrality would be impinged on and the actual amount of time one receives to speak in court is more important than whether both parties received equal time.

Incompatibilities between different antecedents of procedural justice

Participants' stories reveal that the antecedents of procedural justice sometimes conflict. In particular, incompatibilities seem to exist between participation and neutrality and between respect for rights and concern for needs. This means that in some cases, the positive effect of the perceived care for one antecedent of procedural justice is neutralised by the perceived lack of care for another antecedent.

Incompatibilities between participation and neutrality

As explained above, some participants felt that certain ways of participation by victims and offenders to the criminal proceedings prevent judges from judging cases in an impartial manner. This finding could possibly explain, at least in part, why studies into participation of victims in criminal proceedings (e.g. by means of victim impact statements) often find that victims who participated in criminal proceedings are not significantly more satisfied than victims who did not and that victim participation in criminal proceedings only positively affects perceptions of procedural fairness to a limited degree (see De Mesmaecker, 2007). Explanations that have been proposed to account for this finding are that victims are disappointed about the fact that their input did not have an effect on the sentence (Erez *et al.*, 1994); that victims are simply not eager for increased participation in criminal proceedings (Davis and Smith, 1994); that victims are disappointed that their victim impact statements are edited before the sentencing hearing to delete those passages that are deemed inadmissible (Booth, 2012); and that victims lack legal standing in court (Henley *et al.*, 1994). This study suggests an additional explanation: it could be that victims who participated feel good about this chance for participation in itself but at the same time feel that the neutrality of the judge was affected, which lowers perceptions of procedural fairness.

Incompatibilities between respect for rights and concern for needs

A number of situations were described above in which participants felt that they had been treated in an unfair manner while in fact the legal procedures had been applied correctly. People also thought they had rights that in reality did not exist. The fact that they thought they had these rights indicates that they experienced a certain need; the fact that certain procedural rules had to be respected meant that the authorities could not pay heed to these needs. One concrete example is that the police, when arresting a 19-year-old living with his parents, are not obliged to call the suspect's parents to inform them that their son has been arrested. Another example is that the police cannot decide to return stolen goods to victims. The police's adherence to legal rules and respect for each party's rights, then, sometimes implies that litigants' (emotional, practical, informational) needs cannot be met. Comparable findings were reported by Aertsen and Hutsebaut (2010), who performed a study on how the parents of victims of fatal traffic accidents experience the criminal justice system. The results of their study too demonstrate that litigants struggle with a number of procedural rules because the authorities' adherence to those rules – that is, their adherence to those principles that determine the factor 'respect for rights' – prevents their needs from being met. For example, the authors found that the parents found it hard to accept procedures stipulating which victims have a right to read the file, or specifying that victims need to pay for a copy of the file. These examples and those reported on in the previous chapters illustrate Meares' (2013) stance that 'very little of constitutional criminal procedure promotes the kind of dignity concerns that people tend to care about. Indeed, much of the law is even at odds with these concerns' (1884). There is quite a gap between what codes of criminal procedure prescribe and what people feel they should prescribe.

The effect of procedural fairness on (future) willingness to cooperate with the police and defer to the law

The results of this study confirm one of the basic premises of procedural justice theory, i.e. that there is a relationship between the quality of the treatment that people receive from the police and their willingness to report future victimisation, or cooperate with the police. However, while in its current form procedural justice theory mainly stresses that *future* willingness to cooperate is influenced by the degree to which the police treat people with respect, this study shows that perceptions of fair treatment also affect people's willingness to cooperate at the time of arrest, when reporting the crime, and during interrogation. For example, one victim said that she was prepared to tell the police her complete story despite this being difficult for her because she had been treated very well. A number of offenders said that if the police act with force when making arrests, then arrestees are more likely to resist; where the police behave in a polite manner, offenders are more likely to calmly go to the police station with them.

Interestingly, the data suggest that fair treatment by the police is more important with a view to securing short-term cooperation and compliance, that is, during interrogation or at the time of arrest, while future willingness to obey the law actually depends more on the manner in which one was treated in court than on the manner in which one was treated by the police. A number of respondents explicitly mentioned a relationship between how they were treated in court and their will and strength to conform to the law in the future. They argued that being treated patronisingly and disrespectfully in court lowered their self-esteem, which did not, as procedural justice theory proposes, make them less *willing* to conform to the law, but made it more *difficult* for them to do so. The loss of self-esteem, they explained, made it hard for them to take up their lives again. In other words, the effect of unfair treatment on deference to the law is not just such that people are not *willing* to obey the law; it seems that their self-identity is hurt so badly that they no longer have the strength to carry out their job properly or find a job or to take care of themselves, which in turn increases the chance of future wrongdoing.

Closing remarks: procedural justice theory in a changing penal landscape

Departing from a value-based perspective on human motivation (see Tyler, 2009), procedural justice theories have convincingly demonstrated the beneficial effects of principles of procedural justice to regulatory approaches. While police departments and court systems strive to implement the principles of procedural justice (see Tyler and Jackson, 2013), contemporary changes in the administration of criminal justice provide new challenges, but also new opportunities, for procedural justice research. One such challenge is posed by the international financial crisis that has been holding the global economy in its grip for some years. Police departments and criminal justice systems have been and still are facing considerable budget cuts and monetary constraints (Millie and Bullock, 2012; Sindall and Sturgis, 2013). While law-enforcing strategies based on principles of procedural fairness instead of deterrence have been advanced as relatively inexpensive (Schulhofer *et al.*, 2011; Hough, 2013), times of financial austerity are not conducive to police departments and court systems being able to implement policy changes.

Another development in law enforcement that is of particular relevance to procedural justice research is the increasing 'technologisation' of policing. The nature of the most basic form of interaction between citizens and the criminal justice system – i.e. the daily and routine contact between citizens and the police – undergoes changes as police departments implement the use of new technologies such as wearable cameras. While police officers say that wearing such cameras makes them more circumspect in the execution of their duties and thus more likely to 'go by the book' (Goold, 2003), it is not clear how this affects citizen perceptions of procedural fairness. In fact, citizen–police interactions may become less natural and more constrained because of the use of these technologies, and going by the book may imply an impersonal and detached approach. This might be an undesirable development, considering that the main reason for people to have contact with the police is to receive help (Tyler and Huo, 2002) and that victims, when asked to define desired victim–police relationships, use such words as 'connection' and 'customer service' (Elliott *et al.*, 2012).

Meanwhile, the nature of adjudication too is considerably different today than it was at the time procedural justice theory was developed. Ever more cases are being dealt with by means of alternative methods of dispute resolution – one of the most notable evolutions that comes to mind is the implementation of restorative justice practices such as victim–offender mediation and Family Group Conferencing. While procedural justice theory was developed to account for people's experiences with authorities and thus with binding dispute resolution procedures, new methods of adjudication such as mediation are often dispute resolution procedures of a non-binding nature. Procedural justice scholars have already started to look into this issue, demonstrating the importance of principles of procedural justice to these non-binding dispute resolution procedures (e.g. Lind *et al.*, 1983; Wemmers and Cyr, 2004, 2006; Tyler *et al.*, 2007; Hollander-Blumoff and Tyler, 2008; Van Camp and Wemmers, 2013). Some have even found that such dispute resolution procedures are considered more procedurally fair than traditional arbitration and court procedures (Shapiro and Brett, 1993; Barnes, 1999). Yet little research is available so far on the implications for procedural justice theory of the other major evolution in adjudication that has taken place and changed the penal landscape in recent decades, i.e. the increasing use of methods of plea bargaining. In the United States, 90 to 95 per cent of criminal cases are now dealt with by plea bargaining (Lippke, 2011; Stuntz, 2011; Pollock, 2012) and countries such as Belgium deal with a considerable number of cases by means of penal mediation – this implies that defendants do not face court if they come to an agreement (e.g. on compensation or taking therapy) with the prosecutor. Both developments have resulted in the judges' role becoming less vital while that of the public prosecutor is ever more crucial (see also Simon, 2007, on how the 'war on crime' has radically transformed and expanded the traditional role of the prosecutor at the expense of judges). This evolution affects not only the relationship between the legal authorities but also the relationship between litigants and those legal authorities; procedural justice researchers will need to look into the consequences of these changes for the way citizens perceive each of the legal authorities individually and the criminal justice system as a whole and as such for the interpretation of the key concepts of procedural justice.

Finally, despite several studies demonstrating that those dealing with the legal system have considerable doubts as to whether the legal authorities exercise their authority in a fair manner (e.g. Tyler, 1990, 1998), citizens have also been found to be rather reluctant to accept profound changes to the administration of criminal justice. This is evinced by the rather slow pace at which alternatives to court-based litigation make their way into the criminal justice realm and the scepticism with which these alternatives are approached by individual victims and offenders as well as the public. Evidence suggests, for example, that the public is more likely to support restorative justice-based interventions after crime if these are combined with some form of punishment (Gromet and Darley, 2006) and that people are generally not in favour of replacing court-based litigation with restorative justice-based practices but of combining both (De Mesmaecker, 2011; Van Camp and Wemmers, 2011). In other words, though those who personally encounter the criminal justice system at times describe it as unfair, and despite low levels of public confidence in criminal justice existing in different countries (Roberts and Hough, 2005), citizens do seem to endorse the system – one of the participants in this study spoke of a 'necessary evil'. This too is a phenomenon that procedural justice researchers may want to look into, as it suggests that other than procedural justice concerns play a role when citizens consider the viability of the criminal justice system.

These and other developments and evolutions in the administration of justice may be expected to have implications for the way legal authorities can communicate procedural fairness to those who encounter the criminal justice system in person and to citizens in general. Indeed, while this book has focused on the procedural justice judgements of those who became personally involved with the system, the majority of citizens never encounter the system in person. Still, procedural justice theory has been found to provide a framework for understanding their opinions about the fairness of the system too and to be an important determinant of the general public's level of confidence and trust in the system. The current study has extended our understanding of how procedural justice is interpreted by those personally encountering the criminal justice system; the use of a qualitative research design has contributed greatly to this achievement. Future research may want to employ similar techniques to also extend our understanding of how the key concepts of procedural justice are interpreted by the public at large.

References

Aertsen, I. and Beyens, K. (2005). "Restorative justice and the morality of law: a reply to Brochu." In Claes, E., Foqué, R. and Peters, T. (eds), *Punishment, Restorative Justice and the Morality of Law* (101–17). Antwerp: Intersentia.

Aertsen, I., Christiaensen, S., Hougardy, L. and Martin, D. (2002). *Vademecum politiële slachtofferbejegening.* Ghent: Academia Press.

Aertsen, I. and Hutsebaut, F. (2010). *Kinderen als slachtoffer van het verkeer. Onderzoek naar de noden, behoeften en ervaringen van verkeersslachtoffers en hun nabestaanden.* Brussels: ASP.

Allen, J. and Monk-Turner, E. (2010). "Citizen perceptions of the legitimacy of traffic stops." *Journal of Criminal Justice,* 38 (4): 589–94.

Arrigo, B.A. and Williams, C.R. (2003). "Victim vices, victim voices, and impact statements: on the place of emotion and the role of restorative justice in capital sentencing." *Crime and Delinquency,* 49 (4): 603–26.

Barnes, G.C. (1999). "Procedural justice in two contexts: testing the fairness of diversionary conferencing for intoxicated drivers." Unpublished dissertation, University of Pennsylvania.

Baumert, A. and Schmitt, M. (2009). "Justice-sensitive interpretations of ambiguous situations." *Australian Journal of Psychology,* 61 (1): 6–12.

Bies, R.J. (1987). "Beyond 'voice': the influence of decision-maker justification and sincerity on procedural fairness judgments." *Representative Research in Social Psychology*, 17: 3–14.

Bies, R.J. and Moag, J.F. (1986). "Interactional justice: communication criteria of fairness." In Lewicki, R.J., Sheppard, B.H. and Bazerman, M.H. (eds), *Research on Negotiations in Organizations* (43–55). Greenwich: JAI Press.

Blader, S.L. and Tyler, T.R. (2003a). "A four-component model of procedural justice: defining the meaning of a 'fair' process." *Personality and Social Psychology Bulletin*, 29 (6): 747–58.

——(2003b). "What constitutes fairness in work settings? A four-component model of procedural justice." *Human Resource Management Review*, 13 (1): 107–26.

Booth, T. (2012). "'Cooling out' victims of crime: managing participation in the sentencing process in a superior sentencing court." *Australian and New Zealand Journal of Criminology*, 45 (2): 214–30.

Bradford, B., Jackson, J. and Stanko, E.A. (2009). "Contact and confidence: revisiting the impact of public encounters with the police." *Policing and Society*, 19 (1): 20–46.

Carr, P.J., Logio, K.A. and Maier, S. (2003). "Keep me informed: what matters for victims as they navigate the juvenile criminal justice system in Philadelphia." *International Review of Victimology*, 10 (2): 117–36.

Colquitt, J.A. (2001). "On the dimensionality of organizational justice: a construct validation of a measure." *Journal of Applied Psychology*, 86 (3): 386–400.

Colquitt, J.A., Conlon, D.E., Wesson, M.J., Porter, C.O. and Ng, K.Y. (2001). "Justice at the millennium: a meta-analytical review of 25 years of organizational justice research." *Journal of Applied Psychology*, 86 (3): 425–45.

Cotti, A., Magalhães, T., da Costa, D.P. and Matos, E. (2004). "Road traffic accidents and secondary victimisation: the role of law professionals." *Medicine and Law*, 23 (2): 259–68.

Cropanzano, R., Stein, J.H. and Nadicis, T. (2011). *Social Justice and the Experience of Emotion*. New York: Routledge.

Davis, R.C. and Smith B.E. (1994). "Victim impact statements and victim satisfaction: an unfulfilled promise?" *Journal of Criminal Justice*, 22 (1): 1–12.

De Cremer, D. and Tyler, T.R. (2007). "The effects of trust in authority and procedural fairness on cooperation." *Journal of Applied Psychology*, 92 (3): 639–49.

De Mesmaecker, V. (2007). "Afdalen in de kloof tussen slachtoffers en straftoemeting. Participatie aan de rechterlijke besluitvorming door slachtoffers van misdrijven." *Panopticon*, 4: 6–22.

——(2011). "Perceptions of justice and fairness in criminal proceedings and restorative encounters: extending theories of procedural justice." Unpublished dissertation, University of Leuven.

——(2012). "Antidotes to injustice? Victim statements' impact on victims' sense of security." *International Review of Victimology*, 18 (2): 133–53.

De Mesmaecker, V., Kranendonk, P.R. and Malsch, M. (2013). "De variabiliteit van slachtofferbehoeften. De invloed van de gepercipieerde intentie van de dader op de behoefte aan procedurele rechtvaardigheid en actieve participatie." *Panopticon*, 34 (2): 80–99.

Elliott, I., Thomas, S. and Ogloff, J. (2012). "Procedural justice in contacts with the police: the perspective of victims of crime." *Police Practice and Research: An International Journal*, 13 (5): 437–49.

——(2013). "Procedural justice in victim–police interactions and victims' recovery from victimisation experiences." *Policing and Society.* Available at www.tandfonline.com/doi/abs/10.1080/10439463.2013.784309#.Um6DAlO2b1I.

Englebrecht, C.M. (2011). "The struggle for 'ownership of conflict': an exploration of victim participation and voice in the criminal justice system." *Criminal Justice Review,* 36 (2): 129–51.

Erez, E., Roeger, L. and Morgan, F. (1994). *Victim Impact Statements in South Australia: An Evaluation.* Adelaide: Office of Crime Statistics.

Erez, E. and Tontodonato, P. (1992). "Victim participation in sentencing and satisfaction with justice." *Justice Quarterly,* 9 (3): 393–418.

Fetchenhauer, D. and Huang, X. (2004). "Justice sensitivity and distributive decisions in experimental games." *Personality and Individual Differences,* 36 (5): 1015–29.

Folger, R. (1977). "Distributive and procedural justice: combined impact of 'voice' and improvement on experienced inequity." *Journal of Personality and Social Psychology,* 35 (2): 108–19.

Gollwitzer, M., Schmitt, M., Schalke, R., Maes, J. and Baer, A. (2005). "Asymmetrical effects of justice sensitivity perspectives on prosocial and antisocial behavior." *Social Justice Research,* 18 (2): 183–201.

Gonzalez, C.M. and Tyler, T.R. (2007). "Why do people care about procedural fairness? The importance of membership monitoring." In Törnblom, K. and Vermunt, R. (eds), *Distributive and Procedural Justice: Research and Social Applications* (91–110). Aldershot: Ashgate.

Goold, B.J. (2003). "Public area surveillance and police work: the impact of CCTV on police behaviour and autonomy." *Surveillance and Society,* 1 (2): 191–203.

Greenberg, J. (1993). "The social side of fairness: interpersonal and informational classes of organizational justice." In Cropanzano, R. (ed.), *Justice in the Workplace* (79–103). New Jersey: Lawrence Erlbaum Associates.

Greenberg, M.S. and Ruback, R.B. (1992). *After the Crime: Victim Decision Making.* London: Plenum Press.

Gromet, D.M. and Darley, J.M. (2006). "Restoration and retribution: how including retributive components affects the acceptability of restorative justice procedures." *Social Justice Research,* 19 (4): 395–432.

Henley, M., Davis R.C. and Smith, B.E. (1994). "The reactions of prosecutors and judges to victim impact statements." *International Review of Victimology,* 3 (1/2): 83–93.

Herman, S. (2010). *Parallel Justice for Victims of Crime.* Washington, DC: National Center for Victims of Crime.

Heuer, L., Blumenthal, E., Douglas, A. and Weinblatt, T. (1999). "A deservingness approach to respect as a relationally based fairness judgment." *Personality and Social Psychology Bulletin,* 25 (10): 1279–92.

Heuer, L., Penrod, S., Hafer, C.L. and Cohn, I. (2002). "The role of resource and relational concerns for procedural justice." *Personality and Social Psychology Bulletin,* 28 (11): 1468–82.

Hoekstra, R. and Malsch, M. (2003). "The principle of open justice in the Netherlands." In van Koppen, P.J. and Penrod, S.D. (eds), *Adversarial versus Inquisitorial Justice: Psychological Perspectives on Criminal Justice Systems* (333–46). New York: Plenum Press.

Hollander-Blumoff, R. and Tyler, T.R. (2008). "Procedural justice in negotiation: procedural fairness, outcome acceptance, and integrative potential." *Law and Social Inquiry,* 33 (2): 473–500.

Holmvall, C.M. and Bobocel, D.R. (2008). "What fair procedures say about me: self-construals and reactions to procedural fairness." *Organizational Behavior and Human Decision Processes*, 105 (2): 147–68.

Hough, M. (2013). "Procedural justice and professional policing in times of austerity." *Criminology and Criminal Justice*, 13 (2): 181–97.

Kautt, P. (2011). "Public confidence in the British police: negotiating the signals from Anglo-American research." *International Criminal Justice Review*, 21 (4): 353–82.

Kool, R. and Moerings, M. (2004). "The victim has the floor: the victim's right to be heard in writing or orally in the Dutch courtroom." *European Journal on Criminal Policy and Research*, 12 (4): 46–60.

Krehbiel, P.J. and Cropanzano, R. (2000). "Procedural justice, outcome favorability and emotion." *Social Justice Research*, 13 (4): 339–60.

Lemonne, A. and Vanfraechem, I. (2010). "Evaluatie van de voorzieningen ten behoeve van slachtoffers van inbreuken: de belangrijkste bevindingen." In Vanfraechem, I., Lemonne, A. and Vanneste, C. (eds), *Wanneer het systeem de slachtoffers ontmoet. Eerste resultaten van een evaluatieonderzoek aangaande slachtofferbeleid* (13–118). Gent: Academia Press.

Lerner, M.J. (1980). *The Belief in a Just World: A Fundamental Delusion*. London: Plenum Press.

Lerner, M.J. and Montada, L. (1998). "An overview: advances in belief in a just world theory and methods." In Montada, L. and Lerner, M.J. (eds), *Responses to Victimizations and Belief in a Just World* (1–8). London: Plenum Press.

Lind, E.A., Kanfer, R. and Earley, P.C. (1990). "Voice, control, and procedural justice: instrumental and noninstrumental concerns in fairness judgments." *Journal of Personality and Social Psychology*, 59 (5): 952–59.

Lind, E.A., Lissak, R.I. and Conlon, D.E. (1983). "Decision control and process control effects on procedural fairness judgments." *Journal of Applied Social Psychology*, 13 (4): 338–50.

Lind, E.A. and Tyler, T.R. (1988). *The Social Psychology of Procedural Justice*. New York: Plenum Press.

Lippke, R.L. (2011). *The Ethics of Plea Bargaining*. Oxford: Oxford University Press.

Lissak, R.I. and Sheppard, B.H. (1983). "Beyond fairness: the criterion problem in research on dispute intervention." *Journal of Applied Social Psychology*, 13 (1): 45–65.

Maass, A., Merici, I., Villafranca, E., Furlani, R., Gaburro, E., Getrevi, A. and Masserini, M. (2000). "Intimidating buildings: can courthouse architecture affect perceived likelihood of conviction?" *Environment and Behavior*, 32 (5): 674–83.

Malsch, M. (2009). *Democracy in the Courts: Lay Participation in European Criminal Justice Systems*. Aldershot: Ashgate.

Malsch, M., de Keijser, J., Kranendonk, P.R. and de Gruijter, M. (2010). "Het verhoor op schrift of op band? De gevolgen van het 'verbaliseren' van verhoren voor het oordeel van de jurist." *Nederlands Juristenblad*, 37: 2402–7.

Malsch, M. and Nijboer, J.F. (2005). "De ideale rechtbank: openbaarheid en gerichtheid op de buitenstaander." In Malsch, M. and Nijboer, J.F. (eds), *De zichtbaarheid van het recht: openbaarheid van de strafrechtpleging* (19–49). Deventer: Kluwer.

Maxwell, G. and Morris, A. (2002). "The role of shame, guilt, and remorse in restorative justice processes for young people." In Weitekamp, E.G.M. and Kerner, H.-J. (eds), *Restorative Justice. Theoretical Foundations* (267–84). Cullompton: Willan Publishing.

Mazerolle, L., Antrobus, E., Bennett, S. and Tyler, T. (2012). "Shaping citizen perceptions of police legitimacy: a randomized field trial of procedural justice." *Criminology*, 51 (1): 33–64.

Meares, T. (2013). "The good cop: knowing the difference between lawful or effective policing and rightful policing – and why it matters." *William and Mary Law Review*, 54 (6): 1865–6.

Merryman, J.H. and Pérez-Perdomo, R. (2007). *The Civil Law Tradition. An Introduction to the Legal Systems of Europe and Latin America*. Stanford, CA: Stanford University Press.

Mikula, G. (1974). "Nationality, performance, and sex as determinants of reward allocation." *Journal of Personality and Social Psychology*, 29 (4): 435–40.

Mikula, G., Scherer, K.R., and Athenstaedt, U. (1998). "The role of injustice in the elicitation of differential emotional reactions." *Personality and Social Psychology Bulletin*, 24 (7): 769–83.

Millie, A. and Bullock, K. (2012). "Re-imagining policing post-austerity." *British Academy Review*, 19: 16–18.

Mohiyeddini, C. and Schmitt, M. (1997). "Sensitivity to befallen injustice and reactions to unfair treatment in a laboratory situation." *Social Justice Research*, 10 (3): 333–52.

Mulcahy, L. (2007). "Architects of justice: the politics of courtroom design." *Social and Legal Studies*, 16 (3): 383–403.

Murphy, K. and Cherney, A. (2012). "Understanding cooperation with police in a diverse society." *British Journal of Criminology*, 52 (1): 181–201.

Murphy, K., Hinds, L. and Fleming, J. (2008). "Encouraging public cooperation and support for police." *Policing and Society*, 18 (2): 136–55.

Murphy, K., and Tyler, T. (2008). "Procedural justice and compliance behaviour: the mediating role of emotions." *European Journal of Social Psychology*, 38 (2): 652–68.

Murphy, K., Tyler, T. R. and Curtis, A. (2009). "Nurturing regulatory compliance: is procedural justice effective when people question the legitimacy of the law?" *Regulation and Governance*, 3 (1): 1–26.

Ohbuchi, K., Sugawara, I., Teshigahara, K. and Imazai, K. (2005). "Procedural justice and the assessment of civil justice in Japan." *Law and Society Review*, 39 (4): 875–92.

Orth, U. (2002). "Secondary victimization of crime victims by criminal proceedings." *Social Justice Research*, 15 (4): 313–25.

Peak, K.J. (2004). *Justice Administration. Police, Courts, and Corrections Management*. New Jersey: Prentice Hall.

Pemberton, A., Winkel, F.W. and Groenhuijsen, M.S. (2008). "Evaluating victims' experiences in restorative justice." *British Journal of Community Justice*, 6 (2): 99–119.

Pollock, J.M. (2012). *Crime and Justice in America. An Introduction to Criminal Justice*. Oxford: Elsevier.

Reeves, H. and Dunn, P. (2010). "The status of crime victims and witnesses in the twenty-first century." In Bottoms, A. and Roberts, J.V. (eds), *Hearing the Victim: Adversarial Justice, Crime Victims and the State* (46–71). Cullompton: Willan Publishing.

Roberts, J.V. and Hough, M. (2005). *Understanding Public Attitudes to Criminal Justice*. Berkshire: Open University Press.

Rock, P. (1993). *The Social World of an English Crown Court: Witness and Professionals in the Crown Court Centre at Wood Green*. Oxford: Clarendon Press.

Schmitt, M., Gollwitzer, M., Maes, J. and Arbach, D. (2005). "Justice sensitivity: assessment and location in the personality space." *European Journal of Psychological Assessment*, 21 (3): 202–11.

Schmitt, M. and Mohiyeddini, C. (1996). "Sensitivity to befallen injustice and reactions to a real life disadvantage." *Social Justice Research*, 9 (3): 223–38.

Schmitt, M., Neumann, R. and Montada, L. (1995). "Dispositional sensitivity to befallen injustice." *Social Justice Research*, 8 (4): 385–407.

Schulhofer, S. J., Tyler, T.R. and Huq, A.Z. (2011). "American policing at a crossroads: unsustainable policies and the procedural justice alternative." *Journal of Criminal Law and Criminology*, 101 (2): 335–74.

Shapiro, D.L. and Brett, J.M. (1993). "Comparing three processes underlying judgments of procedural justice: a field study of mediation and arbitration." *Journal of Personality and Social Psychology*, 65 (6): 1167–77.

Simon, J. (2007). *Governing through Crime: How the War on Crime Transformed American Democracy and Created a Culture of Fear*. New York: Oxford University Press.

Sindall, K. and Sturgis, P. (2013). "Austerity policing: is visibility more important than absolute numbers in determining public confidence in the police?" *European Journal of Criminology*, 10 (2): 137–53.

Stanko, E.A. and Bradford, B. (2009). "Beyond measuring 'how good a job' police are doing: the MPS model of confidence in policing." *Policing*, 3 (4): 322–30.

Strang, H. (2002). *Repair or Revenge: Victims and Restorative Justice*. Oxford: Clarendon Press.

Strang, H. and Sherman, L.W. (2003). "Repairing the harm: victims and restorative justice." *Utah Law Review*, 2003 (1): 15–42.

Stuntz, W.J. (2011). *The Collapse of American Criminal Justice*. Cambridge, MA: Belknap Press.

Sunshine, J. and Heuer, L. (2002). "Deservingness and perceptions of procedural justice in citizen encounters with the police." In Ross, M. and Miller, D.T. (eds), *The Justice Motive in Everyday Life* (397–415). Cambridge: Cambridge University Press.

Sunshine, J. and Tyler, T. (2003). "The role of procedural justice and legitimacy in shaping public support for policing." *Law and Society Review*, 37 (3): 513–48.

Sweeney, P.D., McFarlin, D.B. and Cotton, J.L. (1991). "Locus of control as a moderator of the relationship between perceived influence and procedural justice." *Human Relations*, 44 (4): 333–42.

Szmania, S.J. and Mangis, D.E. (2005). "Finding the right time and place: a case study comparison of the expression of offender remorse in traditional justice and restorative justice contexts." *Marquette Law Review*, 89 (2): 336–58.

Tatar II, J.R., Kaasa, S.O. and Cauffman, E. (2012). "Perceptions of procedural justice among female offenders: time does not heal all wounds." *Psychology, Public Policy, and Law*, 18 (2): 268–96.

Thibaut, J. and Walker, L. (1975). *Procedural Justice. A Psychological Analysis*. New Jersey: Lawrence Erlbaum Associates.

——(1978). "A theory of procedure." *California Law Review*, 66 (3): 541–66.

Tyler, T.R. (1987). "Conditions leading to value-expressive effects in judgments of procedural justice: a test of four models." *Journal of Personality and Social Psychology*, 52 (2): 333–44.

——(1990). *Why People Obey the Law*. Princeton, NJ: Princeton University Press.

——(1994). "Psychological models of the justice motive: antecedents of distributive and procedural justice." *Journal of Personality and Social Psychology*, 67 (5): 850–63.

——(1998). "Public mistrust of the law." *University of Cincinnati Law Review*, 66 (3): 847–76.

——(1999). "Why people cooperate with organizations: an identity-based perspective." *Research in Organizational Behavior*, 21: 201–46.

——(2003). "Procedural justice, legitimacy, and the effective rule of law." *Crime and Justice*, 30: 283–358.

——(2009). "Legitimacy and criminal justice: the benefits of self-regulation." *Ohio State Journal of Criminal Justice*, 7 (1): 307–59.

——(2011). *Why People Cooperate: The Role of Social Motivations*. Princeton, NJ: Princeton University Press.

Tyler, T.R. and Blader, S.L. (2000). *Cooperation in Groups: Procedural Justice, Social Identity, and Behavioral Engagement*. Philadelphia, PA: Taylor & Francis.

——(2001). "Identity and cooperative behavior in groups." *Group Processes and Intergroup Relations*, 4 (3): 207–26.

——(2003a). "The group engagement model: procedural justice, social identity, and cooperative behavior." *Personality and Social Psychology Review*, 7 (4): 349–61.

——(2003b). "Social identity and fairness judgements." In Gilliland, S., Steiner, D.D. and Skarlicki, D.P. (eds), *Emerging Perspectives on Values in Organizations* (67–96). Greenwich, CT: Information Age Publishing.

Tyler, T.R., Degoey, P. and Smith, H. (1996). "Understanding why the justice of group procedures matters: a test of the psychological dynamics of the group-value model." *Journal of Personality and Social Psychology*, 70 (5): 913–30.

Tyler, T.R. and Huo, Y.J. (2002). *Trust in the Law: Encouraging Public Cooperation with the Police and Courts*. New York: Russell Sage Foundation.

Tyler, T.R. and Jackson, J. (2013). "Future challenges in the study of legitimacy and criminal justice." In Tankebe, J. and Liebling, A. (eds), *Legitimacy and Criminal Justice: An International Exploration*. Oxford: Oxford University Press.

Tyler, T.R. and Lind, E.A. (1992). "A relational model of authority in groups." In Zanna, M.P. (ed.), *Advances in Experimental Social Psychology vol. 25* (115–91). London: Academic Press.

Tyler, T.R., Rasinski, K.A. and Spodick, N. (1985). "Influence of voice on satisfaction with leaders: exploring the meaning of process control." *Journal of Personality and Social Psychology*, 48 (1): 72–81.

Tyler, T.R., Sherman, L., Strang, H., Barnes, G.C. and Woods, D. (2007). "Reintegrative shaming, procedural justice, and recidivism: the engagement of offenders' psychological mechanisms in the Canberra RISE drinking-and-driving experiment." *Law and Society Review*, 41 (3): 553–86.

Van Camp, T. (2011). "Is there more to restorative justice than mere compliance to procedural justice? A qualitative reflection from the victims' point of view." Unpublished dissertation, Université de Montréal.

Van Camp, T. and Wemmers, J.-A. (2011). "La justice réparatrice et les crimes graves." *Criminologie*, 44 (2): 171–98.

——(2013). "Victim satisfaction with restorative justice: more than simply procedural justice." *International Review of Victimology*, 19 (2): 117–43.

van den Bos, K. (2001). "Uncertainty management: the influence of uncertainty salience on reactions to perceived procedural fairness." *Journal of Personality and Social Psychology*, 80 (6): 931–41.

van den Bos, K. and Lind, E.A. (2002). "Uncertainty management by means of fairness judgments." In Zanna, M.P. (ed.), *Advances in Experimental Social Psychology vol. 34* (1–60). London: Academic Press.

van den Bos, K., Wilke, H.A.M. and Lind, E.A. (1998). "When do we need procedural fairness? The role of trust in authority." *Journal of Personality and Social Psychology,* 75 (6): 1449–58.

van Dijk, J., van Kesteren, J. and Smit, P. (2007). *Criminal Victimisation in International Perspective: Key Findings from the 2004–2005 ICVS and EU ICS.* Den Haag: Boom Juridische Uitgevers.

Vermunt, R. and Steensma, H. (2001). "Stress and justice in organisations." In Cropanzano, R. (ed.), *Justice in the Workplace: From Theory to Practice* (vol. 2) (27–48). Mahwah, NJ: Lawrence Erlbaum Associates.

——(2003). "Physiological relaxation: stress reduction through fair treatment." *Social Justice Research,* 16 (2): 135–49.

Vermunt, R. (2002). "Employee stress, injustice, and the dual position of the boss." In Gilliland, S., Steiner, D. and Skarlicki, D. (eds), *Emerging Perspectives on Managing Organizational Justice* (157–76). Greenwich, CT: Information Age Publishing.

Weisman, R. (2009). "Being and doing: the judicial use of remorse to construct character and community." *Social and Legal Studies,* 18 (1): 47–69.

Weiss, H.M., Suckow, K. and Cropanzano, R. (1999). "Effects of justice conditions on discrete emotions." *Journal of Applied Psychology,* 84 (5): 786–94.

Wells, W. (2007). "Type of contact and evaluations of police officers: the effects of procedural justice across three types of police–citizen contacts." *Journal of Criminal Justice,* 35 (6): 612–21.

Wemmers, J.-A.M. (1995). "Victims in the Dutch criminal justice system: the effects of treatment on victims' attitudes and compliance." *International Review of Victimology,* 3 (4): 323–41.

——(1996). *Victims in the Criminal Justice System.* Amsterdam: Kugler.

——(1999). "Victim notification and public support for the criminal justice system." *International Review of Victimology,* 6 (3): 167–78.

Wemmers, J.-A.M. and Cyr, K. (2004). "Victims' perspectives on restorative justice: how much involvement are victims looking for?" *International Review of Victimology,* 11 (2/3): 259–74.

——(2006). "What fairness means to crime victims: a social psychological perspective on victim–offender mediation." *Applied Psychology in Criminal Justice,* 2 (2): 102–28.

Winkel, F.W. and Vrij A. (1995). "Coping with burglary: the effects of a police service on victims' emotional readjustment." In Davies, G., Lloyd-Bostock, S., McMurran, M. and Wilson, C. (eds), *Psychology, Law, and Criminal Justice: International Developments in Research and Practice* (363–73). Berlin: de Gruyter.

Winkel, F.W., Vrij, A., Koppelaar, L. and van de Steen, J. (1991). "Reducing secondary victimisation risks and skilled police intervention: enhancing the quality of police–rape victims' encounters through training programmes." *Journal of Police and Criminal Psychology,* 7 (2): 2–10.

Wright, M. (2002). "The court as last resort: victim-sensitive, community-based responses to crime." *British Journal of Criminology,* 42 (3): 654–67.

Zimbardo, P.G. (2007). *The Lucifer Effect: How Good People Turn Evil.* London: Rider.

Index

For Product Safety Concerns and Information please contact our EU
representative GPSR@taylorandfrancis.com
Taylor & Francis Verlag GmbH, Kaufingerstraße 24, 80331 München, Germany

www.ingramcontent.com/pod-product-compliance
Lightning Source LLC
Chambersburg PA
CBHW050515280326
41932CB00014B/2329